PATRIARCHAL STRUCTURES AND ETHNICITY IN THE ITALIAN COMMUNITY IN BRITAIN

To my husband Giuseppe Settimio Medaglia

DAMES
Dansk Center for Migration
og Etniske Studier

CENTRE FOR RESEARCH IN ETHNIC RELATIONS

ERCOMER
EUROPEAN RESEARCH CENTRE
ON MIGRATION & ETHNIC RELATIONS

Patriarchal Structures and Ethnicity in the Italian Community in Britain

AZADEH MEDAGLIA

Routledge
Taylor & Francis Group
LONDON AND NEW YORK

First published 2001 by Ashgate Publishing

Reissued 2019 by Routledge
2 Park Square, Milton Park, Abingdon, Oxon, OXl 4 4RN
52 Vanderbilt Avenue, New York, NY 10017

Routledge is an imprint of the Taylor & Francis Group, an informa business

A Library of Congress record exists under LC control number:

ISBN 13: 978-1-138-71105-1 (hbk)
ISBN 13: 978-1-138-71103-7 (pbk)
ISBN 13: 978-1-315-19996-2 (ebk)

Contents

List of Figures

Figure		**Page**

List of Tables

Acknowledgments

I would like to thank Professor Sylvia Walby, Phyllis Sellick OBE, Professor Fereydoun Adamiat, Seán J. Hawkes, Andri Soteri, Yassamine Mather, Dr.Yik-Koon Teh and Farideh Sajjadi. Without their guidance and support, this book would not have been possible.

Introduction

Since the 1980s, much interest has been shown in such disciplines as sociology, anthropology and history in Italy and in Italian Diaspora communities throughout the industrialized world. This book focuses on the forms and specificities of gender relations within the Italian community in Britain.

Italian migration to Britain started over 150 years ago and the present population consists of approximately 220,000 people, spread geographically across the country. The patriarchal traditions and belief systems that Italian migrants brought over with them from Italian village communities were rigid and strongly held. However, life in modern British towns has posed new challenges and led to some major adaptations.

Italians constitute an ethnic group although they are European, white and Christian. Their ethnicity is signified by their use of Italian language, their social customs and their religion (Roman Catholicism). They are now quite integrated but little assimilated into British society. In other words, they fully participate in most aspects of British social life, while retaining strong ethnic particularities and solid attachments to their mother country and its culture; at the same time, they remain on the margins of decision making at the national level. As a non-racialized ethnic group, they do not share the sometimes traumatic experiences of black or non-Christian ethnic groups.

This book highlights the debates on theorizing patriarchy and on changes in gender relations in the Italian community. These changes identify: the way in which women have adapted to their new social, cultural and economic environment; their role in the integration of the family; their position within the household as dictated by the Italian culture; the impact of paid employment on their role within the reproductive sphere; their changing subjectivities; the stumbling blocks on their path to integration; their conflicts, differences and similarities with their second and third-generation daughters.

Walby (1990) studies and compares changes in the form and degree of patriarchy in Britain in the 19th and 20th centuries through examining the six patriarchal structures of paid employment, household production, culture, sexuality, violence and the state. She distinguishes between private and public patriarchy and identifies the structures of employment and the state as the main sites of women's oppression in the 20th century. Due to the multi-cultural nature of British society, the aforementioned theory cannot be universal. This book tests Walby's theory against the Italian community in Britain. The theoretical application aims at determining the specificities, the form and the degree of patriarchy within the six structures, the balance between the structures, their different modes of interaction and inter-structural causal relations.

Italian women are not confined to the household any more; the majority are in full-time paid employment, equally divided between the mainstream and ethnic job markets. However, most are still segregated into less qualified, low remunerated jobs. They are still burdened with the double shift, i.e. both paid employment and household chores. Their sexuality is influenced and regulated by the Italian Catholic Church which assumes both pastoral and socio-cultural roles within the community. The impact of Italian education and media on gender relations is marginal; this is because Italian children use the British educational system and Italians as a whole are mainly exposed to British media. Ethnic Italians have a particular relationship with the British and Italian states: they live in Britain and benefit from the whole range of social services offered by the British State. Yet, the overwhelming majority feel primarily Italian as opposed to British, they have Italian citizenship and expect the Italian State to make regular contributions in order to improve Italian cultural and educational facilities within the Diaspora communities. Due to the reluctance of the interviewees to discuss the subject and lack of adequate secondary data it has proved difficult to assess the extent of domestic violence within the Italian community.

The structure of sexuality is the main site of patriarchy within the Italian Diaspora, and public and private patriarchy co-exist throughout the Italian way of life. Italian immigrants live within both British and Italian structures. Gender relations take on their particular configurations and mutate according to the Italians' ease of movement within these different social institutions. Religion and its interplay with ethnicity play a crucial role in regulating Italian gender relations and way of life.

The *Way of Life* is defined as the ensemble of distinguishable social, familial and sexual customs i.e. ideas and behaviour shaped by cultural and religious beliefs over an extended period of time and preserved within the institution of the family. The Italian way of life encompasses ethnic Italian attitudes and subjectivities about appropriate gender roles and representation. It is strongly influenced by the importance of the family at the centre of life, a philosophy which has been steadfastly reinforced by the teachings of the Catholic Church throughout the ages. The Church exerts a great influence on the other constituents of the Italian way of life, namely sexuality and household production. The cultural variations of their religious practice set the Italians apart even from the English or Irish Catholics. The *Way of Life* created at the intersection of the structures of culture, sexuality and household production is independent from the underlying economic structure of society to a significant extent. In an Italian immigrant family, individual interests are merged in the general interest of the family group. It is not unusual for the Italian mother to sacrifice her own life aspirations in order to provide better opportunities for her family. Children adopt deferential filial attitudes and harbour feelings of immense gratitude towards their parents who strive to build a better future for them. The second-generation Italian is more culturally integrated than her/his parents' generation, yet

> the Italian teenager cannot find a group in society, besides his own family one, with which to identify, therefore he remains isolated and lonely. His condition could be described with, and compared to, the condition of an adopted child. He always feels the nostalgia to know his parents' motherland though he does not really care about it. He has good relationships with English society which receives and accepts him in its house, though he remains conscious of being an adopted child (Bottignolo, 1985, p. 204).

Within the familism of the Italian immigrants, women generally occupy a more unequal standing. A large percentage of them work outside the home and yet they are almost exclusively responsible for the household work. First-generation Italians teach their traditional outlook to their children, thus perpetuating the weak position of women within the community in general, and the family specifically. Due perhaps to the strong influence of the Catholic Church, divorce rates and the number of female-headed households are low. Women may not have easy access to abortion due to community and family pressure. Close friendships between women are very common amongst the Italians. It is not of course suggested that lesbianism is encouraged; far from it, since Catholicism strongly condemns homosexuality. Pre-marital and extra-marital sexual relationships are still heavily tainted by the double standard:

> In Mediterranean cultures... women are traditionally seen as being in one of two categories: 'fallen' or 'not yet fallen'. The implication is that women's sexuality is inevitable and dangerous. It is not defined as a lack, as in post-Victorian northern Europe. The only way to preserve the family honour is thus the total subservience of women to male control. Here men project onto women a rabid and ever-present sexuality, which leads to irrational jealousy (Holloway, cited in Crowley and Himmelweit, 1992, p. 244).

The main argument of this book is as follows: the form and degree of patriarchy within the structures of employment, household production, culture, sexuality, violence and the state are ethnically specific, as is the balance between the structures. The structure of sexuality is identified as the main site of women's oppression and the Roman Catholic Church as an institution which reinforces sexual patriarchy.

The findings in this book are based on qualitative analysis carried out at an individual and an institutional level within the Italian community, and quantitative analysis of a survey. Questionnaires, interviews, secondary data, historical analysis, field trips to Italy and participant observation have all been used as investigative methods in this research, thus applying methodological triangulation. The quantitative findings are limited to the sample of 66 women used in this study.

I chose England, in particular London, as the main site of research because it accommodates the biggest concentration of Italians in Britain. The terms Britain, UK and England have sometimes been used interchangeably in this book. The reason for this is that for the average Italian, the word 'Inglese' (English) is generally devoid of any regional and national nuances and is equivalent to 'British'. In addition, the sample was gathered in England and there are no reasons for thinking there are significant differences amongst Italians in different parts of Britain.

I chose the subject of patriarchy because, having been born and raised in a patriarchal society, I have been subjected for most of my life to patriarchy in both its public and private forms. Themes of womanhood, women's oppression, women's acceptance of their plight, women's direct or indirect cooperation with men to maintain the patriarchal status-quo have always represented a most important intellectual preoccupation for me and have therefore constituted an obvious and natural subject for research.

On several occasions I have been told by other academics that my not being Italian could constitute a weakness for the study and that as an Iranian, I should naturally be researching the Iranian community. I find the suggestion that *it would have been most natural for me to investigate the Iranian community* as objectionable, Eurocentric, and usually directed from Western academics to non-Western researchers. The developing countries are indebted to many Western social scientists for having meticulously and most usefully researched various aspects of their societies and I believe researchers from developing countries should have an equal opportunity to investigate aspects of Western societies. Wider multicultural horizons can only enrich social investigations.

The choice of the Italian community as the main area of my research was due to the combination of several factors:

- With Britain increasingly becoming a multicultural society, any research relating to one of its ethnic components would be of use and interest. Awareness of the existence of culturally diverse groups of people and of their needs and potentialities can guide policy makers in their decisions. In addition, an appreciation of multiculturalism will lead to a more natural integration and a reduction in racial tensions.
- The progress of European unification has been slow and arduous but it is a reality. The further consolidation of the European Union necessitates a better understanding of its component societies. European unification has also a significant bearing on women's socio-political and economic standing. A study of the female component of the Italian community, especially in an era of lively interest for Italian studies in general, would therefore be a useful and welcome contribution to the field.
- The study of a white Christian ethnic group is interesting since the particularities of such groups, which are sometimes called 'invisible' ethnic groups, tend to go unnoticed. Such a subject matter could instigate other investigators to conduct further research on parallels between white and black ethnic groups.
- I am familiar with the Italian community through my husband who is Italian. This has helped me to circulate easily within the community.
- To my knowledge there is no other sociological study exclusively on gender relations within the Italian community and the present could form the basis for further research in this area.
- Gathering a representative sample, geographical distances to reach interviewees, difficulties of access, availability of proper statistics, time and resources, the response rate and the reliability of the interviewees are some of the methodological issues which set the boundaries to this research. The subject of research is a minority ethnic community within the politically and culturally dominant Anglo-Saxon Protestant community. The elements of racism and ethnic nationalism come into play. Ethnic nationalist feelings might be felt strongly by some Italian women because of actual or perceived discrimination in the host country or as a result of perceived cultural differences. The same women who are oppressed within their community might well be ready to defend its patriarchal ways or try to dissimulate them; hence the possibility of an ambivalence in women's attitudes towards patriarchy. Women may prefer their sheltered lives within the patriarchal family, to life in the threatening, culturally different host society.

This book is organized as follows:

- Chapter 1 reviews the spectrum of feminist theorization of women's subordination, establishes the theoretical framework of the research and identifies key structures of gender relations.
- Chapter 2 reviews the definitions and functions of religion and specifically investigates the relation of the Catholic Church with ethnicity and gender. It explores the major theoretical approaches to ethnicity, the relation between theories of gender relations and ethnicity, with emphasis on non-racialized Italians.
- Chapter 3 retraces the brief history of the Italian community in Britain, from the Middle-Ages to the 20th century; also, it reviews a study on the Italian women in Scotland, drawing parallels with the Italian women in England.
- Chapter 4 focuses on the quantitative analysis of the collected data using SPSS (Statistical Package for Social Sciences); the theory of patriarchy is tested against the various Italian social structures.
- Chapter 5 analyzes the interviews conducted at the Italian institutional level.
- Chapter 6 analyzes the social and cultural developments in Italy since the First World War, emphasizing the consequences for gender relations; the results are used to draw comparisons with the Italian community in Britain.
- Chapter 7 recapitulates the conclusions.

1 Theories of Gender Relations

PART I: FEMINIST THEORIZATION OF WOMEN'S SUBORDINATION

Liberal Feminism

Liberal feminist theory explains women's subordination in terms of gender stereotyping and confinement of women to gender specific roles in the market place and society in general. In other words, unequal access to voting, legal representation, education, job-training programs and paid employment are at the root of unequal gender relations. More recently, lack of access to pregnancy benefits, maternity leave and childcare centres have been theorized as gender subordinating.

Already in the 18th century, Mary Wollstonecraft (1759-1799) identified unequal access to education as the main cause for women's subordination. In the 19th century, John Stuart Mill and Harriet Taylor Mill theorized that unequal gender relations are the consequence of unequal access to civil liberties, economic and educational opportunities. The quintessential contemporary liberal feminist, Betty Friedan (1965), argued that women's subordination was a result of their confinement to the home. However, she did not contest the minor role men play in the private sphere. Moreover, she did not address issues of race, class and sexual orientation and concentrated instead on white, middle-class, suburban, heterosexual housewives. She failed to consider the difficulties of the double day without the introduction of major structural changes. Nearly twenty five years later however, in her book 'Second Stage' (1981), she recognized that the structural configuration of institutions and public values which favour men and impede women's progress, play an instrumental role in women's subordination.

Liberal feminists have been criticized for emphasizing gender-neutral humanism over gender-specific feminism. Elshtain (1981) argues that not all differences between men and women can be attributed to cultural gender stereotyping, ignoring nature completely. Furthermore, it has been claimed that liberal feminists overestimate the number of women who want to be like men and relinquish their roles as wives and mothers:

> There is little evidence that the family and the feminine role within it has lost any of its appeal as the central, prime and overwhelming attraction and responsibility for women. Whether women have successful careers or not, they remain just as committed to finding and keeping a man and to upholding the traditional divisions between the sexes (Coward, 1992, p. 9).

The liberalism paradigm has been criticized as being male biased:

- *Normative dualism* overvalues mental activities at the expense of bodily functions. Throughout the western philosophical tradition men have tended to become the ones closely associated to the world of the mind and 'culture' whereas women have become connected to the world of bodily functions and reproduction.
- *Political solipsism* is the belief that the rational, autonomous individual is essentially isolated, with interests different and sometimes in opposition to those of other individuals in the community; this concept is alien to female life experience of interdependence and nurturing.
- *Abstract individualism* is a conception of reality according to which every rational individual is entitled to equal rights regardless of sex, race or class. Women's reproductive functions however, generate different needs such as pregnancy leave, maternity and other related services (Jaggar, 1988).

I believe criticising *normative dualism* on the basis of its excessive overvaluing of mental activities is contradictory: if feminists truly believe that bodily functions are as important and valuable as mental functions, why do they struggle to gain access to positions where 'mental' activity counts (e.g. in public life)? Why are they not satisfied with childbearing which is the ultimate bodily function?

Marxist Feminism

In contrast to liberal feminism, Marxist feminism emphasizes the material and the social structure, when theorizing unequal gender relations. In 'The Origin of the Family, Private Property and the State' (1845), Engels argues that from the earliest pre-capitalist times, human societies have been characterized by a 'natural' sexual division of labour which itself probably originated from the division of labour in the sexual act. Thus in primitive societies, men specialized in controlling the tribe's animals and providing food, while women occupied a strong position within the household as the main centre of subsistence production (bedding, clothing, simple tools).

Why did men end up going out hunting while women stayed home? One answer is that women became pregnant and their lack of mobility dictated they should stay at home. However, this is not convincing because women were not pregnant all the time, all their life. They could have stayed home for the last few months of their pregnancy when their mobility was drastically reduced and the rest of the time go out doing what men did. Another answer is that most women are physically weaker than men and thus the physically more demanding job of hunting and gathering food was left to men. With the invention of agriculture and the domestication of animals, men succeeded to expand production, raise a surplus and accumulate wealth. It became profitable to own slaves and the first form of class society came into existence. At the same time, this process led to the devaluation of women's work, production and status within society. With their wealth increasing, men exerted pressure to convert the hitherto matrilineal and matrilocal societies into patriarchal ones and this constituted what Engels calls 'the world-historic defeat of the female sex' (cited in Tong, 1993, p. 48).

The emergence of private property and the patriarchal society marked the shift to monogamous family structure which insured the secure and orderly transfer of the father's patrimony to his children. Engels concludes that the domination of women by men within the monogamous family, where man controls the property, is simply the class division between the propertied and the propertyless and this ancient struggle continues into modern times. Only through the dissolution of the institution of private property and subsequently that of monogamy as a male supremacist economic institution, will the oppression of women ever cease. He goes on to argue that the working class woman does not experience oppression as much as the bourgeois woman, for entry into the labour market has rendered the proletarian woman less dependent on her husband for survival.

Alison Jaggar (1988) has criticized Engels for basing his explanation of the original sexual division of labour on the division of labour in the sexual act, a deterministic argument which implies that, apart from the institution of private property, the institution of heterosexuality is also instrumental in the oppression of women. I would add, why should the division of labour in the sexual act put women and not men at a disadvantage? Certainly women, with their capacity for reproduction, could have been in a privileged position.

Although early Marxist feminists have not directly addressed women's sexual and reproductive concerns and have attempted to theorize gender oppression through the nature and function of women's work, they go beyond Engels' explanation of women's oppression by trying to prove that the job of reproducing the labour force is not 'unproductive'. With the advent of capitalism and the transfer of goods production from the private household to the public workplace, women became responsible for the unremunerated production of simple use-value, childcare and heavy domestic duties; even when they were engaged in paid employment in the public sphere, they still carried the burden of the double day. Other Marxist feminists such as Mariarosa Dalla Costa and Selma James (1973) have made the claim that women's domestic work is already a productive work which creates surplus value and leads to their direct and indirect exploitation: it is reproducing labour which in turn creates surplus value.

Marxist feminists have also drawn attention to the fact that even when women are engaged in paid employment, they usually end up doing women's work such as nursing, cooking, clerking and teaching; since their work is undervalued, they also receive lower salaries than men, regardless of their knowledge and skill. Elshtain (1981) has criticized Marxist feminism on the grounds that it has overlooked the family as a haven which could provide love, security, comfort and diversity of life perspective. This criticism is especially valid in the case of racial and ethnic minorities for whom the family is a nucleus of solidarity and comfort in the face of hostility from the dominant cultural group.

Marxist feminists have condemned the family as an economic unit, not as an emotional one:

> In truly socialist society, men marry women, but these women are their equals; heterosexual couples have their own biological children, but these children are regarded as everyone's social children; and people set up individual households even though little in the way of cooking, cleaning, and/or child care goes on in them. Far from rejecting Elshtain's family, then, many a Marxist feminist has actually embraced it as a description of the family under authentic socialism (Tong, 1993, p. 63).

Michele Barrett counts among the theorists who have given a new direction to Marxist feminism. She criticizes Marxism for its economism and for not placing sufficient emphasis on the significance of ideological processes and culture. She stresses the considerable role of familial and domestic ideology in women's oppression:

> The oppression of women under capitalism is grounded in a set of relations between several elements. Of these perhaps the most crucial are the economic organization of households and its accompanying familial ideology, the division of labour and relations of production, the educational system and the operations of the state. Yet the continuance and the entrenched nature of this oppression

> cannot be understood without a consideration of the cultural processes in which men and women are represented differently -created and recreated as gendered human subjects-. Nor can it be understood without an analysis of sexuality and gender identity, and the complex question of the relationship between sexuality and biological reproduction as it affects both men and women (Barrett, 1988, pp. 40-41).

Alison Jaggar has criticized Marxist feminists because they have said too little about women's oppression by men. They consider men to be secondary oppressors at best, the primary oppressor being Capital. She has further criticized Marxist feminists for having rarely discussed issues related to sex. She says that when they do take up such issues, it is only to apply the analogy of employer-employee to pimp/prostitute and husband/wife relations. According to Jaggar, they do this in order to

> link the Marxist treatment of women's sex-specific oppression with Marxism's main theoretical system, incorporating domination both by class and by gender in the same explanatory framework (cited in Tong, 1993, pp. 63-64).

Despite its limitations, Marxist feminism has contributed to the understanding of the relation between the institutions of capitalism and family: capitalism needs the free reproduction work of women at home and it keeps them generally segregated in the most boring and low-paid jobs, once they enter into the labour market.

Radical Feminism

Radical feminism is a phenomenon generated by the 1960s women's liberation movement. It maintains that 'gender oppression is the oldest and most profound form of exploitation which predates and underlies all other forms including those of race and class' (H. Eisenstein, 1983, p. xix).

The term 'patriarchy' was first used to point out that in many parts of the world, men exert control over women (Millett, 1977). In traditional societies, this is done through the constraints of religious beliefs and social customs, and in modern, industrialized societies, by engineering consent among women themselves and conditioning them to accept a system of cultural sex-role stereotyping. However, not only in traditional societies do religious beliefs influence women's social position: for example, Catholicism still plays an important role in controlling women in a highly industrialized country such as Italy or within the Italian Diaspora in Britain (see Chapters 4 and 5).

Another prominent radical feminist, Shulamith Firestone, regards romantic sexual love as a patriarchal structure that perpetuates the rule of man over woman with the latter's full participation and consent. She argues:

> Unless revolution uproots the basic social organization, the biological family - the vinculum through which the psychology of power can always be smuggled- the tapeworm of exploitation can never be annihilated. We shall need a sexual revolution much larger than -inclusive of- a socialist one to truly eradicate all class systems (cited in H. Eisenstein, 1983, p. 17).

According to Brownmiller (1977), the genital difference that gave men the phallic power to rape women is the secret of patriarchy. Rape, she argues, is a crime committed by a few men, with tacit acceptance of many. Both the possibility and the actuality of rape have been the principal mechanisms to force women into submission.

Although Brownmiller's view of rape is a form of deterministic biological materialism (which would imply that the structure of human genitals must change in order for rape to stop), she contradicts herself by claiming optimistically that women 'could deny rape a future', through feminist organization and self-defence techniques. I argue that men can rape because, apart from their phallic power, most have a superior physical force. Sheer masculine force is applied in rape, domestic violence and battering. Both men and women become aware of their disparity in physical force, early in their life. Such awareness gives confidence to men and intimidates women. Confidence extends to all spheres of human life and helps men to materialize their ambitions. Intimidation poisons women's consciousness, is present throughout their life cycle and impedes them from materializing their lives' 'projects'.

Radical feminism theorizes that regardless of class, race and education, women form an exploited and subordinated sex class. I argue that the idea of a sex class is a mirage:

> They live dispersed among the males, attached through residence, housework, economic condition and social standing to certain men -fathers or husbands - more firmly than they are to other women (de Beauvoir, 1952, p. xxii).

By the mid 1970s, a group of feminists (Adrienne Rich, 1976, 1981; Susan Griffin, 1981) developed a perspective that came to be known as woman-centred analysis, advocating the possibility that femaleness was normative, while maleness was a deviation. One source of this new perspective was lesbian-feminism. Radical-lesbians put forward the concept of the primacy of women, of 'woman identified woman'. They theorized that women are subordinated because they direct their primal commitments, including sexual love, towards men rather than women. According to radical-lesbians, heterosexuality is a patriarchal concept inculcated and enforced on women. I criticize this argument on the following grounds:

- The argument implies that, in the absence of patriarchy, all or most women would be lesbians; there is no reason to assume this.
- Why should compulsory heterosexuality apply only to women? In our present society where patriarchy does not oppress men, all or most men should be homosexuals, which is obviously not the case.

Radical feminists have thought that the system of sex-role stereotyping has severely damaged women's psyche, to the point that not only men attribute all undesirable characters to women, women themselves internalize the denigrating values that men have about them. Radical feminism forwards the argument that the oppression of women is at the root of all other oppression, racial, economic and political. It often identifies psychology as a major locus of power, frequently at the expense of underlying social and economic factors which help to shape it. Moreover, radical feminism is characterized by a universalism that generalizes the experiences of women, ignoring the specificities of race, class and culture.

Some of the most important contributions of radical feminism have been towards the theorization of reproduction, mothering and sexuality. Shulamith Firestone (1974), argues that the relations of reproduction rather than those of production are the driving force in history; as long as biological reproduction remains the rule rather than the exception and the family prevails as the main economic unit, nothing will change fundamentally for women. However, once women are no more obliged to reproduce biologically, there would be no reason for them to stay at home: they would enter into public life, en masse and on a par with men.

According to many radical feminists, socially constructed sexual roles (male dominance and female submission) are as instrumental as socially constructed reproductive roles, in causing and perpetuating women's subordination. In this context, there have been heated debates amongst feminists on the subjects of pornography, heterosexuality, lesbianism and sadomasochism: feminists such as Dworkin (1981) and Mckinnon (1987) have condemned pornography on the grounds that it is an especially pernicious factor in promoting male dominance. It intentionally degrades and subordinates women. Other feminists (mainly liberal feminists) have condemned the censorship of pornography on the grounds of preserving civil liberties. The opponents of sadomasochism claim that it reproduces patterns of domination and submission not only at the sexual level but also at the political level; the advocates of sadomasochism claim that it eroticizes pain which, within certain limits, could be sexually stimulating. I argue that sadomasochism would reproduce unequal power relations within both heterosexual and homosexual contexts. The inequality would not remain constrained to sexuality and could eventually infiltrate other structures of private and public life.

Psychoanalytic Feminism

Psychoanalytic feminists have revised Freud's theory of human sexuality, attempting to strip it of its repressive thoughts and using its liberating aspects. Freud's theory of sexuality is based on the principal that boys and girls, from infancy onwards, go through successive stages of psychosexual development: oral, anal, phallic and finally genital when they reach puberty. During the phallic stage, the three or four year old child develops the Oedipus and castration complexes which boys and girls resolve differently. Their future 'normality' or typicality will depend on the successful resolution of these complexes. Freud has been criticized from many feminists quarters:

- Betty Friedan has argued that Freud's ideas were shaped by his Victorian culture and that he has universalized common traits of his own culture. She has accused him of biological determinism encapsulated in his phrase 'anatomy is destiny' (cited in Tong, 1993, p. 144). According to Friedan, Freud condemns women to a destiny of procreative life; he concentrates on the hypothesis that women' discontents stem from their physical lack of a penis rather than from lack of social, economic and cultural privileges; he thus makes women believe that they are deficient.
- Firestone has praised Freud's innovative openness in talking about sexuality but has criticized him for ignoring the pathological power relations within the nuclear family.
- Millett has found the concept of 'penis envy' egocentric. She has argued that instead of celebrating woman's power to give birth, neo-Freudians interpret it as a pathetic attempt to possess a substitute penis:

> Freudian logic has succeeded in converting childbirth, an impressive

> female accomplishment.... into nothing more than a hunt for a male organ (cited in Tong, 1993, p. 145).

- Alfred Adler (1927), Karen Horney (1973) and Clara Thompson (1964) are amongst psychoanalytic feminists who have rejected biological determinism. Adler recognized the repressing role of patriarchy in thwarting women's endeavour for superiority and power and in their developing neurosis. Horney pointed out that women's feelings of inferiority stem from the realization of their social subordination. She asserts 'women do not want to be men because they are enamoured of the penis; they want to be men because men are in control of society' (cited in Tong, 1993, p. 148). Adler, Horney and Thompson all believed that women's feelings of guilt, inferiority and self-hatred were products of patriarchal culture and its use of biology, not biology itself. Dorothy Dinnerstein (1978) and Nancy Chodorow (1978) have theorized that male dominance is the result of men and women not sharing mothering equally.

Dinnerstein has described current gender relationships as having been marked by six characteristics:

- Female erotic impulsiveness is muted (female eroticism being totally oriented towards male pleasure).
- There is excessive male sexual possessiveness. I argue that sexual possessiveness is not exclusive to men. Women stand to forfeit more in social and economic power, should they lose their men; consequently female sexual jealousy and possessiveness is anything but rare.
- For most women, sexual excitement and personal sentiment are tied; but this is not the case for men. Dinnerstein explains the difference as follows: the woman feels guilt about abandoning her mother for a one-night-stand; only a very deep, meaningful, binding relationship equivalent to the one she had with her mother could justify her rejection of the mother in favour of a man. The man, on the other hand, fearing a woman would overwhelm him once again and shatter his ego by withdrawing from him, will try to keep himself distant and unemotional when having intercourse.
- Women are denied personhood and are viewed as 'it's in contrast to men who are considered as 'I's.
- The female body is hated and denigrated.
- There is a tacit agreement between men and women that men should go out into the public world and that women should stay at home.

Dinnerstein attributes all six of these gender arrangements to women's sole responsibility for child rearing. She fails to account for economic realities as partial causes for gender inequality.

Like Dinnerstein, Nancy Chodorow believes that woman's oppression has its roots in her monopoly on motherhood. Chodorow wonders why women want to mother. She has rejected the two standard explanations of instinct and socialization. Instead, she has identified the pre-Oedipal mother/son and mother/daughter relationships as the cause of the differing psychosexual development of boys and girls, with social implications of inequality: boys and girls enter the Oedipal stage differently; the boy separates from his mother more abruptly and less painfully, because he can identify with his powerful and prestigious father. In contrast, the daughter's symbiosis with her mother never really breaks (because she is female like her mother and over-identifies with her). This differentiated process eventually results in the woman's overdeveloped and the man's underdeveloped capacity for relatedness. Chodorow's argument that the boy separates more easily from the mother is in direct contrast with Dinnerstein's theory, which postulates that the man is frightened to establish meaningful relationships with a woman because he has been traumatized in infancy by his mother's abandonment.

In their identification of the root cause of women's oppression, both Dinnerstein and Chodorow can be criticized on the following grounds:

- Dinnerstein theorizes on the basis of men and women's infant experiences; why is it that the woman selectively remembers her mother's all-encompassing love while the man only remembers his mother's unpredictability and withdrawal? With the gradual changes in sexual morality, women engage in casual sex and may enjoy it just as much as men do. Dinnerstein's theory is not scientifically verifiable.
- They have focused too much on psychological dynamics, ignoring largely the material transformations of society.
- They have concentrated on white, capitalist, middle-class, heterosexual family. This is a criticism that is directed at psychoanalysis in general; it does not take culture, ethnicity and race into account. One example is the frequent use of western mythology in psychoanalytical theory, overlooking the fact that it is not necessarily related to the collective memory of all the cultures in the world; one cannot assume theories derived from western mythology would be universally applicable.
- Dual parenting may actually exacerbate women's oppression by giving men even more power (both in public *and* private spheres). Juliet Mitchell (1975) believes that the attribution of social and symbolic

gender roles is buried very deep into our unconscious. Our psyches, she argues, may be too set in their ways for a reformist measure such as dual parenting, to jolt them into a new state of being.

Socialist Feminism

Socialist feminism is closely linked to Marxism and radical feminism. It uses a feminist version of the Marxist method to provide feminist answers to feminist questions (Mitchell cited in Jaggar, 1988, p. 124). In other words, it requires the use of historical materialism as originally developed by Marx and Engels, but transforms its gender-blind character by applying it to gender issues identified and made visible by radical feminists. The latter draw attention to the systematic domination of women by men both within and outside the labour market, and point out that men of all classes enjoy women's free domestic and sexual services. According to socialist feminists, capitalism, male domination in both public and private spheres, racism and imperialism are all closely intertwined. What distinguishes socialist feminism and at the same time links it to Marxist and radical feminisms, is its attempt to theorize women's subordination by identifying categories of productive activity hitherto not considered economic (e.g. procreation, sexual and emotional satisfaction), and by explaining them in economic terms. To overcome the limitations of both Marxist and radical feminisms, socialist feminists have developed dual-systems theory and unified-systems theory. The first is based on the tenet that patriarchy and capitalism are two separate, autonomous forms of social relations whose dialectic intersection oppresses women in a particular way (Mitchell, 1975; Hartmann, 1979). Unified-systems theorists (Zillah Eisenstein, 1979, 1986) on the other hand, regard capitalism and patriarchy as two inseparable dimensions of the same phenomenon. Juliet Mitchell refutes the monocausal explanation of women's oppression and links woman's status to her role in production (economic factors) *and* reproduction (psychological factors).

Heidi Hartmann, a dual-systems theorist, has attempted to combine a traditional Marxist analysis of capitalism with a materialist analysis of patriarchy. She defines patriarchy as 'a set of social relations between men which have a material base, and which, though hierarchical, establish or create interdependence and solidarity among men that enable them to dominate women' (cited in Tong, 1993, p. 180). In capitalist countries, Hartmann argues, men exert this control through the institutions of monogamous heterosexual marriage, reproduction, employment and the state: capitalism and patriarchy eventually collude to subordinate women, to the benefit of both. Sylvia Walby (1990) has developed dual-systems theory to include the full range of patriarchal structures. In her analysis of patriarchy, she identifies six structures namely waged work, housework, sexuality, culture, violence and the state. Her usage of the concept of patriarchy has been criticized for being essentialist, reductionist, with no dynamics of change (Pollert, 1996), universalist and not flexible enough to deal with variations in gender inequality in different times and spaces, in particular with regard to class and ethnicity (Humphries, 1977; hooks, 1984). However, Walby's work does analyze change and gendered struggle (Walby 1986, 1990, 1997). Acker (1989) criticizes Walby's theory of patriarchy on the grounds that it has set up system boundaries between patriarchy, capitalism and racism instead of treating all social relations as gender relations. Walby (1997) argues that these conceptual distinctions are necessary in order to analyze interconnections between the diverse sets of social relations. The theory of patriarchy has been criticized for having neglected to 'allow, for instance, for the fact that in most societies some women have power at least over some men as well as other women' (Yuval-Davis, 1997, p. 7). The critique does not however identify such societies nor specify the number of such empowered women and the nature of their power. While Walby's theory needs to be developed in order to deal more efficiently with issues of ethnic difference, it does clearly address the articulation between patriarchy, capitalism and racism in order to highlight the importance of social and economic power relations.

Existentialist Feminism

Simone de Beauvoir (1952), the pioneer of existentialist feminism, adopted the ontological and ethical tenets of existentialism previously developed by Sartre.

According to Sartre, each subject, in the process of self-definition, seeks to overpower other beings which it sees as 'Others'. Moreover, while each subject considers itself free and transcended, it views the Other as immanent and enslaved. Simone de Beauvoir applies this Sartrean principle to Man as 'Self' and Woman as 'Other'. In order for the Self or the Man to remain free, the Other must be subordinated. While Woman is in no way the only Other to be oppressed, her kind of oppression is unique in the sense that historically it has never been reversed or contested and besides, this sense of Otherness has been internalized by Woman herself. Moreover, de Beauvoir argues, if Woman feels to be the unessential never to become the essential, it is because she herself fails to bring about change. De Beauvoir describes the basic trait of Woman as being 'the Other in a totality of which the two components are necessary to one another' (de Beauvoir, 1952, p. xxiii).

But why is woman the inferior Other? De Beauvoir looked beyond biology as sufficient answer. She also rejected Freud's suggestion that civilization could be simply reduced to the product of repressed or sublimated sexual impulses. She was not satisfied with Marxist theories which contend that the oppression of women is rooted in a society where one class exploits the labour of another and would last until capitalism is overthrown; she did not see an end to women's oppression in socialist countries; she contested Engels' argument which traces men's will to power to the institution of private property and women's oppression to the beginnings of capitalism:

> If the human consciousness had not included the original category of the Other, the invention of the bronze tool could not have caused the oppression of woman (de Beauvoir, 1952, p. 64).

De Beauvoir's own explanation comes through an examination of the data of prehistoric research and ethnography, in the light of existentialist philosophy. She explains the disadvantage of woman as being the continual handicap of childbirth, child rearing, menstruation, which prevent her from engaging in creative activities; meanwhile Man as Homo Faber, has transcended his animal nature and also engages in warring activities where the mere confrontation of danger and risking of life confer prestige and superiority. This is how, de Beauvoir explains, Man got a head start in life, as the Self. She identified social roles and the socialization of women into passive feminine roles as the principal mechanisms of control of the Other by the Self. The roles of wife and mother block women's freedom.

Elshtain (1981) criticizes de Beauvoir for having treated the body, especially the female one, in a negative way, as an unavoidable degenerating object which limits the freedom of each conscious subject. Elshtain believes that this approach could alienate a woman who is perfectly happy in her Being-in-Itself state and does not wish to transcend herself beyond the body into the world of the mind. Elshtain also criticizes de Beauvoir for embracing and perhaps glorifying male norms: denigrating woman's body and character and deploring her association with nature; valorizing man's body and character and revering his association with the construction of culture.

Postmodern Feminism

Postmodern feminists, frequently referred to as French feminists, reject fixed, traditional assumptions about truth and reality as being phallologocentric (originating mainly from the male thought), and advocate plurality, multiplicity and difference. According to postmodern feminists, gender identities are fluid and constantly changing. Much of postmodern feminism has been informed by the work of the French philosopher Foucault (1981, 1989) who has enhanced feminist understandings of the control of women's sexuality and bodies. According to Foucault, bodies and sex are not biologically essentialist entities but rather social constructions which are produced as effects of power within dominant discourses. Foucault emphasizes the disciplining and subordinating power of discourse but does not explain the nature and origins of discursive formations. Furthermore he does not appreciate how new powerful discourses may liberate us from bigoted, intolerant ones i.e. scientific discourse may have liberated people from religious discourse of sin, heaven and hell (Ramazanoglou, 1997).

Despite the diversity in their theories and politics, Helene Cixous (1981), Luce Irigaray (1985) and Julia Kristeva (1986) are categorized together under the label 'Postmodern', because they all draw their philosophical inspirations from the existentialist, psychoanalytic and deconstructionist streams of thought, and especially from the philosophers Jacques Lacan (1977) and Jacques Derrida (1976, 1981).

From Simone de Beauvoir's existentialist theory of feminism, they adopt the concept of woman as Other, but emphasize the positive aspects of being the Other: openness, plurality, diversity and difference rather than the traditional negative connotations of Otherness such as inferiority, rejection, marginality. The major theme of deconstruction is in fact this emphasis on the positive side of Otherness.

From Lacan and Derrida, postmodern feminists got their understanding of language as a dominating, logocentric, phallocentric and binary structure. Lacan (1977) identifies the series of interrelated signs, roles and rituals in every society as 'The Symbolic Order'. Every child internalizes this order through language which constricts thought and its different interpretations and meanings. 'Regardless of whatever differences of content and style distinguish postmodern feminists one from the other, in general they believe that the woman, the Other, the feminine, has been left unthematized and silent, in the gap that continually blocks union between language and reality' (Tong, 1993, p. 223).

Helene Cixous (1981) is primarily a novelist who theorizes that a dichotomous conceptual order constrains women to exist and function in man's world, on his terms. Phallocentric language, she claims, determines women's place in the world. She praises feminine writing, like feminine sexuality, as open, multiple, varied, very much in contrast with male sexuality and writing which she finds ultimately boring. It is of course presumptuous to claim that male writing is boring. After all, it was male writing and its cultural prevalence which first enticed women to enter the public world. Luce Irigaray (1985) is a psychoanalyst who agrees that girls, unlike boys, never completely resolve the Oedipal phase; however, she opines that from the 'Imaginary' (the pre-Oedipal stage), before entering the 'Symbolic Order' which is phallocentric, women have untapped possibilities to enter selfhood and language without any mediation from men. Julia Kristeva (1986) does not fully accept the ideas put forward by Cixous and Irigaray according to which the feminine is identified with biological woman and the masculine with biological man; because, she argues, upon entry into the Symbolic Order, boys and girls are free to identify with either parent and become either more feminine or more masculine. Therefore, boys can end up writing in a feminine mode and girls in a masculine mode. Kristeva wants society to come to terms with the marginal, the different, the abject, the feminine being aspects of it.

Postmodern feminism can be criticized for:

- the neglect of a full range of patriarchal institutions such as the state, the economy, religion.
- creating endless possibilities of diversity which make analysis of power and inequality problematic.
- the complexity of its style of writing which makes it almost exclusively a subject for academics.
- valuing the female over the male.
- making philosophical assumptions which may lead to chaos and anarchy.

Conclusion

Liberal feminism has pointed to the analytic significance of educational and political reforms without which later feminist struggles would not have had a future. However, it has neglected racial and ethnic differences. Despite its limitations, the gains and achievements of later feminists would have been almost impossible without the educational and legal reforms prompted by liberal feminism. Liberalism, as Zillah Eisenstein has predicted, is by no means out of date and may even have the 'radical future'. Marxist feminism has rightly indicated the economic and material exploitation of women but has disregarded women's sexual, reproductive and ethnic concerns. Radical feminism has formulated the right questions about the role of sexuality and violence in unequal gender relations; but it has not come up with the right answers. Psychoanalytic feminism, while rightly addressing gender issues such as motherhood and child rearing, has again neglected ethnic differences. Existentialist feminism has undervalued female difference and has neglected issues of race and ethnicity. Postmodern feminism has celebrated female difference while disregarding a whole range of patriarchal institutions (state, economy, religion) which influence patterns of gender relations.

I regard dual-systems feminists' theorization of unequal gender relations and in particular Walby's system of patriarchal structures as the most comprehensive explanation of women's oppression. The six patriarchal structures (employment, household production, culture, sexuality, violence and state) explain the material, social, cultural and sexual basis of unequal gender relations and expose the articulation of capitalism and patriarchy in the oppression of women. Although Walby's theory does not sufficiently develop issues of ethnicity, its explanatory tools are flexible enough to evaluate patterns of unequal gender relations and trajectories of change within the ethnic Italian community in Britain.

PART II: STRUCTURES OF GENDER RELATIONS

Paid Employment

Women have traditionally engaged less than men in paid employment and are segregated in less remunerated jobs. Although the mass entry of women into the labour market after the Second World War was hailed as emancipation, in practice, gender inequality has not diminished remarkably in terms of pay and job quality.

Since the 1940s, in the industrialized world and more specifically in Britain and the USA, there has been a drastic shift away from manufacturing industries towards service industries, and women's part-time employment has played a major part in these changes (Dex, 1985, pp. 177 - 178; Walby, 1990, p. 26). What is significant about part-time work, however, is that it is highly exploitative and heavily gender specific.

Part-time jobs are notably segregated from full-time jobs, they are dead-end because there are no promotions. They are mainly categorized as unskilled even when some part-time jobs, such as those in welfare services, involve quite complex responsibilities. They lack most of the advantages that accrue to people in full-time employment such as sick pay, maternity pay or pension schemes. They are lower paid with more intense working hours. Moreover, a large number of women who come back to the labour market after a period of childbearing and child rearing, experience downward mobility. Therefore, despite women's mass entry into the labour market, analysis of the jobs typically open to women demonstrate that their new conditions are far from emancipatory.

Sexual division of labour and women's lower quality jobs have been theorized differently:

- Functionalists explain gender inequality in paid employment on the basis of the 'human capital' theory drawn from modern neo-classical economics. The theory argues that women's inferior human capital (skills, training, qualifications, job experience) results ultimately in wage differentials with men. 'Human Capital' theory has been criticized on both empirical and theoretical levels: Treiman and Hartmann (1981) demonstrated in their empirical survey that worker characteristics did not play a significant role in wage differentiation. Instead, they claimed, the principal reason for wage differentials was job segregation. Theoretically, the 'Human Capital' theory can be criticized because of its assumption of a perfect labour market in which employers reward employees according to their worth. It ignores the institutionalized power relations which allow men to have their jobs designated as 'highly skilled' and therefore much better paid.
- There are four Marxist and Marxist-feminist variations of theorizing gender relations in paid employment: Marx himself had little to say about women's employment specifically. However, two of his main theses namely the 'Deskilling' thesis and the 'Industrial Reserve Army' have been picked up by Harry Braverman, who in his 'Labour and Monopoly Capital' (1974), argues that these two theoretical arguments are still relevant to the understanding of women's employment in the 20th century. The 'Deskilling' thesis asserts that capitalism, in its relentless pursuit of profit, tries to reduce the number of highly paid skilled workers by dividing the simplified work among a large number of unskilled workers. The 'Reserve Army' thesis argues that as capitalism develops, it draws more and more workers into its system, only to expel them in times of crisis, when they are surplus to production requirements. Braverman argues that capital penetrated the

domestic economy, took over the production of commodities previously produced within the family and thus created a supply of women (reserve army) who took over most of the unskilled part-time jobs. Braverman's analysis can be criticized on the grounds that the categorization of a job as skilled is by itself problematic. Traditionally, men have been able to have their jobs classified as skilled, through powerful institutions such as trade unions. On the other hand, women's jobs, particularly part-time ones, have been categorized as unskilled or semi-skilled even when they involve complex competencies. Braverman fails to explain why it is women who are used as cheap and unskilled labour and the reason why they accept disadvantageous terms. He overlooks the fact that women's paid employment, albeit unskilled and low-paid, provides them with an independent income which may open a range of new social opportunities. In short, Braverman stresses economic factors at the expense of political and ideological ones, thus ignoring the family, the state and the processes of social reproduction. In her early work (1978), Veronica Beechey applies Marx's concept of a 'reserve army' to women, not like Braverman as a long-term reserve of labour, but as a latent, flexible reserve which could be brought into the labour market cyclically in times of economic boom, only to be sent home during recession. However, in 'A Matter of Hours' (1987), Beechey warns that statistically, the concept of a disposable reserve army, may not be as useful as previously thought, because of the employers' system of restructuring and reorganizing, which can reduce full-time employees' working hours or have them rehired by private contractors to do the same jobs under worse terms and conditions. Beechey and Perkins (1987) further criticize Marxist analyses of the labour process for failing to use Marx's arguments within the context of 20th century labour market characterized by new labour restructuration and gender relations in production processes. The 'Family Wage' theory as introduced by Humphries (1977), considers women as basically full-time home-makers who, by taking care of the family (the young, the sick, the old), help control the supply of labour, enable the family to raise its standard of living through a higher family wage and reinforce the solidarity of the working class. This theory can be criticized on the grounds that it justifies higher wages for men and the confinement of women to the private sphere; it also ignores female-headed families and does not explain the reason why, in order to control the supply of labour, women and not men should remain outside the market. The Marxist segmented labour theory argues that capitalists segment the labour market based on ethnicity and gender so that the divided working class is too weak to resist the demands of capitalism. However, this theory does not explain where these ethnic and gender divisions come from. Generally, Marxist accounts of gender relations in paid work over-concentrate on the capital/labour relation, neglecting the theorization of gender as an independent source of inequality.

- Dual-systems theorists use the analytical tools of patriarchy and class analysis to understand and explain gender relations: Hartmann (1979) argues that sexual segregation, achieved through the influence of state-protected exclusively male trade unions, is central to the understanding of gender relations. A vicious cycle is created when men's access to better jobs and the so-called family wage enable them to marry women who need their financial support, on more favourable terms; these women become full-time housewives and lose their opportunities to get marketable qualifications. Walby goes beyond Hartmann's analysis and develops the dual-systems approach to gender and employment. She maintains there is much more tension between the interests of capitalism and patriarchy as hitherto assumed by Hartmann: 'If women are working for capitalists they have less time to work for their husbands' (Walby, 1990, p. 41). Periods of struggle between the two (capitalism and patriarchy) include women's massive entry into the munitions factories during the two World Wars. Each time the State intervened in favour of patriarchy, to remove women from men's work or to limit their scope of employment. The role of ethnicity and racism has been hitherto neglected in the analysis of gender and paid employment (Carby, 1982; hooks, 1984). An example of the role of racism in the theorization of sexual division of labour is the changing gender composition of the textile industry in post-war Britain:

> Between 1970 and 1982 the percentage of workforce that was female declined from 51 per cent to 42 per cent... This appears to be the result of the hiring of black male workers to work a night shift in order to utilize the capital machinery on a more intensive basis.... Only black men would take jobs at the wage rates on offer, because racial discrimination in the labour market closed the more lucrative forms of employment to them. The change in the gender composition of the textile workforce is then directly related to the changing racial composition, with an increase in the employment of black men and a decrease in the employment of white women. This change in the gender composition of cotton textiles then, can be explained only in the context of the intersection of racist structures with those of patriarchy and capitalism (Walby, 1990, pp. 44-45).

There are significant variations of forms of both patriarchy and capitalism and their articulation over time and space (both regionally and internationally). For example the specific form of gender inequality in capitalist Muslim fundamentalist societies is different from that prevailing in the developing countries where the new international division of labour concentrates women in assembly line factories, or that which exists in different regions and different ethnic minorities in Britain. The role of the State as an agency to solve key conflicts between the capitalist and patriarchal forces is highly instrumental but has been changing over the years in Britain, through the two World Wars and after legislation such as the 1970 Equal Pay Act and the 1975 Sex Discrimination Act. Generally, due to feminist struggle, the State has become relatively more favourable to women, compared to the pre-franchise period. In short, women have entered the labour market in increasing numbers after the Second World War. However their concentration has been in lesser-skilled, lower-paid and mainly part-time jobs. The wages gap has diminished only slightly. Feminist struggles have succeeded in securing more of the state protection as exemplified by the Equal Pay Act or the Sex Discrimination Act which are still far from being truly effective. Within the public sphere, women are still subordinated to men not only in terms of pay or type of job, but also through sexual harassment and violence (Walby, 1990).

Household Production

Women's expropriation of labour in the household has been theorized differently:

- The Parsonian functionalist conceptualization of gender relations within the 'family' is in terms of sex roles: Men playing the instrumental external role and women assuming the expressive, ideological, internal function. The relations between men and women are also conceived as being different but equal. Parsons and other noted functionalists such as Goode (1963) and Smelser (1959), are all in agreement that the small nuclear family of working husband, home-maker wife and dependent children is functionally suited to industrialized societies. The functionalist theorization of the family as a consensual unit can be criticized on the following grounds: it ignores the power relations within the household and conceives of the family as a functional, harmonious unit with a sexual division of labour which is ultimately in the best interest of the individual members of the family and society as a whole. According to Parsons, men's instrumental role and women's expressive one must be kept separate, in order to avoid conflict between the occupational structure and the kinship system. Parsonian functionalism does not recognize women's work at home as proper labour but rather as an ideological cultural activity. Oakley (1974) has demonstrated that women's housework is just like any other work, even when not remunerated. Pahl's (1984) suggestion that ideology is very important in determining the sexual division of labour, is parallel to the position of the functionalists who regard women's role within the household as ideological and cultural and insist that male and female roles (respectively instrumental and expressive) must remain separate lest conflict arises between the occupational structure and the kinship system.

- Amongst the liberals Young and Wilmott (1975) argue that women are now more likely to go into paid employment, therefore the two sexes' roles are converging. The liberals consider the household as a consensual unit, leaving no theoretical space to explain power relations or changes in power relations. They identify divisions of tasks within the household, but fail to link them to a wider social inequality.
- Among the Marxists, Engels is the first to attempt theorizing gender inequality and women's subordination. In his base/superstructure model of society, reproduction together with production constitute the base: with the advent of class society there came the world historic defeat of the female sex, the development of the monogamous family and the domination of men over women in both production and reproduction spheres. According to Engels, this domination would only disappear with the advent of socialism. Althusser (1971) views the family as an ideological site to socialize children for the capitalist state, ignoring women's work within the household as an important economic activity. Other Marxists, such as James and Dalla Costa (1973), argue that women create exchange value in the capitalist system by cooking, cleaning, keeping house and taking care of labourers who would in turn enter the market to produce surplus value for the capitalists. Barrett (1988) undertakes a non-economistic analysis of gender and attaches much importance to the role of ideology which is rooted in the family, a central institution for the oppression of women. Although Barrett does not make capitalism the main causal element behind women's oppression, she believes capitalist developments are implicated. Black feminists argue that for black women, the family is less of a site of oppression and more a haven of solidarity and resistance to white racism (hooks, 1984). However, for

some ethnic women, the solidarity that their families offer against white racism outweighs the oppression of patriarchy.

- The strength of Radical feminism in theorizing gender relations within the household lies in its stress on the important notions of power and inequality between the sexes. Its weakness is in ignoring the variations across time, space, class and race. However, there are variations among the radical feminists themselves as to the importance they attach to the particular material site of gender inequality and women's subordination. For example Firestone (1974) sees reproduction and therefore the household as the main site of oppression; Brownmiller (1977) considers rape as central and Adrienne Rich (1981) sees institutionalized heterosexuality as the main culprit. Some feminists (Shorter, 1975; Young and Wilmott, 1975) have hailed the use of contraception pills or the application of modern medicine to childbirth as important moves in the emancipation of women. Others (Ehrenreich and English, 1979) argue that the development of modern obstetrics constitutes an increase in male control over women's bodies and reproduction, one of women's few bases of power. Hilary Rose, in her article 'The Politics of Reproductive Science and Technology', condemns the recent reproductive technologies such as amniocentesis, In Vitro Fertilization (IVF), gene therapy and artificial insemination as innovations which subject women to more repression, cruelty and humiliation rather than emancipation. She criticizes amniocentesis and gene therapy, comparing them to the Nazi eugenics programs (cited in Stanworth, 1987, p. 165). Not all radical feminists see reproduction as the main site of women's oppression. Adrienne Rich considers children as a source of joy to women and criticizes the patriarchal state which, by failing to help mothers, converts the blissful experience of motherhood into an institution of oppression, thus perpetuating gender inequality.
- Heidi Hartmann's dual-systems theory (1979) incorporates both the materialism of Marxist analysis and the radical feminist concept of patriarchy. It can, however, be criticized on the grounds that it lacks historical and cultural specificity. Carol Brown (1981), in an attempt to rectify this flaw, has produced a historical analysis of the household and examined the value of children to mothers and fathers over the last century. She has concluded that in the 19th century, children had a high economic value for their families, hence custody of the children went to the male patriarch upon divorce. Today, by contrast, children are an economic drain and custody generally goes to the mother.

Over the years, there have been significant changes in the domestic division of labour and in household composition. Many women do less housework because some of the productive work previously done under relations of patriarchy is now being done by the state or under capitalist relations of production. The composition of the household has changed in the industrialized world: fewer people are married than two decades ago, people are marrying later and the divorce rate is rising (Walby, 1987, p. 83). The first no-fault divorce law in the Western world was instituted in California in 1970. Family and divorce reform laws followed in Britain in 1973 (Walby, 1990). The no-fault divorce law had the unintended effect of impoverishing women and the children in their care because it treated them as equal to men, disregarding a long history of established gender inequality. Another component of the divorce revolution is the changing social attitude towards the divorced who are no longer considered exceptional or socially deviant. Finally, fewer households are composed of the typical male breadwinner and female full-time housewife. Despite the increase in the number of women in paid employment men have not moved to any significant extent towards sharing domestic tasks with their working wives.

Culture

> The term culture is defined very broadly in sociology. It is most commonly used to delineate the symbolic aspects of human society so as to include beliefs, rituals, customs, conventions, ideals or artistic endeavours. In this usage, culture contrasts with the biological aspects of human behaviour, on the one hand and society or social institutions on the other (Abercrombie, Warde, Soothill, Urry, Walby, 1991, p. 395).

Culture may be taken as constituting the 'way of life' of an entire society and this will include codes of manners, dress, language, rituals, norms of behaviour and systems of belief. Raymond Williams, having stressed the extreme difficulty in defining words which involve ideas and values, as exemplified by dictionary definitions of culture such as: 'advanced development of the human powers' or 'evidence of intellectual development (of arts, science, etc.) in human society' (Oxford Dictionary of Sociology), proceeds to identify three broad categories of usage for the word culture:

> (i) the independent and abstract noun which describes a general process of intellectual, spiritual and aesthetic development... (ii) the independent noun,

> whether used generally or specifically, which indicates a particular way of life, whether of a people, a period, a group, or humanity in general...(iii) the independent and abstract noun which describes the works and practices of intellectual and especially artistic activity. This seems often now the most widespread use: **culture** is music, literature, painting and sculpture, theatre and film (Williams, 1983, p. 90).

The latter use of culture does of course distinguish between high culture and popular culture which has come under the scrutiny of research with the post-modernists. Some sociological theorists (Bilton et al., 1987; Giddens, 1989; Walby, 1989, 1990) tend to analyze the cultural as a sphere structured through the specific institutions of media, education, religion. Other feminists (Cixous, 1981; Irigaray, 1985; Kristeva, 1986; Mitchell, 1975) have drawn on Lacan's innovative and radical psychoanalytic theory emphasizing culture rather than biology. Lacan himself was no feminist and his theoretical stance can sound as biologically deterministic as Freud's:

> It seems to condemn all women to being the unconscious symptom of men's hysteria, to being the symptom of male neurosis about their symbolic castration by their fathers, their fear of being feminine (cited in Crowley and Himmelweit, 1992, p. 201).

According to Lacan, 'woman' within patriarchal societies has no position outside language, and within language she can represent only the 'lack', the negative 'not man', because she indeed lacks the 'phallus' which is the crucial signifier of power. Drawing on this argument, some feminists (Spender, 1980; Spivak, 1987) have argued that by challenging and changing the language that defines women as inferior and which has denigrated them until now, there is the possibility of changing women's position in society. In challenging the language of sexism, women are encouraged to refuse to identify with negative representations of femininity, to begin constructing their own language, to be more authoritative in the use of language and to acquire the conviction and seriousness men convey in their speech. Terms such as sexual politics, male chauvinism, sexual objectification, oppression, sisterhood are examples of critical feminine language.

> Language helps form the limits of our reality. It is our means of ordering, classifying and manipulating the world. It is through language that we become members of a human community.... Yet it is ironic that this faculty which helps to create our world also has the capacity to restrict our world. For having learnt

> a particular language and had access to being 'humanized' we have also been 'socialized' in the process, we have also learnt to confine our way of looking at the world to a particular cultural world view. Having learnt the language of a patriarchal society we have also learnt to classify and manage the world in accordance with patriarchal order and to preclude many possibilities for alternative ways of making sense of the world (Spender, 1980, p. 3).

Although Spender admits she does not suggest that modifying the language would create employment for women or help reduce their economic dependence, she nevertheless argues that economic independence alone is no guarantee for psychological and emotional liberation. She concludes:

> Both language and material resources have been used by the dominant group to structure women's oppression, and they are interconnected. One cannot be transformed without the other if women are to be liberated and patriarchy is to be prevented from persisting (Spender, 1980, p. 6).

Studies of language as a site of patriarchy seem to have largely concentrated on European languages and ignored the existence of non-European languages which, at least in syntax do not appear to be patriarchally constructed. If we are to universalize the theorization of patriarchy, we ought not to adopt a Eurocentric approach towards the study of language. The non-European Persian language is an example. Although Persian is replete with words and expressions which denigrate women and womanhood, the language is grammatically gender blind: for example, in Romance languages the presence of one male amongst an infinite number of females is sufficient to impose the use of masculine pronouns, endings and structures; in Persian however, there are no grammatical distinctions between the two genders. A semantics example would be: whereas in most European languages, 'Man' is meant to designate 'human beings', in Persian there is no such overlap and 'human being' has its own neuter signifier. There may be many other gender blind languages and the claim that language is a universal patriarchal structure should be used with caution. However, the non-patriarchal structure of a language does not guarantee the non-patriarchal nature of a social system which uses that language.

The French feminists, notably Irigaray (1985), argue for the revival of an essential femininity that has been repressed. Irigaray suggests that women should completely reject the patriarchal rationality so alien to them. She and others like Kristeva (1986) and Cixous (1981) glorify things to do with women and assert that masculine culture and rationality, while dominant, is not a superior way of being. However, by rejecting rationality as the French feminists suggest, women could not hope to infiltrate the rational public life which is at present predominantly male. Furthermore, if we endorse the lack of rationality as an essentially feminine trait, how do women hope to make inroads into scientific fields?!

The post-structuralist and post-modernist model analyzes culture as 'ways of life' and 'resistances' with numerous sub-cultures. Postmodern debates have dominated the social science and cultural fields for the past two decades. Postmodernism follows the era of modernity which was ushered in by Descartes and the Enlightenment philosophers, when Reason was considered to be the source of knowledge and the key for human progress. Modernity emerged in everyday life through new technologies, means of communication, transport, mass consumption, modern art. The post-structuralists' approach to gendered subjectivity and culture concentrates on difference (following Derrida, 1976, 1981) and discourse (Foucault, 1981; Rabinow, 1984). They focus on forms of and nuances of representation of gender in cultural contexts such as film, literature and media. Foucault looks at institutions and is concerned about the operation of power in the construction of subjectivity. He believes that we can only understand the world through our ideas about it and it is, therefore, impossible to gain pure insight into the reality of society simply because what we perceive of it is structured by existing discursive arguments. When challenging prevailing ideas, feminists have to challenge the institutions that constitute the power base of those particular discourses and which, through their practices, justify the exclusion of women.

Psychoanalytic theory is another approach to gendered subjectivity. While Freud's original position on women is widely believed to be misogynist and biologistic as epitomized by his phrase 'anatomy is destiny', some feminists (Mitchell, 1975; Chodorow, 1978) have tried to rescue those elements they deem useful for feminist theory, from Freud's theorization of sex: Chodorow identifies the reproduction of mothering as the key to understanding the differentiation in male and female subjectivities and women's oppression. At some point in the process of growing up, Chodorow explains, boys have to sever emotionally from their loving mothers in order to identify with their distant father and become masculine. Girls never have to go through this traumatic break and they grow into nurturing adults with the capacity to mother children themselves. Mitchell sees the ideology of patriarchy as deeply entrenched in people's culture and unconscious.

The culturalists, identified with the Centre for Contemporary Cultural Studies at the University of Birmingham and characterized by their interdisciplinary fields of research along with relatively leftist ideological orientation, have used different models of culture which shift away from the orthodox Marxist assumption of the mechanistic economic determinism (Franklin et al., 1991; Hall and du Gay, 1996). The breakdown of the historical distinction between high and popular culture brought about by post-structuralism, the feminist concerns addressing identity, subjectivity and sexuality, the theories of ethnicity and racism have all contributed to developments within cultural studies. In short, due to the influence of critical theory, psychoanalysis, post-structuralism and post-modernism and especially Foucault's discourse theory, cultural studies have introduced new challenges to the traditional understandings of culture. These include:

- A model of culture derived from Marxist Althusserian framework which emphasizes the cultural within Marxist frameworks but does not go far enough to address feminist issues such as unequal power relations within sexuality, reproduction and violence.
- A model of culture that has its origins in structuralism and has two strands. One strand is influenced by the work of Claude Levi-Strauss. It takes sexual difference and sexual division of labour for granted and thus establishes patriarchy as natural. The second strand, influenced by the work of Ferdinand de Saussure (who had proposed a structural analysis of language as a system of signs) emphasizes that meaning is understood in relation to other signs rather than referring to existing objects.
- A third model of culture inspired by post-structuralism, understands culture in terms of ways of life (e.g. working class as opposed to bourgeois), subcultures, resistances.

Finally, Walby (1990) argues that although there have been significant changes in the formation of gendered subjectivities, a dichotomy is still part of the popular culture wherein masculinity is more valued than femininity.

Sexuality

There have been deep and bitter divisions amongst feminist activists as to the role sexual power and pleasure play or should play in women's lives, as to whether sexuality is an instinctive drive biologically inherent in all human beings or socially constructed, and as to whether the so-called 1960s 'sexual revolution' has been really liberating for women. Some of the important issues tackled under the rubric of sexuality encompass the divisions between lesbianism and heterosexuality, sexual desire and freedom in pornography and in lesbian sado-masochism.

Freud's account of sexuality, according to which the sexual drive underlies all other social constructs, is biologically deterministic. He argues that boys and girls are initially attracted to their mothers, but at some stage in their development boys sever this tie due to their fear of castration by their fathers. Girls break off, driven by 'penis envy' translated into the desire for a child which only a man can give them. As for homosexuality, Freud believes that all people were originally bisexual only becoming heterosexual during the course of 'normal' development. I argue that Freud's suppositions are based mainly on Western mythology rather than scientific falsifiable research. Inevitably, his conclusions are Eurocentric (Eysenck, 1986; Gellner, 1988). Furthermore, why should women have 'penis envy' as opposed to men having 'womb envy' in their desire for a child that only a woman can give them? And again, how can 'normal' development be universally defined?

Symbolic Interactionists, on the other hand, consider sexuality as being a social rather than an instinctual construct, and contend that there is no proper 'normal' path of sexual development instigated by an underlying instinctual force (Plummer, 1975; Jackson, 1978). Instead, they argue, becoming sexual consists of a learning process usually starting with adolescence and not at birth as suggested by orthodox Freudians. Within the symbolic interactionist framework (Plummer, 1975), homosexuality is described as a sexual development going through four stages: sensitization to the idea that one is gay, labelling by others, coming out as a gay and finally stabilization in a homosexual role. According to this view, the homosexual person can stop the homosexual behaviour at any stage before being permanently stabilized into the role. In criticism of this view, one can argue that the homosexual person can stop the homosexual behaviour at any stage before being stabilized into the homosexual 'role', but it is doubtful whether she/he could repress the homosexual feelings. Repression would of course be at a high emotional and psychological cost. The symbolic interactionist view does not account for systematic gender inequality in sexual relations and therein lies its theoretical weakness.

Foucault, too, argues that sexual desires are not biological essences, but are constructed as a discourse in relation to other discourses and therefore their meaning cannot be fixed. He further claims that the growth of institutional powers (medical, psychiatric, psychotherapeutic, religious) which sustain the sexual discourse, leads to greater control over people and greater repression rather than greater liberalization. However, Foucault does not address the implications of gender and class inequalities for sexual discourses.

The issue of diversity of sexual practices (heterosexuality, homosexuality, pornography) is mainly tackled by the radical feminists. On the issue of lesbianism, feminists are divided: the liberal humanists see lesbianism as a free choice for women; others see it as the only possible way for women to eradicate gender inequality. The lesbian feminists who call on all women to put an end to heterosexual practice, argue that it is specifically through sexuality that the oppression of women is maintained.

> In the couple, love and sex are used to obscure the realities of oppression, to prevent women identifying with each other in order to revolt, and from identifying 'their' man as part of the enemy. Any woman who takes part in a heterosexual couple helps to shore up male supremacy by making its foundations stronger (Jeffreys, 1990, p. 292).

Furthermore, Jeffreys theorizes sexual pleasure as the eroticization of subordination. She claims that women's subordination is sexy for both men and women and that is why it is tolerated by the latter. Jeffreys argues that women are constantly assured through powerful institutions such as the media or the medical, psychiatric and psychotherapeutic bodies, that they can be liberated in the public sphere as long as they remain traditional and passive in the bedroom. In Britain, these radical ideas were first put into writing in 1979, in the 'Political Lesbian' paper published by the Leeds Revolutionary Feminist Group. The writers attracted tremendous hostility, were accused of 'telling women what to do' and became characterized as 'authoritarian cadres'. The attacks originated from non-feminists but also from convinced heterosexual feminists imbued with the traditions and liberal ideas of the 1960s sexual revolution. In 1980, Adrienne Rich published her article 'Compulsory Heterosexuality and Lesbian Existence'. In this paper, which is less offensive to heterosexual women than the 'Political Lesbian', Rich compares heterosexuality to political systems of oppression like capitalism and the caste system, designed to produce and maintain a class of inferior status. Her paper seems to allow heterosexual women to continue their relationships with men while politically sharing in the lesbian continuum.

> I mean the term lesbian continuum to include a range - through each woman's life and throughout history - of woman-identified experience; not simply the fact that a woman has had or consciously desired genital sexual experience with another woman (Rich, cited in Jeffreys, 1990, p. 296).

Radical feminists are right to use sexuality as an analytic conceptual tool to theorize women's subordination and have posited the right questions. However, they have come up with the wrong answers. My criticisms of Radical lesbian theorization are the following:

- Even if women sever their sexual relations with men, they would still remain bound in unequal gender relations with their fathers, brothers and sons.
- The elimination of heterosexuality will not guarantee the elimination of unequal power relations between and amongst lesbians. Just as women may and do undermine each other over winning a man in a heterocentric world, lesbians might engage in unequal power relations over another woman. In a separatist lesbian world, the whole range of negative feelings and actions deriving from unequal relations of power would soon emerge.
- By abandoning heterosexual sex, women could not prevent the incidence of rape. It might even increase due to a vindictive backlash from the male community.
- If heterosexuality is all about power, why have gay men relinquished this power? Have they done so consciously? If so, on what material basis? Should we not allow for some biological considerations when theorizing homosexuality and heterosexuality?
- *'The concept of difference, institutionalized as heterosexuality, rests on a value system where one is superior and the other inferior, one is dominant and the other dominated'* (Jeffreys, 1990, p. 297). However, even if all women became lesbians and consequently all men became gay, the 'difference' would still persist between gay men and lesbian women. What guarantee is there that gay men would not then feel superior to lesbian women? In fact 'difference' will never disappear. It is universal and exists in sex, culture, race, age and education.
- Jeffreys does not explain the construction of lesbianism. How did lesbians become lesbian? Was it through biology or ideology? How did they escape the mechanisms of eroticization of subordination? Surely, not all lesbians in the world have access to radical-lesbian feminist literature.
- According to radical lesbian analysis, heterosexuality relies upon the prevention of bonding between women. This argument is ethnocentric because in some very patriarchal societies (e.g. the Middle-East), bonding among women is quite strong and in fact indispensable to the society they live in:

> By establishing and maintaining ties of support and assistance, women widen their social world and find compensation for their relative isolation

from the rest of society (Altorki, 1986, p. 118).

Another thorny sexual issue which divides feminists is pornography, including sado-masochistic pornography. Attitudes about representations of erotica have oscillated from acceptance to rejection over the years. Some contend that pornography and obscenity in the media are responsible for violent aggressive actions against women (Dworkin, 1981; MacKinnon, 1987). Others warn against censorship, which would never be totally effective anyway, and argue that access to pornography does not have any long-term behavioural effect on men (The Feminist Anti-Censorship Taskforce FACT, an alliance of mainly liberal American feminists). Andrea Dworkin (1981) argues that the consumption of pornography by men, in whatever form, is violence against women and is symptomatic of the way women are treated in patriarchal societies.

Despite the liberalization of private forms of control over women's sexuality and greater tolerance for alternative sexual behaviour, there has been a move towards the public control of women's sexuality: there has been an expansion of pornography inciting sexual hatred and abuse of women; and the sexual double standard still persists. Moreover, many ethnic women still suffer the most archaic forms of male oppression, thus being victims of both private and public patriarchy.

Violence

Male violence against women encompasses murder, rape, sexual assault, wife battering, child sexual abuse and sexual harassment. It cuts across boundaries of nationality, race, religion and class.

> A comprehensive analysis of available evidence indicates that rape, child sexual abuse and sexual harassment are perpetrated primarily by males. Furthermore, an analysis of the four most serious crimes of violence about which the police gather data reveals that nine males are arrested for every one female arrested. This male predominance must be explained not only for rape and other sexual exploitation, but for all other crimes of violence as well (Russell, 1984, p. 228).

As Liz Kelly (1988) notes, a vital part of feminist work has involved finding and introducing terms such as battered women, domestic violence, sexual harassment, incest survivor, that convey women's experiences which have hitherto gone unnoticed, unheard and ignored. There are several theoretical approaches to the analysis of male violence:

- Biological explanations of male violence have been generally rejected; however as noted by Caroline Ramazanoglou (1989), men are on average larger and stronger than women and they might use their superior force against women in societies where ideology legitimizes violence. Ramazanoglou's argument weakens when we consider that women could nevertheless show forceful aggression towards other women who happen to be weaker than themselves.
- The conventional liberal approach theorizes male violence as abnormal acts of deranged males whose own psychological development has been hindered by traumatic childhood experiences and disrupted family backgrounds. West, Roy and Nichols' (1978) account of rape are examples of a typical liberal approach to male violence. Within this approach, the State is criticized for its inefficiency in dealing with such criminals. Liberal accounts of male violence are criticized on the grounds that there is plenty of empirical evidence suggesting that rapists, for example, are not generally psychologically disturbed or come from disrupted family backgrounds (Gelles, 1972; Wilson, 1983). I also argue that numerous women have had traumatic childhood experiences; why do *they* not turn into violent sexual offenders as often as men?
- The Marxist account of male violence shifts the level of analysis to that of social structure and as such is an improvement on the liberal approach which accounts for violence as aberrant acts perpetrated by psychologically deranged individuals. Class analysis theorizes violence as the frustration generated in men who are at the bottom of class hierarchy. However, as noted by Walby (1990), it cannot explain why it is that the lowest in the class hierarchy, namely women, are not the most violent of all in society. Another version of class analysis is put forward by Amir (1971) who suggests that men in the lowest social strata develop a deviant sub-culture of violence, valuing machismo and physical superiority, as a result of their alienation from the main culture. The incidence of male rape, which is not uncommon although rarely reported, could be in part explained by the sub-culture theory. By 1975, Anthony Scacco argues, 'the sexual domination of other males had become a fashionable street means to show off one's machismo' (cited in Russell, 1984, p. 71). The arguments of the class analysis proponents are based on the notion that violent men are disproportionately drawn from the lower social strata. Walby (1990) argues that the evidence to support this claim is shaky: Pizzey's (1974) study reveals that men who batter their wives come from all social strata; Russell's (1984) research concludes that in the case of marital

rape, husbands were drawn from all social strata; and finally the

> majority of rapes are not reported to the police and those which are reported are more likely to be the ones a white police force in a racist society is most likely to believe (Walby, 1990, p. 133).

- Radical feminists argue that male violence is a form of social control over women. Susan Brownmiller, in her study of rape (1976), contends that not all men rape but the terror those few who do disseminate, is sufficient to intimidate all women. Thus women live in fear of sexual assault and may very well curtail their activities, night-time work, travel, etc. Other radical feminists (Hamner and Saunders, 1984) blame the welfare state for not providing enough resources for women to enable them to leave their violent partners, and they condemn the criminal justice system for not providing adequate police protection.
- Finally, O'Briens' (1975)

> examination of divorce petitions showed that men's violence was more likely to be cited if the husband was less educated than his wife, if the husband had a lower occupation than the woman's father, if there were disputes over the adequacy of the husband's income, if the husband was dissatisfied with his job, and if the husband had failed to complete high school or college (cited in Walby, 1990, p. 136).

One of the most comprehensive studies of sexual exploitation and male violence is the one carried out in San Francisco in 1978 by Diana Russell. A random sample of 930 women were interviewed in depth about their experience of male violence: forty four % of the women interviewed had been a victim of rape or attempted rape at some time in their lives (Russell, 1984, p. 283); 38% of the women reported at least one experience of incestuous and/or extra-familial sexual abuse before reaching the age of 18 years; 28% reported at least one such experience before reaching 14 years of age (Russell, 1984, p. 183). Such data do not exist in Britain and could be used as best estimates of the extent of violent crime against women in Britain.

Sexual harassment also appears on the continuum of male violence against women. Although males can also become victims of sexual harassment, women are more sexually harassed. It has been suggested that rape, child sexual abuse and sexual harassment are interrelated and although no major research has been undertaken in this respect, many adult males appear to act out their anger originating from childhood sexual abuse and traumas. The discernible pattern for women is that they appear to internalize their anger and usually become prostitutes, drug addicts or other victims (Russell, 1984). Due to lack of adequate data, it is difficult to measure changes in male violence. Both first and second waves of feminist campaigns have been instrumental in opening up legal (e.g. Sexual Offences Amendment Act 1976) and practical (e.g. refuges for battered wives, rape and incest crisis lines) routes of escape for female victims of violence. However, despite the State being the main arbiter and regulator of the level of violence, its inefficiency and infrequency of intervention indicates 'that this is more a shift in the locus of control and legitimization of violence than its elimination' (Walby, 1990, p. 149).

State

> We can specify the State in terms of a body of institutions which are centrally organized around the intentionality of control with a given apparatus of enforcement at its command and basis. Coercion and repression are then to be seen both as forms of control and as back-up. Different forms of the state will involve different relationships between the control/coercion twin which is the residing characteristic of the state (Yuval-Davis and Anthias, 1989, pp. 4-6).

The State has also been identified as that body of centralized social institutions which has coercive power, is patriarchal, capitalist and racist; it is engaged with gendered political forces, its actions have gender-differentiated effects and its structure is highly gendered. It does not have a monopoly over legitimate coercion since individual men use coercion and violence against women without any effective intervention on behalf of the State (Walby, 1990).

According to the Marxist-feminist analysis, the Capitalist State aims predominantly to preserve the dominant class relations and assist the accumulation of capital. This is achieved through upholding the structure of the nuclear family (the significant site of reproduction of labour power). The unanswered question is why should the State, in its efforts to fulfil the needs of capital, reinforce male and not female dominance and privilege?

Mary McIntosh (1978), in her Marxist analysis of the state and gender relations, points out the State's quasi-benevolence and non-interference in the exercise of criminal law towards women. She argues that

> far more men are convicted of crimes than women, and far more men are sent to prison and other forms of harsh institutions, and for far longer terms (cited in Kuhn and Wolpe, 1978, p. 257).

This contradicts McIntosh's other argument which asserts that the State does not provide any protection for women against violent crimes such as rape or domestic violence. McIntosh explains this contradiction by stating that, in the two latter cases the assumption is these female contexts are too private and personal to be subject to criminal sanction. This illustrates that the State cannot act as a coherent or a non-contradictory entity. The same institution (the criminal justice system) is both benevolent towards women and misogynist.

The radical feminist approach characterizes the State as a patriarchal body which institutionalizes masculine interests. Within this framework, the State is not central to the analysis of politics and power relations because the radical feminist theme of 'the personal is political' encompasses not only the politics of the State but all forms of gender interaction (sexuality, housework, paid work, conversation, etc.). However, in one radical feminist study (Hamner and Saunders, 1984), the State has been viewed as the instrumental patriarchal agency that through a policy of non-intervention in violence against women, colludes with men to subordinate women. This argument fails to consider the contradictory nature of State practices and the fact that the State should not be conceptualized as monolithic.

In contrast to the above approaches which imply that the State incorporates dominant groups and acts in their interests, liberal feminists draw on the liberal views advanced by John Stuart Mill and Jeremy Bentham and define the State as a neutral arbiter. In their view, the State is pluralistic, although different interest groups can influence its different institutions. Furthermore, liberal feminists believe that, through their initiatives, the State is the right vehicle to promote gender equality by ratifying legislation beneficial to women (Pizzey, 1974; Kirkpatrick, 1974).

Zillah Eisenstein's dual-systems theory (1979) synthesizes Marxism and radical feminism and contends that capitalism and patriarchy need each other in order to survive. Their fusion is at the level of the State which incorporates patriarchal interests represented by male capitalists.

Walby criticizes Eisenstein's theory on the grounds that it underestimates the tension between patriarchy and capitalism and the significance of feminist struggle in changing the position of women in paid employment. The State is both capitalist and patriarchal but

> the actions of the state should not simply be read off from the interests or logic of the system; rather, there is a degree of autonomy of the political struggle from the material base of patriarchy and of capitalism. This political struggle is important in determining the state's actions (Walby, 1990, p. 159).

The single most important political change has been the parliamentary franchise of 1918 and 1928; there has been an end to the legal exclusionary practices in employment (1975 Equal Pay Act) and education; divorce has been facilitated (1949) and there is the decriminalization of abortion (1967 Abortion Act) and contraception. However, despite the undeniable benefits of these transformations for women and their entry into the public sphere, their position there is not much improved: The equal opportunity legislation has only had a marginal impact on women's position. Female-headed families receive low levels of state benefits; there is an increased circulation of pornography due to the relaxation of censorship. What has occurred is really more a change in the form of patriarchal control (Walby, 1990).

2 Interplay of Religion and Ethnicity

PART I: RELIGION

Definitions of Religion and Major Sociological Perspectives

It has proved difficult, inconsistent and contradictory to capture the meaning of religion and the diversity of religious experience within a single concept (Hamilton, 1955). A sociological approach to the analysis of religion would examine empirical data, observing socially structured individual or group behaviour, categorizing and ultimately theorizing. This procedure alone would not, however, exhaust the understanding of religion and its symbolic content. Talcott Parsons (1961) speaks of the involvement of religion in three of the four general systems constituting human life, namely the physiological system of the organism, the personality system of the individual, the social system of the group and the system of culture. According to Parsons, the cultural values of society are internalized in the personality system, via religion as a central force. Hence a more accurate, working definition of religion would involve an interdisciplinary understanding of sociology, anthropology, psychology, history, philosophy and mythology. Moreover, with the spread of postmodernism and despite its rejection of all-embracing theories of metaphysics, the study of religion has become increasingly concerned with cultural diversity.

Most Marxist accounts of religion are based on historical materialism and couched in terms of economic interest, mode of production and class struggle. Marx described religion as 'the opium of the people' and suggested that it had a narcotic effect on revolutionary consciousness. However, the social opium theory cannot account for social conflicts inspired by religion and religious imagery of revenge, martyrdom and return (e.g. Iran's 1978 revolution). According to Engels' classical Marxist theory of religion, the dominant class couches its interests in religious terms and controls the means of cultural production through educational institutions. It thus insures that subordinate classes absorb the dominant ideology as their own and experience the world through the mental categories of the ruling class. Marx and Engels' alternative theory of ideology emerges in the preface to the *Critique of Political Economy* (1971), where it is asserted that each distinctive class possesses its own ideology giving expression to its interests and thus producing class solidarity. This theory appears to be in contradiction with the dominant ideology thesis expressed in *German Ideology* (1964) which regards religion as being an integrating social cement. Turner (1983) offers two solutions to this apparent contradiction: firstly, he regards religion as the mechanism that legitimates the privileged social position of the dominant class and gratifies the subordinated classes' yearning for consolation and revenge. The same religion thus fulfils the psychological needs of all the classes. Secondly, he argues that subordinated classes have split class consciousness. That is to say they simultaneously produce their own culture and absorb that of the dominant class which possesses and controls the means of mental production.

Turner criticizes the classical Marxist theory of religion on following grounds:

- It fails to explain convincingly the mechanism of ideological transmission to the distinct classes of society, thus exaggerating the degree to which the subordinated classes actually absorb the dominant ideology.
- It underestimates the power of coercive measures in imposing the values of the dominant ideology.
- It portrays the class structure as being a simple, dichotomous system consisting of privileged and under-privileged classes.

Durkheim focused on institutions such as religion, education, family, politics and the economy as basic functional components of society. He considered religion to be the most fundamental social institution, its main function being to integrate members of any society and generate sentiments of solidarity, belonging and common purpose (Durkheim, 1965; Turner, 1983; Thompson, 1990; Ashley and Orenstein, 1995). In 'The Elementary Forms of the Religious Life'(1965), the last major work published during his lifetime, he examined the totemic religion of the Australian aborigines, because they represented, in his opinion, the most basic systems of religious and social organization. According to Durkheim, all religions make a fundamental distinction between the sacred -violations of which result in severe punishment- and the profane being what is used in a utilitarian manner. From the study of the elementary religion of the aborigines, he then deduced the structural principles that link the sacred and the profane in more complex societies. Beliefs and rites also constitute magic which at times resembles religion. However, magic is sought by clients for its utilitarian properties, whereas religion is adhered to by a moral community. Religion is thus defined as

> a unified system of beliefs and practices relative to sacred things, that is to say, things set apart and forbidden- beliefs and practices which unite into one single moral community called a Church, all those who adhere to them (Durkheim, 1965, p. 62).

However, Durkheim saw the institution of religion, along with other social institutions, in a state of drastic change, bringing about disunity and social pathology.

Weber was largely concerned about the individuals' drive for salvation in the traditional religions, and the articulation of this quest with the practical exigencies of daily life. He suggested a causal relationship between the rise of Protestantism and the capitalist organization of industrial society (Weber, 1976). Weber rejected Marxist reductionist interpretations of religious beliefs. However, he based his own sociology of religion on social stratification and dichotomies of privileged and non-privileged groups. While regarding conceptions of a supernatural order as ubiquitous, Weber theorized that religions of salvation, compensation and revenge are only compatible with the non-privileged groups who have a sense of personal unworthiness. Dominant social groups, enjoying high social status and consequently a high sense of individual worth, are indifferent to religious notions of sin, humility and salvation. The latter groups are, however, well aware of the political importance of religion as a social control device:

> The bureaucratic class is usually characterized by a profound disesteem of all irrational religion, combined, however, with a recognition of the usefulness of this type of religion as a device for controlling the people (cited in Turner, 1983, p. 82).

Freud (1934) defined religion as the materialization of Man's need to exorcise his fears of the unknown and most particularly death. Erich Fromm (1934) defined religion as a provider of consolation to the deprived of the Earth, and relief to the privileged who might suffer from feelings of guilt regarding their superior station in life. De Grazia (1963) theorized religion as the ultimate projection of the internal child's need for powerful paternal figures. Barbara Hargrove (1979) offers an operational definition of religion:

> Religion is a human phenomenon that functions to unite cultural, social, and personality systems into a meaningful whole. Its components generally include (1) *a community of believers* who share (2) a common *myth* that interprets the abstractions of cultural values into historic reality through (3) *ritual behaviour*, which makes possible personal participation in (4) a dimension of experience recognized as encompassing something more than everyday reality- *the holy*. These elements are united into recognizable *structures* that undergo *processes* of change, development, and deterioration (Hargrove, 1979, p. 12).

In order to avoid ethnocentricity, some sociologists have tried to define religion in terms of the most recognizable functions it performs in all societies (Luckmann, 1967):

- *Integrative function*: Religion provides a unified system of meaning and a rationale for the structure of society and the individual's station in it. Through a shared re-enactment of rituals, it brings people together in their understanding of the structure of their world.
- *Reinforcement of social moral codes*: Religion bestows divine character and authority to social moral codes, restores equilibrium in society, is capable of provoking shared enthusiasm and provides a psychological sense of security in times of crisis and in hostile environments.
- *Latent functions*: Robert Merton (1957) distinguishes between the manifest (with intended consequences) and latent (with unintended consequences) functions of religion. Maintenance of class and gender and ethnic distinctions constitute the latent function of religion.
- *Political function*: Until recently, Marxist oriented social and political analysis had significantly de-emphasized the role of religion in politics. However, the religiously oriented political events in Northern Ireland, Iran, Poland, Yugoslavia and Israel exemplify the power of religion in contemporary politics.

One can also define Religion in terms of its structural universal elements: all religions are composed of a community of believers. They are based on myths and rituals, they differentiate between the 'sacred' and the 'profane', they constitute a security valve for human fears and frustrations (McGuire, 1987; Durkheim, 1965).

To define religion by a single, comprehensive concept proves problematic due to its complex and contradictory nature. My definition of religion is thus eclectic: religion is a belief system invented by humankind out of fear of death and the unknown and in order to establish material and moral order in a chaotic, incomprehensible and often hostile world. Its role cannot be determined by single comprehensive concepts. Religion is contradictory by nature and so are its functions: it has an integrative capacity and serves as social cement to unify communities, but paradoxically, it can serve a potentially divisive role in times of crisis and conflict. It reinforces moral codes, acts as a form of social control, advocates commonality, provides solace to the underprivileged of the world and at the same time maintains class, gender and ethnic distinctions. It can have a narcotic effect on the masses and be used by the dominant classes to dampen revolutionary consciousness, just as it can create dissent, and have revolutionary effectiveness in the hands of the dispossessed and the discontented.

Relation of Religion with Race and Ethnicity

Rohit Barot (1993, 1994) explains how the idea of racial superiority and races as fixed types, with their own culture and religion, first developed in Europe: Christianity came to be considered as the religion of the superior white race whereas Islam and Hinduism were attributed to inferior races (see Roberts, 1985; Mann, 1988). Religion can thus be implicated in systems of cultural dominance and enhance aggressive forms of nationalism (e.g. Ireland, Israel, Yugoslavia).

In the context of economic and social oppression, various ethnic groups have made use of religion and ethnic churches in order to provide centres of interaction in alien, racist and hostile environments. Multi-ethnic countries such as the United States and Britain are cases in point: the relationship of the specific communities with their respective churches has been noted to be dynamic from one generation to the next, depending on the socio-political position of the particular ethnicity. Thus, second-generation immigrants have been seen to distance themselves from their ethnic roots, including religion, only for the third generation to come back to religion in search of a cultural identity, in an increasingly meaningless mass society (Glazer and Moynihan, 1963).

In the industrialized world, the underprivileged members of society in terms of class, race and ethnicity have sought solace from their sufferings in a diversity of cults and off-shoot denominations. Such institutions have provided hope for people with minimal social and political opportunities, helped maintain their identity and served as a defence against dominant groups. The American black churches originating in the slavery period exemplify the mutual effects of race and religion: black churches made the miseries of slavery more tolerable and at the same time clandestinely developed ideas of freedom, equality and eventually rebellion. They stood against the racism and discrimination of the white churches and became an important bulwark in the psychological survival of black people within an endemically racist society. They provided their black congregations not only with solace and spiritual guidance in their search for meaning, but also with alternative social institutions. Such an alternative social structure was made necessary given the segregation imposed by the white social structure. Thus black churches began functioning as centres for mutual aid, professional business advice, group recreation, communication, socialization, education and welfare agency for the poor and the ill. In the 1960s, they played a very important political role under the leadership of Martin Luther King. Black theology has also lent itself to an interpretation of the gospel which is more relevant to the black ghetto than to white communities (Cone, 1969).

The Italian Church in Britain is another example of a functional ethnic church. Italian churches have traditionally served their community through a wide network of spiritual and material assistance thus strengthening the foundations of the Italian community and culture.

Religion and Gender Relations

'Gender ideology' (a belief system that explains how and why men and women differ) is instrumental in perpetuating gender inequality. This ideology is in part based on religious principles which vary to the extent they legitimize female inferiority (Saltzman Chafetz, 1990):

> Patriarchy is inextricably tied up with deep religious roots and ramifications, not only because of the widely perceived (rightly or wrongly) absolutist rule of a divine father -which must be rejected- but also because of the inherent patriarchal structure of all historical religions. Wherever one looks in the world, religious institutions are dominated by men. Women are largely invisible, or at least marginal to the public positions of power, authority and hierarchy. There are hardly ever official 'spokeswomen' of religious institutions whereas at the grass roots level women almost everywhere form the majority of participants in ordinary, day to day religious life (King, 1993, p. 23).

The frequent androcentric structure of religion and the disadvantageous asymmetrical treatment of women in religious teaching institutions have recently come under scrutiny and criticism. However, although historical religions are frequently misogynist in doctrine, the social and political positions of women differ considerably in societies and communities where different religions are practised (King, 1993, 1995).

Being embedded in religious systems, gender ideologies are typically inflexible and resistant to change. Major world religions sanction and legitimate male supremacy but at the same time provide specific protective measures for women, within an unequal relationship. They may be seen to symbolically reward women for their obedience and in particular sexual chastity. This symbolic idealization might set limits to women's aspirations and life projects and eventually come to be internalized and perpetuated by women themselves. They become resigned to the 'feminine' roles religion assigns to them (Daly, 1968).

The institutions of religion and family have maintained strong ties throughout the ages. Life cycle events such as birth, baptism, puberty, sexual mores, marriage, divorce and death are tied to some form of religious ceremony in almost all communities. Religion has traditionally provided moral and ethical guidelines for family life. With the exception of theocracies where religion rules in both private and public realms, religious ethical guidelines are usually directed to private morality, including the family's sexual activity. It is within this regulated private domain that religion has usually reinforced gender inequalities. By emphasizing the role of women as being primarily *wife* and *mother*, religious ideology often indirectly limits the entry of women into public life. By controlling women's sexuality, religious communities usually set their boundaries and reproduce the patriarchal authority of their moral codes within the family. Contraception, abortion, pre-marital sex, marriage, divorce, sexual orientation, even the dress code have thus come to be regulated by religious institutions commonly ruled by men, to the disadvantage of women. Since the 1980s there has been a resurgence of religious fundamentalism in many political guises, with disadvantageous repercussions for women in all cases (McDowell and Pringle, 1992).

As with all analysis of social data, gender has now become a critical category in the study of religion, its language, practice, experience and symbolism. This critical task implies the development of cross-disciplinary feminist theory involving a wide spectrum of religious studies, history and anthropology. Ursula King (1995) even suggests a tentative definition of religion as being

> something experiential and personal, especially in relation to the personal experience of women and the different forms in which that experience finds its historical and contemporary expression (King, 1995, p. 3).

Most traditional world religions are rich with symbolic ascendancy of the woman while they socially denigrate her and condemn her to a low religious status. Women usually occupy the lowest rungs of the ladder in terms of power and authority. Occasionally they may have enjoyed high spiritual and moral authority as saints, shamans, healers, nuns and mystics in both traditional and tribal religions, but they have never been accorded institutional authority. However, in primitive and non-institutionalized religions (shamanism, spiritualism) women hold higher positions of authority. None of the founders of the traditional religions were women and they are all ruled by an absolutist divine Father. The patriarchal structure of these highly institutionalized religions has relegated women to powerless and subservient positions. Mostly, it has excluded them from advanced learning and teaching. Thus, Hindu women were not allowed to study the Vedas, Jewish women were forbidden to study the Talmud and Christian women had, for a long time, no access to theological schools (Baker, 1993; Sharma, 1994; King, 1995). Weber designates monastic misogyny as one reason for women's low religious status:

> The fact that a prophet such as the Buddah was glad to see clever women sitting at his feet and the fact that he employed them as propagandists and missionaries, as did Pythagoras, did not necessarily carry over into an evaluation of the whole female sex. A particular woman might be regarded as sacred, yet the entire female sex would still be considered vessels of sin (Weber, 1993, p. 239).

The quest for religious meanings has traditionally resided within the realm of men, while women have been allowed to transmit androcentric religious values to younger generations through the combination of cultural and customary views (Afshar and Maynard, 1994).

In practice, the relation between religion and gender inequality differs according to the structure and nature of the Church, the political and social history, including the history of feminist movements, in each particular country.

The patriarchal nature of Christianity is one of the foci of this book. Simone de Beauvoir (1952) identifies the Christian religion and its Church as being one of the most virulent oppressors of women throughout history. She argues that for the first time in the history of humankind, it is in Catholicism and in the cult of the Virgin Mary, that the Mother kneels in front of the Son and admits her inferiority. In 'The Church and the Second Sex' (1968), Mary Daly explores the long history of Catholic patriarchy and misogyny:

> The Judaic-Christian tradition has served to legitimate sexually imbalanced patriarchal society. Thus, for example, the image of the Father God, spawned in the human imagination and sustained as plausible by patriarchy, has in turn

> rendered service to this type of society by making its mechanisms for the oppression of women appear right and fitting. If God in 'his' heaven is a father ruling 'his' people, then it is in the nature of things and according to divine plan and the order of the universe that society be male dominated (cited in Schneir, 1995, pp. 262-263).

Daly identifies the women's liberation movement as playing a key role in overthrowing a culture which endorses patriarchal, oppressive religious symbols.

Thirty three percent of the world's population is Christian, of which around 900 million are Catholic and 400 million are Protestants. Women make up to 70% of active churchgoers (Ruether cited in Sharma ed., 1994, p. 267). Because of the various Christian denominations and the particularities of each society, it is an impossible task to give a general account of how the Church has shaped women's lives. However, it is clear that in every country, they constitute the wide base of a hierarchical pyramid. Since the late 19th century, the United States of America have been the 'pace-setter' for radical changes in women's religious status. American women won the rights of full citizenship in 1921 but it was not until 1956 that two major Protestant denominations, Methodist and Presbyterian, changed their regulations with regard to women's ordination (McGuire, 1987). In time, other Protestant churches from all over the world followed suit, until in November 1992 the Church of England itself finally voted for the ordination of women (McCutcheon, 1996). The Roman Catholic and Orthodox Churches have so far strongly resisted granting equal religious rights to women.

Catholicism, Protestantism and Gender

There are doctrinal differences between Catholicism and Protestantism with implications for gender issues and patriarchy. Thus in Britain, the patriarchal system of a Catholic ethnic community (the Italian community) differs with that of the mainstream Protestant majority. It is noted that not all Catholics in Britain are Italians and not all Britons are Protestant. Nevertheless, Protestantism is the established state religion in Britain and it has fundamentally shaped the British culture and way of life. In the United Kingdom, in 1995, there were 2.0 million formally registered Catholics and 4.1 million members of the Protestant Churches (Social Trends, 1997, p. 224). Since the Reformation led by Martin Luther in the 16th century, a great many Protestant denominations have been formed throughout the world (McGuire, 1987). These hold a wide spectrum of theological beliefs which are sometimes mutually exclusive. A detailed study of the various denominations and their beliefs is outside the scope of the present book and the emphasis will be on the Church of England, which is the official English State denomination. The Church of England is the mother church of the Anglican Communion. It originated from the conflicts between the State and the Roman Catholic Church, in the Tudor period. Luther's ideas of Reformation had reached England from the Continent; people resented papal taxes and submission to a distant Italian Pontiff; circumstances were ripe for schisms that were to shatter the unity of Christendom. The Act of Supremacy issued by Henry VIII in 1534 declared the Monarch to be the Supreme Head of the Church in England. Under Elizabeth I, the Church of England separated definitively from papal authority which had been restored during the brief reign of Mary Tudor (1553-58). There is no single authority linking the independent churches of the Anglican Communion throughout the world, although all recognize the leadership of the Archbishop of Canterbury (Whitaker's Almanack, 1995). The Church of England is Protestant and reformed and it is often called a comprehensive Church because of the wide range of theological positions it represents. The most radical are the Evangelicals who consider themselves the heirs of the 16th century reformers. Their central doctrinal tenet is access to God without the mediation of a priest. They recognize only two sacraments, namely Baptism and Holy Communion. Anglo-Catholics, as their name suggests, are closer to Roman Catholics. They emphasize tradition, ritual and the central place of the priest as dispenser of grace through the seven sacraments. The liberals lie somewhere in the middle; they generally have looser concerns about doctrine and practice, including ordination of women, and adapt more easily to the cultural norms of society (McGuire, 1987; Barr-Hamilton, 1996; Hawkes, 1996; McCutcheon, 1996).

Doctrine in Catholicism and Protestantism

Doctrine is defined as the law of God, that which cannot be changed. The most outstanding doctrinal disagreements between the Roman Catholic Church and most Protestant churches including the Church of England concern 1) Papal supremacy, authority and infallibility 2) the Marian dogma 3) The Sacrifice of the Mass and the Trans-Substantiation, which is the transformation of bread and wine into the Body and the Blood of Christ 4) The number of the sacraments (McCutcheon, 1996).

The Second Vatican Council, inaugurated by Pope John XXIII in 1962, introduced reforms in canon law or practice of the Catholic religion.

Examples are: performing mass in the vernacular, priests facing the people when saying Mass, allowing altar girls and women to distribute communion, encouraging ecumenism (Daly, 1982; McCutcheon, 1996). However, the Council did not introduce any changes on doctrinal matters.

Canon Law and Gender Issues

All Christian churches differ on canon law, to a greater or lesser degree. For Catholics, practice consists of the ecclesiastical laws laid down by the Catholic Church and ultimately the Pope. For Protestants, practice is the way Christians interpret the Bible.

Regarding gender issues (marriage, divorce, contraception, abortion, ordination of women, homosexuality) the official practice of both the Catholic and Protestant churches is in many instances similar. Both religions advocate the sanctity of marriage and condemn pre-marital sex, homosexual acts and abortion. However, the Protestant religion provides the believer with a wider space for individual practice (Hargrove, 1979; Barr-Hamilton, 1996). Feminists and both Catholic and Protestant Churches have been engaged for decades in debates over these gender issues and their patriarchal nature.

Marriage and Divorce

Marriage is a sacrament in Catholicism. In the Encyclical Letter of Pius XI, Christian marriage is so described:

> Let us recall this immutable, inviolable, and fundamental truth: matrimony was not instituted or re-established by men but by God; not men, but God, the author of nature, and Christ our Lord, the Restorer of nature, provided marriage with its laws, confirmed it, and elevated it; and consequently those laws can in no way be subject to human wills or to any contrary pact made even by the contracting parties themselves. This is the teaching of the Church; it is the solemnly defined doctrine of the Council of Trent, which uses the words of Holy Scripture to proclaim and establish that the perpetual indissolubility of the marriage bond, its unity and its stability, derive from God Himself (cited in Fletcher, 1970, p. 23).

Although the Anglican church does not officially recognize divorce, there are variations in attitude amongst Anglican clergymen as to blessing the marriages of divorced partners (Frank, 1967).

Contraception

Pope Pius XI, in his Casti Connubii encyclical (1930), re-affirmed the uninterrupted Christian tradition

> that any use of matrimony whatsoever in the exercise of which the act is deprived, by human interference, of its natural power to procreate life, is an offence against the law of God and of nature, and those who commit it are guilty of a grave sin (cited in McReavy, 1968, p. 2).

In 1930, the Lambeth Conference of Anglican bishops, which has considerable moral authority but cannot legislate as the Pope can, reversed its previous disapproval of contraception (McReavy, 1968):

> It must be recognized that there is in the Catholic Church a very strong tradition that the use of preventive methods is in all cases unlawful for a Christian. We acknowledge the weight of that testimony, but we are unable to accept that tradition as necessarily final. It must be admitted that it is not founded on any directions given in the New Testament. It has not behind it the authority of any Ecumenical Council of the Church ...... In our judgement the question which they should put to themselves is this: Would conception be for any reason wrong? If it would clearly be wrong, and if there is good moral reason why the way of abstinence should not be followed, we cannot condemn the use of scientific methods to prevent conception, which are thoughtfully and conscientiously adopted (Lambeth Conference Report, 1930, pp. 90-91).

Abortion

Abortion is strongly condemned in Christianity. However, in Catholicism, it acquires the rank of a mortal sin which could heavily weigh on the Catholic woman's conscience and would have to be expiated through the sacrament of Confession. In Italy where a Christian government, solidly connected with the Vatican, was in power for more than 40 years, this resulted in strict anti-abortion laws which prevailed until 1978 (Kaplan, 1992).

In Britain the separation of Church and State has made it easier for the government to introduce laws which dissent from the practice of the Church. Thus the Abortion Act of 1967 made abortion legal in Britain (Walby, 1990). There is no sacrament of Confession in Protestantism, therefore the Protestant woman is not overburdened by 'sin' to the same extent as the Catholic believer (McCutcheon, 1996; Barr-Hamilton, 1996).

Ordination of Women

Two major American Protestant denominations (Methodist and Presbyterian) began changing their regulations in favour of the ordination of women in 1956. The Church of England followed suit in 1992. However, the Roman Catholic Church has steadfastly refused to give into pressure and grant equal religious rights to women (King, 1995; McCutcheon, 1996).

Homosexuality

Both religions condemn homosexuality. However, while the Protestant churches and clergy, including the Archbishop of Canterbury, have consistently shown flexibility in engaging in dialogue regarding homosexuality and in accepting homosexual clergymen/women, the Catholic church condemns homosexuality as a perversion and a mortal sin (Barr-Hamilton, 1996; McCutcheon, 1996).

Divine authority is mediated differently in Catholicism and Protestantism. For Catholics, the Church, with the Pope at its pinnacle, is the sole interpreter of the Holy Bible. Religious tradition overtakes reason and the text of the Bible itself. Traditional Catholicism binds the believer to God through doctrine and the sacraments of the Church (Ashley and Orenstein, 1995). Thus the Church and the Pope dominate Catholic believers through the powers of absolution and ex-communication (power of the keys). Moreover, the Catholic Church appears to be unitary and not fragmented and the ultimate authority lies with the Pope. For Catholics, the liturgy was in Latin, up until the Second Vatican Council in 1962.

On the other hand, starting in the 16th century, Luther and Calvin's Protestant Reformation propagated the doctrine of 'the priesthood of all believers' and thus eliminated the need for professional priestly mediation, the sacraments of the Holy Mother Church and the Mass, in order to gain access to God. The Protestant Church is divided into a number of denominations. The plurality of its churches undermines and relativises authority. It is not represented by an all-powerful figure such as the Pope who holds the 'power of the keys'. The authority of the Protestant Church is thus comparatively diluted and decentralized. The Protestants have used the vernacular since the Reformation of Luther, giving their followers a more independent and rational interpretation of the edicts of the Bible.

The different mediation of authority in Catholic and Protestant religions applies also to gender issues: Catholic women are required to follow the Pope's traditional dictates unquestioningly. Until recently they listened to Mass in Latin. This, along with rituals performed by all-powerful male priests, added to the mystery surrounding religion. According to the Catholic Church, matrimony is a sacrament and thus indissoluble. Sexuality is permitted only in the sanctity of matrimony with reproduction being its main purpose. Human life is sacred from its foetal inception and aborting it is a mortal sin. Ordination of male priests is a sacrament and the Catholic Church strongly opposes the ordination of women. Finally, homosexuality is considered a sinful perversion. Disobedience and opposition to the dictates of the Church on such matters would be met by the threat of ex-communication and eternal damnation. Protestant women, following the doctrine of 'the priesthood of all believers', do not need the mediation of their church to establish a relationship with God, and they do not have the religious equivalent to the Pope. They have been hearing Mass in the vernacular since Luther. Matrimony, confession, ordination are not holy sacraments in Protestant churches. Women may decide on issues of divorce, sexuality, contraception and abortion using reason, their individual special relationship with God and their own interpretation of the Bible. In Protestantism there is no equivalent of the Pope disposing of absolute authority and exerting the power of the keys. Therefore, women do not fear ex-communication. The authority of the Church has become comparatively more diluted due to the multiplicity of Protestant denominations and their varying degrees of conservatism with regard to gender related issues; this has produced a greater lee-way for individual variation and flexibility. The Catholic doctrine is corporatist and anti-individualistic:

> The Popes of the last two centuries have so definitely condemned liberalism, seeking to circumscribe its effects in the economic and social spheres by indirect and direct encouragement of social legislation, and looking forward to the time when it should give place to a corporative organization of society (Fanfani, 1935, p.142).

Catholicism is antithetical to the spirit of Capitalism, the two ideals have always been in conflict with each other for the domination of society:

> Given the aspirations and ends of capitalism, the natural organization of social life in a capitalistic age is that of political and economic liberalism......Once the social organization has adopted the aims of capitalism, it adopts its standards of

judgement, hence its ideas of just and unjust, fitting and unfitting, normal and abnormal (Fanfani, 1935, p. 138).

The 'protestant ethic' on the other hand stressed individualism, self-discipline, thrift and hard work as the means to gain personal wealth and capital accumulation which would in turn signify God's grace and salvation (Weber, 1976). It introduced an element of rationalism in Protestantism which is lacking in Catholicism. Thus Protestantism has an elective affinity with liberalism as well as with capitalism. This liberalism translates into more rationality and flexibility regarding religious, legal and gender issues. On the other hand, Catholicism is less open to criticism and scrutiny, and more rigid, authoritarian, conservative, tradition-oriented, irrational and patriarchal than Protestantism. As such, Catholicism has also been less flexible than Protestant denominations when faced with feminist pressures first originating in the U.S.A during the anti-slavery struggles. It has doggedly stuck to its traditional patriarchal practices which affect women mostly in the structures of culture, sexuality and household production.

For ethnic Italian women, the interplay of religion and ethnicity adds a further dimension to gender relations. Thus Catholic British women's experience of gender relations in Britain differs from that of the Italians. Inevitably British Catholic women have been imbibed in the relatively liberal political tradition and the anti-Papal cultural legacy prevalent in Britain since the Reformation. In Britain, education has never been widely controlled by the Church. It has been far easier for British Catholics to integrate and assimilate in the fabric of the dominant society, than it has been for ethnic Italians. Italians have endured conservative political dictatorships in their motherland, an education system long controlled by the Church, and a degree of discrimination in the host country.

PART II: ETHNICITY

The study of ethnic minorities has been an issue since the early part of the 20th century as evidenced by the classic studies of 'tribal societies' by anthropologists such as Malinowski (1926), Evans-Pritchard (1954), Radcliffe-Brown (1959) and Levi-Strauss (1966). At the time, those isolated tribal societies were viewed as static and homogeneous units. However, the sociological analysis of ethnicities has undergone a huge transformation since the 1950s, due to changes in the social world:

> Ethnic and cultural fragmentation and modernist homogenization are not two arguments, two opposing views of what is happening in the world today, but two constitutive trends of global reality (Friedman, 1990, p. 311).

Definitions of Ethnicity

The various definitions and uses of the term ethnicity have given rise to a degree of conceptual confusion and polemic amongst social scientists:

- The word 'ethnic' is derived originally from the Greek 'ethnikos' meaning heathen or pagan. With the passing of time, it gradually began to designate racial difference and acquired connotations of minority sub-national units and racial inferiority, although majorities are no less ethnic than minorities.
- The Dictionary of Sociology (David and Julia Jary, 1991) defines it as 'shared (perceived or actual) racial, linguistic or national identity of a social group'.
- Yuval-Davis and Anthias (1989) have defined an ethnic group as a people usually having a unity of origin, whether cultural, historical or biological and a common fate.
- The concept of ethnicity has been used to designate differences in social, cultural and linguistic practices. These criteria are, however, not always sufficient to distinguish a 'people' as an ethnic group. To give an example: in a study of ethnic relations in Thailand, Michael Moerman (1965) focused on the ethnic group 'Lue'. He ran into trouble trying to specify how distinctive they were from other ethnic groups: 'since language, culture, political organization, etc., do not correlate completely, the units delimited by one criterion do not coincide with the units delimited by another' (Moerman, 1965, p. 1215). Individual Lues, trying to describe their distinctiveness, mentioned cultural traits identical to those of other neighbouring ethnic groups. They had no exclusive religion, language or customs. Hence Moerman's conclusion that one belongs to an ethnic group if one believes oneself to be a member and acts in ways that validate her/his membership of that group.
- It has been suggested (Eriksen, 1993) that ethnicity is a relationship rather than a group property. Thus, to be able to talk about ethnic groups, these must have a minimum of contact between themselves and an awareness of being culturally distinct.
- Some scholars (Isaacs, 1975) have suggested that ethnicity is a

reflection of 'primordial loyalties'. This argument has been criticized on the grounds that it assumes people have primal static and unchanging loyalties to specific social categories. Anthropologists such as Cohen (1974), Parkin (1974) and Patterson (1977) have demonstrated that peoples' alliances and loyalties alter according to their own best interests. Watson (1977), drawing on the work of Abner Cohen, adopts the 'political' approach to ethnicity:

> Briefly summarised, Cohen argues that alliances based on ethnicity function like 'informal interest groups' and are therefore best seen as political entities; they operate through the idiom of shared 'custom' or what other anthropologists might call 'culture' (Watson, 1977, p. 9).

I have defined an ethnic group as a people to whom most or all of the following conditions apply at any given time: they share the same cultural and historical origin; as part of their common culture, they speak the same language, practice the same religion and have the same customs; their common historical origin makes them believe that they have the same fate and that they are distinctive from other groups. In times of crisis, their loyalty and solidarity is usually directed towards members of their own group.

Ethnic groups may also be ranked hierarchically within a society: the hierarchy could be based on the biological attributes of each ethnic group, hence a degree of confusion between the issues of race and ethnicity may arise. The relationship between ethnicity and racial diversity remains a problematic one. Whereas at one time the idea of different human races was commonplace, today 'Race' exists mainly as a cultural construct without any biological basis, and modern genetics tend not to speak of different races any more. Some social scientists (Miles, 1982) have even suggested to dispense with the term as an analytical concept because the mere usage would perpetuate the legitimacy of an essentialist, non-valid category. The reason for this development is two-fold: the realization that human populations have incessantly interbred throughout the centuries, and the lack of clear boundaries for fixed hereditary physical attributes. Sociologists debate on race relations and study racism only because of the cultural and social relevance of the notion that races exist and personality is linked with hereditary biological attributes. Van den Berghe (1983) does not distinguish between racial and ethnic studies. Michael Banton (1967) refers to race as a categorization of people ('them'), usually based on biological grounds and ethnicity as a group identification ('us'), usually based on cultural attributes. Ethnic discrimination and racism are not always based on a process of racialization i.e. when social significance is attached to particular human features such as black skin; it may rely on the undesirability of alien cultures (Anthias and Yuval-Davis, 1992). Although discrimination on the grounds of race or ethnicity could be identical, it is undoubtedly more difficult for people with different physical traits to assimilate if they wish to escape their ethnicity, or to avoid discrimination and persecution in a racist society.

The relationship between the concepts of ethnicity and nationality is also complex. Nationalists equate cultural boundaries with political boundaries. However, ethnic groups transcend the artificial boundaries of a political state. They have no demand for a state and as soon as they claim one they become by definition a nationalist movement.

Race, nation, minority and ethnic group may at times be used interchangeably; the most comprehensive concept, however, is the term 'ethnic group':

> We see that an ethnic group may or may not be racially different from others in the society of which it is a part. It may or may not think of itself and be thought of by others as a nation. It may or may not be a minority. Whatever the mixture, or in the absence of these three characteristics, ethnic groups are distinguishable culturally; they are identified, by others and by themselves, as separate; and, in the fullest sense, as individuals they join in activities and share beliefs and aspirations that express their distinctiveness. Thus ethnicity is the most inclusive of these four terms (Yinger, 1994, p. 25).

The above definition of 'ethnic group' aptly characterizes the Italian Diaspora community in Britain. Italians are a white minority who reside in Britain without having any territorial claims, while at the same time maintaining solid links with their mother country; they think of themselves as culturally different from the British.

Major Theoretical Approaches to Ethnicity

Within theoretical discussions on ethnicity, two major debates are relevant: The classical debate between Marxists and Weberians; the assimilationist approach versus the hybridization approach. There has been an ongoing theoretical debate on ethnicity between the Marxist and Weberian sociologists:

- Some Marxists argue that it is the capitalist class structure which explains 'racial' and ethnic disadvantage. In other words, ethnic minorities, as an integral part of the proletariat, are exploited by the capitalists (Cox, 1970; Castle and Kosack, 1985). The ruling classes maintain their dominant position by capitalizing on the racially prejudiced ideologies that persist since the colonialist era. The white working classes blame the immigrants and ethnic minorities for their own economic hardships, shortage of jobs or bad social conditions such as inadequate housing, health, etc. The attention of the proletariat is thus diverted from the real causes of its oppression, i.e. the capitalist structure upheld by the state. The capitalists split and weaken the working class by playing one section against the other, i.e. the indigenous workers (both blue-collar and white-collar) against the immigrants who usually occupy the lowest socio-economic positions and are considered inferior by the whites. It is not in the interest of the ruling classes to provide adequate vocational training and education for the immigrants and their children; thus supplies of cheap, unskilled labour remain constant through generations of disadvantaged immigrants (Castle and Kosack, 1985). However, it would be a mistake to consider the Marxist position as a monolithic set of economistic reductionist set of assumptions. Marxist writings have been informed by a vast, heterogeneous spectrum of theoretical models, political arguments and historical analyses, including feminist ones (Hall et al., 1978; Gilroy, 1982; Gabriel and Ben-Tovim, 1978; Phizacklea and Miles, 1980; Phizacklea, 1983, 1990, 1995) which share the basic agreement that the problem of racism cannot be conceptualized as separate from the structural features of capitalist society, while at the same time acknowledging the historical specificity of different 'racisms'. They do disagree on the degree of autonomy of the class and race categories. Annie Phizacklea's *migrant labour model* emphasizes the gender aspect of migration and introduces another layer of segmentation into an already sexually segregated labour market. She suggests that migrant women constitute a reserve army of labour whom the patriarchal ideology and practice categorize as primarily wives and mothers; they provide employers with a powerful weapon to crush organized resistance to exploitation. These women constitute a pool of

> young, female, rural migrants 'reproduced' outside of the confines of the capitalist sector but whose productivity equals or exceeds that of their counterparts in the advanced industrial nations. This development has been described as the migration of capital to labour as opposed to the migration of labour to capital (Phizacklea, 1983, p. 4).

Within the host country, migrant women are caught at the intersection of gender and racial subordination.

- The Weberians argue that competition for scarce resources such as employment, health, housing and education services leads to racial disadvantage among social groups. In other words, identifiable physical or social characteristics of certain ethnic minorities are seized upon by competitive white groups in order to apply social closure and thus exclusion from obtaining scarce social resources. This argument, however, does not theorize the reasons why certain characteristics of particular ethnic groups are seized upon to lead to social exclusion. John Rex, a Weberian, summarizes the complementary position of ethnicity debates with these words:

  > Class theory taken by itself does have considerable limitations. There may be purely ethnic situations where there is no conflict of class interest. People may be assigned to class positions on the basis of racial and ethnic markers. And, finally, the formation of classes-for-themselves may be greatly facilitated by, if it does not actually require, something like ethnic bonding. But to make these points is by no means to say that the elements which are given centrality in class theory, namely the relationship of groups to the means of production and to the control of political and legal power, are not among the most important in the theory of race and ethnic relations (Rex, 1986, p. 81).

  Thus, the Marxist and Weberian positions need not be opposed to each other. In the advanced industrialized societies, especially those with a colonial past, the capitalist class structure creates a relatively attractive labour market for ethnic migrants who are then subjected to institutionalized state discrimination and racism from a white population educated in the colonialist culture.

The Assimilationist Approach

With the political upheavals following the Second World War and the creation of post-colonial states, many of those formerly isolated tribes came into contact with each other and with the international society. Some have continued to develop into nationalist movements. Many members of ethnic groups have migrated from the countryside to metropolitan areas within their own state. Some have migrated from developing countries to Europe and North America. They have come into contact with foreign cultures and been constrained to compete in political and labour markets, sometimes in potentially hostile environments. Regrouping as ethnic minorities in foreign environments and developing social networks provides material and spiritual security and has become the norm all over the world. Previously, ethnicity, gender and religion were theorized as concepts pertaining to 'traditional societies' and did not figure in most accounts of advanced capitalist and socialist societies. However, ambiguous, complex and highly dynamic ethnic groupings have, since the 1950s and 1960s, become a focus of interest for sociologists and anthropologists, hence the notion of ethnicity as a modern phenomena (Glazer and Moynihan, 1963; Cohen, 1974; Isaacs, 1975; Watson, 1975; Yinger, 1994; Smith, 1996).

With the growth of migrant labour in practically all nation-states, ethnic differences have become so visible that it is impossible to ignore them. There has been an explosion of both violent and peaceful ethnic movements all over the world since the Second World War (e.g. ex-European colonies, ex-Soviet Union, Yugoslavia, Canada). Western Europe, where countries are moving towards closer economic, political and cultural integration, is an exception. Sometimes second or third generations of some ethnic groups become assimilated into their host nation. *Assimilation* is defined as a

> process of boundary reduction that can occur when members of two or more societies, ethnic groups or smaller social groups meet. It is a variable, not an attribute (Yinger, 1994, p. 39).

When the process is carried to completion, an assimilated ethnic population is defined operationally as

> a group of persons with similar foreign origins, knowledge of which in no way gives a better prediction or estimation of their relevant social characteristics than does knowledge of the behaviour of the total population of the community or nation involved (Lieberson, 1963, cited in Yinger, 1994, p. 39).

According to Yinger (1994), four separate but interdependent sub-processes constitute Assimilation and determine its extent:

- *Integration*: a process of impersonal contact and interaction within political and economic institutions.
- *Acculturation*: a process of greater cultural similarity between the dominant and the ethnic groups.
- *Identification*: a psychological process whereby individuals from distinctive origins come to share feelings of belonging to the same society.

- *Amalgamation*: when a blurring of genetic distinctions has taken place through extensive inter-marriage.

Assimilation would be hastened when immigrant groups are small, long-term residents and residentially scattered; their return to the homeland is difficult; they share the language, religion and culture of their host country; their biological attributes are the same or very similar to the dominant group; they experience little discrimination; their average level of education is high and they are heterogeneous in class and occupation (Yinger, 1994).

However, the process of assimilation is rarely complete. In their influential study of ethnicity in the United States, Glazer and Moynihan (1963) claim that the celebrated 'American Melting-Pot' never happened and instead Americans continue to use their ethnic networks for social, spiritual and cultural needs. They routinely refer to themselves as Italians, Poles, Irish, Hispanic, etc. Thus, despite the social theorists' prediction at the turn of the century, that ethnicities will gradually vanish in the process of modernization, it is suggested that ethnic movements have in fact surged as a reaction to modernization and some have adopted political traits. Also, powerful assimilative trends are often accompanied or followed by renewed attention to ethnic cultural differences (dissimilation). *Dissimilation* is more likely to happen when the immigrant groups are large, residentially concentrated and periodically renewed; return to the mother country is frequent and easy; there are continuing primordial attachments such as language, religion and culture; their distinctive physical attributes create discrimination against them and they experience feelings of cultural alienation; they have a low average level of education and are homogeneous in class and occupation; there is usefulness in emphasizing ethnicity in the pursuit of power, status and income (Yinger, 1994).

The process of assimilation could, in times of crisis or a perceived great injustice, be rapidly reversed. Examples are the internment of British Italians and Japanese Americans during the Second World War.

In multi-ethnic countries, the particularism of ethnicity and the universalism of assimilation are characterized by both positive and negative aspects. Thus ethnic diversity can become a rallying point for freedom, equality and a source of fresh cultural input, valuable to the dominant culture. It can, at the same time, create ideologies that sanction violence, chauvinism, racism and patriarchy. A moderate degree of assimilation through acculturation and integration will help the harmonization of multi-ethnic societies. On the other hand, undemocratic authoritarian systems could savagely and wastefully repress ethnic diversity in the name of assimilation.

> In spite of identity shifts and high rates of intermarriage in some settings and extensive acculturation and integration in many settings, some ethnic lines will remain sharp and some individuals will think first of their ethnic group when they appraise their own identities. At this period in history, at any rate, it is not a matter of assimilation versus ethnicity, but of assimilation and ethnicity...... That society is most fortunate where ethnicity continues as a minor melody, serving as a counter point to major themes of individual identity on the one hand and identity with the larger society and the world on the other (Yinger, 1994, pp. 343-344).

The Hybridization Approach

The Marxist argument does not explain the persistence of racist ideologies and practice in the post-colonial era, in socialist societies and in countries without any recent colonial tradition. Racialized because of their colour and other biological attributes, blacks have come to be regarded as intruders into authentic Western national life. Paul Gilroy (1993) suggests that blacks in the West, having lived through centuries of colonial experience, stand between two great cultural currents that in today's world, cannot be called mutually exclusive any more. He criticizes the ethnically absolutist discourses that ignore the ethnic minorities' double consciousness and their bilingual, bifocal cultural forms in the post-colonial world. Such discourses view nations as ethnically homogeneous, and the minorities within these nations as mutually exclusive cultural communities. They are based on

> overintegrated conceptions of culture which present immutable, ethnic differences as an absolute break in the histories and experiences of 'black' and 'white' people. Against this choice stands another, more difficult option: the theorization of creolization, metissage, mestizaje, and hybridity (Gilroy, 1993a, p. 2).

Thus, Gilroy concludes, the conceptualization of notions such as nationality, absolute cultural identity and historical memory, which for a long time have been used to silence dissent and political debate, should be revised in favour of notions which reflect fluid cultural intermixture. Gilroy further opines that culture affects and transforms white culture and the two do not remain mutually exclusive in today's multicultural societies. White society has absorbed much of the black way of life as reflected in music, food, fashion and sport on both sides of the Atlantic. Spivak (1987) suggests that fixed identity claims are political manipulations of people. She provides herself as an example of a culturally hybrid product of the post-colonial world: Indian, living in the United States, bilingual, not in exile, not a migrant, critic of the U.S.A's neo-colonialism but at the same time not self-marginalized (interview cited in Landry and Maclean eds., 1996).

Although, as Gilroy suggests, black and white cultures mutually affect each other to produce hybrid people, the balance of the bilateral influence is not clear. Does black culture transform white culture structurally and institutionally, beyond the spheres of music, fashion, sport and food? The hybridization approach does not fully consider all aspects of the fluid nature of identity, and the possibility that changing social circumstances could alter the balance of hybridization. For example if foreign blacks are subjected to some great injustice in some faraway country (e.g. Apartheid in South Africa), the 'hybrid' black Briton might very rapidly reject her/his white cultural heritage and embrace black cultural ideology. The O.J. Simpson case (1995) provides another example: the case unleashed unexpected passions amongst all blacks, including well-integrated, wealthy middle-class ones, largely following racial lines, on both sides of the Atlantic. During any socio-political crisis, the dominant group can be equally quick to victimize the hybrid groups by emphasizing their ethnic heritage. Examples abound: British Italians, German Jews, Japanese Americans during the Second World War and Persian Americans during the 1978 hostage crisis.

Significance of Ethnicity for Theorizing Gender Relations

Contemporary women's movements have been instrumental in forcing social scientists to reconceptualize their previously androcentric theorizations. However, second-wave Western feminism has since been severely criticized for its 'white' homogenized and universalistic assumptions that the notions of family, culture, citizenship, sexuality, the state and the nation mean the same all over the world.

Black feminists (Amos and Parmar, 1981; Carby, 1982; Corea, 1990) have claimed that in positing their priorities for struggle on such issues as legal equal rights, education, abortion and critique of the family, white middle-class *liberal* feminists have not taken into account the particular experiences of black and Third-World women and their internal differentiation in terms of class, religion, culture and nationality. *Marxist* feminist theorizations (James and Dalla Costa, 1973; Barrett, 1980) have recognized the construction of gender through class and economic relations but have not integrated race and ethnicity into their analysis. They have thus overlooked the degree to which racial and ethnic differences alter the experience of oppression and subordination. The essentialist categories of the *radical* feminists (Firestone, 1974; Millett, 1977; Delphy, 1984) have equally come under criticism for failing to incorporate racial and ethnic diversity into their analysis. Radical feminists, by grounding their theorizations on controversial, unalterable antagonisms between all men and women, presuppose the existence of a homogeneous Sisterhood, and render minority women invisible. They fail to note that racism may align some women with some men against other women. With its emphasis on fragmentation and the idea of multiple selves and identities, *postmodernism* has dissipated the conceptualization of grand, rational and unifying theorizations. Postmodernists generally reject the existence of rigid social structures outside our pre-existing knowledge about them (Foucault, 1989; McNay, 1992; Ramazanoglu, 1993); as such they are largely indifferent to issues of race.

> The postmodern position is, broadly speaking, characterized by the view that there is no objective social world which exists outside of our pre-existing knowledge of or discourse about it (Afshar and Maynard, 1994, p. 15).

Much of feminist postmodern work is directed to challenge the hierarchical binary oppositions of western sociology: 1970s feminists have theorized women's oppression in terms of production/reproduction, economic structure/cultural representation, sexuality/motherhood, patriarchy/capitalism. Postmodernist feminists have abandoned grand, general theories which search for the fundamentals of social causation and have instead concentrated on the *'analysis of the local, the specific, the particular'* (Barrett and Phillips, 1992, p. 1). They have used the concept of 'difference' to highlight the variety of voices and meanings in women's lives (Sawicki, 1991). However, there remains the danger that pluralism and cultural relativity could give rise to the notion that anything 'different' is acceptable. It would be wrong and almost racist to defend certain prejudicial misogynist customs in the developing world (e.g. the customs of sati, clitoridectomy, purdah and compulsory veil) as cultural diversity, while knowing that such measures would be totally intolerable for white women in the industrialized world (Felski, 1997). It is the *black feminist* movement (the term 'black' itself encompassing a wide range of different ethnicities) that has in great part been responsible for bringing about the deconstruction of the category 'woman' and destroying the assumption of the unity of women's interests based on the 'white' experience. Black feminists have criticized both Marxist and Weberian theoretical debates on ethnicity for not having taken gender into account when theorizing ethnic disadvantage (Carby, 1982; hooks, 1984). There is now widespread acknowledgement that class, gender, ethnicity and race differentially affect social groups and that it is no longer possible to treat all women as a unitary category in social processes. 'Race' and ethnicity significantly affect women's experiences in the areas of employment, health, education and housing services and their representation in popular culture and the media (Bryan et al., 1985; Modleski, 1991). Black women are not only oppressed by institutions of state powered by white men, they are oppressed by both white men and women. Thus the main sites of oppression may not be identical for black and white women, and again they differ for women within different 'races' or ethnicities.

Role of Women in Ethnic Processes

Grand narratives of nationalist or ethnic theorizations have generally been gender-blind. Nations and ethnic collectivities have been discussed as part of the public political sphere from which women have usually been excluded. Thus the inclusion of women in the production and reproduction of nationalist and ethnic processes has been a recent endeavour.

Women have been described as participating in ethnic processes in five major ways (Yuval-Davis and Anthias, 1989):

Biological Reproducers

Women are very often used by the state for the purpose of reproducing racial, ethnic and national categories. They are the most obvious vehicle for population control. They can be encouraged to reproduce at times when the dominant ethnic majority fears a population decline of the 'right' kind. This is usually done through a combination of religious and ideological discourses (examples are Israel in times of slack immigration and Australia when its 'White Australia' policies were in force). Minority ethnic women can also be discouraged from reproducing, through forced sterilization and massive birth control campaigns by the dominant group. In times of war, women have often been collectively encouraged through both symbolisms such as 'mother of patriot, hero, martyr', and material incentives, to reproduce soldiers for their country (e.g. Fascist Italy and Nazi Germany;

see Koonz, 1987). The gendered character of state population policies affect women's health, their public and private life projects.

Reproducers of Ethnic Boundaries

Ethnic boundaries can be maintained by discouraging female members to marry outsiders. In the Jewish tradition, only children born to a Jewish mother are considered Jewish and in the Muslim community a woman is not allowed to marry a non-Muslim man.

Cultural and Ideological Reproducers

Women are seen as cultural carriers of their ethnic group in so far as they have the task of socializing children, transmitting symbolic cultural customs and keeping the mother tongue alive. Specific cultural codes of dress and conduct are expected from women.

Symbols in Ideological Discourses

Women and the safekeeping of their pure sexuality and honour, have often been used as symbolic markers of ethnic boundaries. A particular ethnic dress code for women (e.g. the wearing of the veil) thus acquires a huge symbolic and political significance, which can be transmitted on a large scale and with immediate effect.

Participants in Political, Economic and Military Struggles

Women have participated in national or ethnic liberation struggles at all times but have often been relegated to secondary positions once they have fulfilled their expected function. Examples of such treatment abound in recent world history: women's participation in the Italian Resistance movement, women's mass entry in munitions factories during the Second World War in Europe, and the Algerian liberation struggle. It is premature to herald the end of the global 'modern' era, but the differential temporality and spatiality of each society should be taken into consideration when theorizing gender and its articulation with processes of nation-building. As such, one cannot ignore the ways in which gender and ethnic processes inform each other (Yuval-Davis, 1997).

Italian Immigrants and Ethnicity

Many observers automatically equate 'immigrants' and 'ethnic relations' with non-European, coloured peoples, thus suggesting that ethnicity is merely a euphemism for race; they further assume that white minorities are easily assimilated and absorbed by the white host societies. Although colour-related racism is the single most significant fact of life for large numbers of ethnic minorities, the example of European, white, Christian Italian immigrants, with their slow rate of assimilation, their intense involvement with their own cultural and political institutions and their fierce loyalty to the mother country, flies in the face of such simplistic assumptions. Referring back to the definition of ethnicity in this book, one can conclude that the Italians form a distinctive ethnic group in Britain: their ethnicity is emphasized through the wide use of Italian language at home. Many second or third generation children attend special language courses partly funded by the Italian government. They have a common geographical origin and are conscious of having a common culture of which they are proud. Their political allegiance lies mostly with the Italian State; they feel it should be responsible for them and criticize it for not doing enough. They strive to establish socio-political ties with the mother country. The majority are practising Roman Catholics; the Italian Church and its various social institutions are highly functional. Ethnic Italians have been able to maintain and perpetuate a system of traditional social customs through numerous formal and informal interest groups (see Chapter 5).

Discrimination against white minorities could be less intense, subtly applied and in some cases barely felt by any white ethnic member. Although one must not forget that ethnic Italians did become the target of discriminatory hostilities during the Second World War they were interned and subsequently deported. Regardless of their class, the Italians' position within the British political and legal power system is not identical to that of the Anglo-Saxon majority.

The slow assimilation of the Italians has been explained by observers in different ways:

> One main characteristic of the Italian community in London seems to be an emphasis on cultural differences between Italianates and other Londoners. Many Italianates are convinced that having an Italian name may be basis enough for some discrimination, even if they are of British nationality and speak English as their mother-tongue...Integration of Italians into English society is very slow; it probably does not become fully effective before the third generation (Garigue and Firth, 1956, cited in Watson, 1977, pp. 252-253).

> Such liberalism [as that of British immigration policy], while it favours and accelerates the adaptation of the immigrant to the new society, functions strangely to permit and legitimise his foreignness. Not being made to feel 'foreign' the immigrant does not need to shed his culture. This is something which does not often occur, even within the Common Market. Here one is not ashamed to be Italian. Even those who were born [in Britain] declare it - and they have to say it in English! (Marin 1969, p. 17, cited in Watson, 1977, p. 253).

Role of Italian Women in the Ethnic Process

Italian non-racialized ethnicity is one reason why Italian women do not suffer much discrimination in the areas of employment, health, education and social services (see Chapter 4).

One particularity of the Italian Diaspora community is that British-Italians exist within two different state structures. None of these two structures exert an all-encompassing power over the collectivity. Italians live in Britain, see their future here and generally have no intention of going back to the mother country. At the same time they are culturally linked to Italy and expect some measures of support from the Italian State in exchange for which they will not break their citizenship ties. As such it would be doubtful that any of these two states could influence Italian women's reproductive rights and schemes by way of reproducing the 'nation' or collectivity. Given the relatively small size of the Italian ethnic community in Britain, its non-racialized minority status, and the fact that it does not in any way threaten the ethnic mix or territorial sovereignty of the dominant majority, any kind of manipulative control of women by either the Italian or British State is highly unlikely.

Most Italian women are practising Catholics. They generally prefer to marry Italian men; they thus remain within the Catholic fold and maintain the ethnic boundaries of the Italian collectivity. However, intermarriage is not infrequent. The fact that both the English and Italians are mainly Christian, white and European makes intermarriage an easier process than for other ethnic groups. Ethnic boundaries may loosen in the future if younger generations do not attach the same importance to ethnic culture including religion.

In the Italian community women are used as cultural and ideological reproducers. They are the ones who socialize children into the Italian culture by speaking Italian at home, by preserving social and cultural customs including culinary ones. They are responsible to uphold the honour of the community and as such are victims of sexual double standard.

Cohabitation and single motherhood are widely discouraged within the community. Again future generations may herald looser allegiance to ethnic social customs and as intermarriage grows, the role of Italian women as cultural reproducers may weaken.

Italian women do not seem to be politically active. From the beginnings of migration their main preoccupation has been to work hard in order to enhance the well being of their families. They have not been active participants in feminist or other political movements in Britain, possibly because they were generally not assimilated in the host country. Their reaction and political allegiance remain to be seen in case of a hypothetical political conflict between Italy and Britain. During the Second World War most Italians, both men and women actively supported Mussolini's regime mainly through financial contributions (see Chapter 3). Future generations of ethnic Italians will almost certainly become politically active in Britain.

3 History of the Italian Community in Britain

PART I: ORIGINS OF THE COMMUNITY

Size and Distribution of Present Community

According to the Italian Embassy (letter dated 31st July 1995), there are approximately 220,000 Italians in Britain, the greatest concentrations being in the South East of England and specifically the Greater London area: 110,000 in London and the surrounding areas, 30,000 in Bedford area, 50,000 in the Manchester and Liverpool area and 30,000 in Scotland.

History of the Ethnic Italian Community: from the Middle-Ages to the Second World War

The Italian migratory movements are quite extraordinary and unique in terms of their scale and their effect on host countries (Foerster, 1919). During the 'imperialist' phase of the Italian presence in Britain in the Middle-Ages, agents of the Vatican monopolised the British wool trade, the so-called 'Lombard' banks controlled the Royal Exchequer under the Tudors and a Venetian trade colony which minted its own currency, set up in London. With the decline of the Italian Renaissance and the consolidation of the British mercantile power, Italians began their journeys to Britain as 'clients' and in search of patronage. The cultural influence of Italy on the British royal courts and the elite was considerable. Numerous craftsmen and artisans such as glass blowers and clock makers, architects, sculptors, artists, musicians and scholars were summoned to Britain. In short, by the 18th century a small colony of artisans, originating from all over Italy but mainly from the North, was established in London, specifically in Clerkenwell. It gradually became a thriving 'Little Italy'.

In the 19th century, another significant migrant group, albeit mostly temporary, was that of the political refugees. In the 1820s, about a thousand Italian exiles whose nationalist struggles against the Austro-Hungarian Empire had forced them to flee, came to London under the leadership of the patriot Giuseppe Mazzini. They were generally well received within the liberal circles of the British society. The political refugees, and especially Mazzini, provided a certain leadership for the embryonic Italian community: in 1841 Mazzini founded the Italian school for poor children which was later closed when he returned to Italy in 1848. St. Peter's Italian church in Clerkenwell was founded in 1864 and took on a very important spiritual role within the Italian colony. Associations such as the 'Italian Benevolent Society' (1861) and the 'Society for the Advancement of Italian Workers in London' -the so-called Mazzini-Garibaldi Club-, flourished in the aftermath of the notion of 'Italianita' (Italian-ness), propagated by the exiled patriots in London. Thus, an infrastructure of impressive dimensions was created with Mazzini as a catalyst, in a Victorian social climate of romantic 'Italophilia' (Watson, 1977, Colpi, 1991).

The first waves of poor, unskilled immigrants arrived in London by the 1830s. They were almost exclusively male, came mainly from the mountainous Tusco-Emilian region, walked their way to England and spread across the British Isles. Population growth combined with improvements in medical care had resulted in a demographic pressure which, coupled with limited agricultural land in the mountainous areas of Northern Italy, left emigration as the only way to relieve economic pressure and extreme poverty. Throughout Italy, inheritance being based on equal shares to each child had resulted in the fragmentation of land and a reduction of agricultural efficiency. The majority of the poor, unskilled immigrants arriving in Britain ended up as street vendors, street entertainers (organ grinders), and artists' models. The last contingents of Italians arriving in Britain in the 19th century were the itinerant craftsmen who originated from specific areas in Italy (figurine makers of Tuscany, mosaic makers of Friuli and knife grinders of Trentino).

The Italians who came to Britain constituted a fraction of a larger exodus heading mainly for the Americas and Australia. It was through the process of 'chain migration' that most immigrants settled in different areas within the British Isles: whenever the pioneer migrants became permanently established in a given location, they sent for their relatives and fellow villagers, thus linking particular areas in Italy to specific Italian communities in Britain. Chain migration was either carried out through personal relationship i.e. when a pioneer migrant instigated the migration of his own relatives and fellow villagers, or through a 'padrone'. The padrone transformed emigration into a business by recruiting young male workers, mainly from his own village or region on an impersonal basis. He would make frequent trips to Italy, organize the whole emigration process including work contracts, transport, accommodation, etc. In exchange for a contract that offered work, food, lodgings and often a lump sum at the end of the agreed period, parents would send their boys off to Britain with the padrone. It was not until the late 1870s that the 'padroni' began bringing female members of the family over. This resulted in a more balanced male-female ratio in the community and consolidated its stability (Colpi, 1991).

Up until 1905, Italian emigration to Britain went ahead, unimpeded by legislation. The Aliens Order of 1905 reinforced by the Aliens Act of 1919, the eruption of the First World War and later the restrictions of the Italian government on mass migration of lower-class Italians lest they would tarnish the prestige of Fascism abroad, reduced it to a trickle, until after the Second World War when the thrust of southern Italian immigration began.

Origins of the Immigrants

The British census of 1861 indicated that most Italian immigrants until that period were from Northern and Central Italy, specifically Liguria, Lombardia and the Tusco-Emilian mountain regions. The Italian census of 1871 indicated that southern Italians made up only 15% of the total number of immigrants in Great Britain (Colpi, 1991, p. 50).

Since the emigrants mainly originated from isolated mountainous communities, the notion of 'campanilismo' (literally the spirit of the bell tower of the church) or localism was very strong amongst them. Customs, dialects and local loyalties, rather than national identity, set them apart.

Growth of the Communities

At the beginning of the migration and throughout the nineteenth century, Italians were mainly concentrated in London and it was not until the 1880s that they gradually spread out to other urban centres in the British Isles, setting up their own residential colonies everywhere they went. In London, by the 1890s, there were already two Italian colonies: that of Clerkenwell and the one in Soho, each with their own sense of identity and system of support services (Marin, 1975; Bottignolo, 1985; Colpi, 1991).

Occupational Patterns

In the 17th and 18th century, the highly educated and skilled Italians who came to Britain in search of patronage from British aristocrats, were well received because there was a growing demand in British society for their particular cultural and artistic skills. With the influx of masses of unskilled or semi-skilled immigrants in mid and late 19th century, Italians had to offer something exotic, distinctive and uncontested, in order to avoid hostility from the local population, trade unions and other immigrant categories. They engaged in street vending and entertaining and with the waning of the popularity of organ grinding, moved into selling chestnuts and ice-creams on the streets. In the late 1880s, in the wake of campaigns against itinerant street pedlars, and because of a more stable male-female ratio in the community, Italians began setting up family-run small catering businesses such as cafeterias, trattorias and ice-cream parlours. At the time, London was the greatest capital in the world; there was a growing demand from rich colonial officers and administrators, for new hotels, restaurants and clubs. Italians met these demands and became increasingly consolidated in the catering sector. A new generation of 'padroni' who would again recruit young Italians for nascent lucrative businesses, emerged (Marin, 1975).

The Advent of the First World War; the Rise of Fascism

Italy joined the Allies in 1915 and no conflict of loyalties was created within the Italian community. There was, however, a huge wave of patriotic fervour and numerous men returned to Italy between 1915 and 1918, to take up arms and defend their mother country. While there, a lot of these young men visited their home villages, got married and returned to Britain accompanied by their brides. There was thus another injection of female migrants into the Italian community. Due to the spirit of campanilismo, Italian families in every community in Britain fervently desired their children to marry someone from the same village or at least the same region, as they themselves had done. Second generation British-born Italians were content enough when their spouses were just 'Italian'.

During the 1920s and 1930s, the Italian community became increasingly consolidated as an integral part of the British society. Mainly self-employed in small service and catering business, Italians not only survived the economic difficulties and the unemployment of the Depression years, they prospered in many instances.

The 1930s saw the rise of Fascism in Italy. Mussolini's government turned its attention towards reorganizing its emigrants along Fascist lines. A huge propaganda program, both cultural and economic, was launched through the Italian embassies and consulates abroad. The main beneficiaries of Mussolini's largesse were the British Italians whom he most wanted to impress: children of the emigrants received generous Christmas parcels from Mussolini, and were sent on free holidays to British or Italian resorts; an Italian school at Hyde Park Gate was underwritten by the Fascist government. The immigrants of every class and occupation were invited to lavish Embassy receptions. The Fascist regime had very cleverly played on the nostalgia and sense of patriotism of the British Italian immigrants and scores of them joined the Fascist party and started to attend the newly founded Fasci (fascist clubs) in London and Glasgow. It has been claimed (Colpi, 1991, p. 88) that they were mostly unaware of the impact of Mussolini's dictatorship in Italy and Europe, and to the majority of them, Fascism was a form of patriotism rather than political involvement. On the other hand, there are those who insist that there was already an anti-fascist nucleus within the Italian community (Alfio Bernabei, lecture on 11.11.93 held at the Federazione Italiana Lavoratori e Famiglie 'FILEF' in Islington).

In November 1935 Britain introduced economic sanctions against Italy, which under the leadership of Mussolini was pursuing an imperialist, expansionist policy in East Africa. There was a frenzy of patriotism amongst the Italian community: as a gesture of support, people were sending in money to the Fasci and women were offering their jewellery and even wedding rings.

On the 10th June 1940 Mussolini declared war on Britain.

The Second World War

Since the mid-1930s there had been a steady increase of hostility towards Italians in Britain. This was due to the Italians' effusive demonstrations of loyalty to Fascist Italy. The golden era of prosperity, popularity, social progress and relative social integration that had characterized the immigrants' lives throughout the 1920s and early 1930s, was rapidly drawing to a close.

The night of 10th June 1940, anti-Italian hostilities burst open: throughout Britain, even in small towns where the few immigrant families considered themselves as fully integrated within the fabric of British life, mobs attacked and ransacked Italian properties, businesses and homes.

The following Daily Mirror article dated 27th April 1940, reflects the prevalent xenophobic popular atmosphere:

> There are more than twenty thousand Italians in Great Britain. London alone shelters more than eleven thousand of them. The London Italian is an indigestible unit of population. He settles here more or less temporarily, working until he has enough money to buy himself a little land in Calabria, or Campania or Tuscany. He often avoids employing British labour. It is much cheaper to bring a few relations into England from the old home town. And so the boats unloaded all kinds of brown-eyed Francescas and Marias, beetle-browed Ginos, Titos and Marios.... Now every Italian colony in Great Britain and America is a seething cauldron of smoking Italian politics. Black fascism. Hot as hell. Even the peaceful, law-abiding proprietor of the back-street coffee shop bounces into a fine patriotic frenzy at the sound of Mussolini's name...We are nicely honeycombed with little cells of potential betrayal. A storm is brewing in the Mediterranean. And we, in our droning, silly tolerance are helping it to gather force (cited in Colpi, 1991, p. 102).

One thousand five hundred Italian males between the ages of 17 and 60 with less than 20 years residency in Britain, were arrested on the night of 10th June 1940. The move was sanctioned by Churchill and recommended by the MI5 which had gathered a list of Italians, and earmarked those suspected to be 'dangerous characters'. The men arrested were from every geographical and socio-economic section of the Italian community. It proved extremely difficult to round up all Italian males fitting the description of potential 'enemy alien', especially in a large city like London, but in total around 4200 men were arrested in two weeks, 300 of whom British born (Colpi, 1991, p. 113).

In the confusion and chaos that the round up had created, numerous innocent anti-fascists, innocuous fascists and British citizens were detained and were soon to perish, while many real fascists escaped the net. A selected group from the arrested men was shipped to the Isle of Man for internment and the rest were put on board the ship Arandora Star, along with German POWs and German Jewish refugees. The destination was Canada. Arandora Star set sail on 1st July 1940, was torpedoed the next morning by a German gunboat and sank within 30 minutes. There was a loss of 700 lives, of whom 500 Italians. Of the survivors, some were hospitalized, some joined other internees on the Isle of Man and around 200 were subsequently shipped to Australia for internment (Colpi, 1991, pp. 115-129). The internments lasted for the duration of the war, after which the Italians either returned to Britain to join their wives and families or settled permanently wherever they were (Isle of Man, Canada or

Australia). The effects of the Second World War and particularly the Arandora Star tragic incident which affected a large number of Italian families in Britain, were devastating for the 'old' British Italian community and left an indelible mark of bitterness and disillusionment on the immigrants' psyche.

Post Second World War Immigration, the New Community

The old chains of migration were re-activated at the end of the Second World War. In addition, the mass influx of southern Italian migrant workers contributed to a fundamental restructuring of the community and led to the creation of a 'new' British Italian community.

The first group of new immigrants were the POWs who, realizing difficulties were awaiting them back home, chose to remain in Britain and take up work in light and heavy industry. A second wave of migration was reactivated through the contacts of the 'old' community (chain migration) and swelled the ranks of the caterers. The third and most important post-war group of immigrants consisted of masses of poor southern Italian peasants who came to Britain as industrial workers. Once again the 'pull and push' model fit the circumstances under which the new migratory influx took place. In post-war Italian Mezzogiorno (southern Italy), poverty, general social distress and literal starvation resulting from an inefficient and overburdened agricultural economy, brought about such a huge mass exodus that it has been described as the 'haemorrhage of the South'. The first waves of this category came not because they particularly wanted to settle in Britain. They came because they had applied to their local employment offices for work anywhere in the world and took up the first opening as soon as it was offered. Such were the economic and social pressures that, despite all the hardships and hostilities Italians had endured in Britain throughout the war years, they were still eager to come.

The post-war reconstruction of Britain with its abundant labour requirements, provided the pull factor for attracting migrants as industrial workers: through 'bulk and group recruitment schemes' and later through the process of 'chain migration' thousands of workers, both male and female, arrived to work in the textile industry, coal mines, foundries, tin-plate factories and most importantly brick making factories.

In the late 1940s there were even inter-governmental agreements between Italy and Britain for the recruitment of Italian labour, to fill shortages within the British industrial sector. Despite resistance from local trade unions, which eventually led to the abrogation of official governmental pacts, the system worked:

> No matter what the moral bleatings of politicians -exploitation, conditions, rights- emigration suits the governments concerned too perfectly for reform. Mediterranean countries, overpopulated, without industries, and never the most stable, must siphon off the hordes of unemployed (the younger the more dangerous)- or explode. For them emigration is a crucial safety valve. The industrial countries of northern Europe have prospered so efficiently that they have exhausted their supply of unskilled labour. For them immigration is the expansion of industry and the continuance of vital services- or, failing it, the collapse of both. The system works (Cornelison, 1980, pp. 299-300).

Between 1948 and 1968, a total of 148140 Italians migrated to Britain, five times the total number of those who had settled here over the entire period of immigration until the eruption of the Second World War. In the 1970s there was a period of return migration and 20% of the inward flow returned to Italy leaving a net immigration of 118558 between 1948 and 1968 (Colpi, 1991, p. 135).

The new migrants were almost all unmarried peasants about to become industrial workers in major urban areas. They underwent dramatic upheavals in their way of life. The most difficult times were endured by the single peasant girls who had been recruited for the textile industry. From their previous sheltered lives in backward southern Italian villages, they had been catapulted into factory life in urban areas, under harsh working and living conditions.

Occupational Patterns in the Present Community

The 'old' community members had already become firmly established in the catering industry and those who reached Britain through the reactivation of the 'old' chain migration, joined in without difficulty. However, often in mixed communities (the new industrial workers) where 'new' migrants attempted to join the rank of caterers, there emerged fierce competition and tension. It is only now, and thanks to second generation Italians for whom the spirit of 'campanilismo' is unimportant, that there is social interaction between the two groups.

However, in the 'new' communities, where there was little competition from the 'old' one (e.g. Bedford), there was again a natural convergence towards the catering sector. While the majority of the 'new' immigrants were engaged in industrial work, some first generation former industrial workers started setting up small, family run Italian bakeries, pizzerie or coffee shops. The Italians who have come to Britain since the 1970s and 1980s are almost all either language students or belong to the professional classes.

PART II: ITALIAN WOMEN IN SCOTLAND

In her 1986 empirical research, Sandra Chistolini has studied the Italian culture within Scottish society at three generational levels, Grandmother, mother and daughter. The cultural characterization of Scottish-Italian women would apply to Italians all over Britain. They have identical ethnic traits and there are no reasons for thinking otherwise.

The reasons motivating women to migrate to Scotland around 1960 were two-fold: poverty and family links. Women could migrate alone, after acquiring a work-permit issued by the British Ministry of Labour, arranged by their employer. Most ended up as domestic servants or unskilled factory workers. In other instances, the whole family decided to migrate, having been enticed and encouraged by friends or relatives who had already migrated and who came back to Italy during the holidays with their success stories. In some cases, the male head of the family migrated first, settled down in the country of adoption and then brought his family over. There were also young Italian men who went back to their home village and came back with their brides. The migrants originated mainly from rural rather than urban areas so their cultural baggage tended to be traditional and patriarchal. The decision to emigrate thus acquired a different meaning for men and women within the household: the man had to overcome financial difficulties, obtain a stable, well-remunerated and preferably independent job, and assure a brighter economic future for the children. His wife was responsible for maintaining the unity of the family. In addition to housework, many women spent long hours working as unskilled factory workers, servants or assistants in family businesses.

Characteristics of Scottish Italian Culture

Chistolini maintains that a solid pillar of the Italian community is the family, where fundamental values of the Italian culture are reproduced. The immigrant Italian family fits into the traditional patriarchal model. Within the structure of this family type, women play the role of guarantors of tradition and providers of a secure space for all family members. The primary socialization of the children within the Italian family is not overwhelmed or threatened by secondary socialization (schools, peer group). At most, an ambivalence is created within the immigrant's psyche but the family and its ethnic connotations always remain as the ultimate protective space. The persistence of this type of family system is in part due to the phenomenon of chain migration so typical of Italian immigration.

The continual influx of migrants from the same village (friends and relatives) has reinforced the rural-traditional concept of familism. Thus the traditionally defined roles of mother, wife, daughter, sister have been preserved by the first generation and transmitted almost intact to the daughters. Daughters are not only emotionally attached to their mothers but they also adopt their values, thus perpetuating the fundamental cultural traits of the Italian community. These observations are consistent with those of a study conducted by J.C. Bertram and H.U. Grunebaum (1981) within three generations of Italian Americans. These authors also observe that for Italian-American women, the main source of information regarding the upbringing and socialization of their children, remains their own mother.

Characteristics of the Italian Family; Way of Life

The family is the children's main agent of socialization before they go to school. An interviewee is quoted:

> You have to be a Scottish person and come here to live with us to really notice the differences... For example we stay at home a lot, the children are in the house a lot.... whereas Scottish children tend to go out a lot, go drinking, go to a pub whereas my children don't do that. Not because they don't agree with it, but just because it is not part of our scene (Chistolini, 1986, p. 193).

and

> We have also different standards than people in Britain ... (Chistolini, 1986, p. 93).

Both these women were born in Scotland. They are of second (48 years old) and third generation (24 years old) yet they refer to themselves as non-British and regard the *Scottish* as a different breed.

One of the most salient characteristics of the Italian family life is illustrated by the way sexuality is internalized through social norms. Religious women are generally less open to the concept of sexual liberation and transmit their own sexual 'double standard' to their daughters. Traditional familism is positively associated with a high level of religiosity just as sexual permissiveness is related to a lower degree of religiosity (Chistolini, 1986; Hobart, 1972). Almost all the participants in Chistolini's study approved of male pre-marital sexual experience while frowning on female sexuality. The following extract from an interview with a 23 year old woman who had migrated to Edinburgh from Central Italy in the 1980s, illustrates the point:

> Men and women are completely different. I will bring up my daughter as I myself was brought up. I did not know anyone but my husband until I got married; I gave the first kiss only to my husband. However, the male is completely different: he goes to the disco, to the bar with his friends. But not the women (Chistolini, 1986, p. 148).

The empirical evidence in Chistolini's research points to Italian women's negative attitude to divorce, abortion and contraception. However, younger immigrants who have a higher level of education and who have been born in Edinburgh, while respecting the religious sanctity of marriage and procreation, are more flexible in their judgement and leave a leeway for special circumstances (e.g. the mother's health). According to one 24 year old Edinburgh-born woman:

> I don't agree with it. I think in certain cases it must be there... I think personally if it is necessary to choose which is going to die the mother or the unborn child and, the mother has got more children to look after... well... that is about the only situation, I think, in which it should be allowed (Chistolini, 1986, p. 196).

First generation Italian parents have some influence on their children's choice of spouses but they admit they cannot always decide for them. There is a definite preference for Italian spouses with whom it is believed there is cultural and religious affinity. The concept of the traditional extended family is still popular in the community, especially amongst first generation mothers who believe their married daughters could continue living with them or at least in the neighbourhood. Such network of relationships creates an ideal structure to maintain traditional social control within the community.

Traditional Gender Division of Labour in the Scottish Italian Community

Chistolini argues that there is a net gender division of labour within the Scottish-Italian community: men work outside the home and women are responsible for the housework. Sometimes women work as assistants in their father or husband's shop and for some, that is a respite from the boredom of staying permanently at home. However, as soon as they get married or have children they tend to become full-time housewives. Within the Italian community, women's work is conceptualized as a vehicle to further the well being of the family, not as an affirmation of independence or self-realization. Women assume the responsibility for all the housework, and in addition, offer assistance at the shop whenever needed. Scottish-Italian women's position in the job market is thus sporadic and marginal and they have no working-class trade unionist consciousness. The job market consists mainly of family catering businesses (fish and chip shops, restaurants, ice-cream parlours, cafeterias, etc.). The reason why Italian women remain within the family business is two-fold:

- They appreciate the security of an economic niche whose success has been proven.
- Their fathers and husbands prefer them to be within control, in a safe and protected environment.

Second-generation women are distinct from first generation ones in that they are not dependent on outside employers for their everyday survival: they help in their own families' businesses. Rarely do they forget that they owe their present economic well being to their parents' enormous sacrifices when they first came to Scotland. This gratitude cements attitudes of respect and tolerance for parents and their traditions. The women's foremost preoccupation is to succeed in their role as wives and mothers.

The Italian way of life encompasses a wide range of concepts such as religious beliefs and customs, clear-cut gender roles and attributes, social customs including cooking, ideas of entertainment, choice of friends, etc. However, prolonged residence in Scotland, a higher level of education, loss of contact with older, more traditional generations, attenuate the more conflictive aspects of the cultural ambivalence that are inevitably present in every Scottish-Italian.

Most Italian immigrants long to go back to Italy (Chistolini, 1986) but nostalgia for the mother country is a defence mechanism for every immigrant in a prosperous host country. When the immigrant feels ambivalent and insecure, she begins fantasising about the country of origin as a haven, where life is rosy and trouble free. The immigrant conveniently forgets that if it really had been so, she would never have emigrated.

Italian Women's Social and Political Life

The majority of Italian women are at best indifferent to social and political public life, which they consider the natural realm of males. When they hold an opinion, it is usually a reflection of that of their male family members. This indifference extends to reading newspapers and keeping abreast of social and political events. This may be due to the women's insufficient knowledge of written English and Italian, lack of time or plain disinterest. Empirical results (Chistolini, 1986) show that women refuse to participate in organized cultural, social and political associations. This is perhaps because they exclude anything not immediately functional for the well being of the family as a whole.

The Italian community in Edinburgh controls the social behaviour of its members through established rules of conduct which everybody, but especially females, must respect in order to acquire psychological security and a sense of belonging. Open conflict between different generations is definitely rare.

The Role of Religion

Apart from its obvious spiritual functions, religion cements social cohesion amongst Scottish-Italian women:

> We Italian women would not meet each other or go anywhere had it not been for Father.... who keeps us somehow united with the Church.
>
> Once a month we get together after Church and have coffee. I also go to the Scottish Church every Sunday. After mass, we get together, and have coffee; we are a group of Italian women. I have made so many friends this way (Translations from Chistolini, 1986, p. 212).

Since 1983, the Italian Church has undertaken to publish an Italian newspaper, *Italiani in Scozia*, in order to preserve the Italian cultural patrimony. In short, Chistolini argues that: within the Italian community in Scotland, first generation women appear to identify completely with the rural-traditional culture of their mother country. Second and third generation women are rarely in direct and open conflict with their parents, to whom they are enormously grateful for their previous sacrifices; nevertheless, they try to strike a balance between the familism inherent in their Italian patrimony and the innovative space offered by the industrial host society into which they have been born. Reaching such an equilibrium comes with ambivalent feelings of 'double belonging': young people practically live a double life with their peers at school, and in their family which offers an indispensable sense of security. As such, the family plays a crucial role within the Italian community in Edinburgh. The role of the Church is also most important: Catholic tenets colour much of the ideological constituents of the Italian way of life, and the observance of religious ceremonies and rituals is functional for women's social cohesion.

First generation Italian women have been instrumental in creating the well being of their families through hard work in catering or in low-paid industrial employment. Outside employment has never prevented them from playing their major role in life, that of wife and mother. Many have gradually developed successful catering businesses and have encouraged their daughters to assist in the family shop. Most Italian women stop working for a few years when they get married and have children. Outside employment is seen as instrumental for the well being of the family and not as a means for independence or self-realization. It is only in the third generation that women begin to further their education, and economically break out from the circle of family business. The absence of women is conspicuous in the social, cultural and political aspects of public life. Italian women in Edinburgh have integrated economically but their emotional and cultural attachment remains mainly to the country of origin.

4 Comparison of Italian and British Social Structures

PART I: RANGE OF STRUCTURES

Gender inequality is the outcome of interaction between the three systems of patriarchy, capitalism and racism. Over the last century there have been major transformations in form and degree within British patriarchal structures. There has been a movement from a private to a public form of patriarchy. In its contemporary public form, patriarchal strategy is segregationist and subordinating and the main site of patriarchy has moved from the household to paid employment and the State (Walby, 1990). However, within the diversity of ethnic communities in contemporary British society, the form, degree and main site of patriarchy are not homogeneous. The theoretical starting point for this book is to compare the patriarchal systems of mainstream Anglo-Saxon British society with those of the Italian ethnic community.

Strong elements of Italian ethnic identity pervade the Italian community. Italians are characterised by an ensemble of distinguishable social, familial and sexual customs, ideas and behaviour which have been preserved within the institution of the family. Their way of life encompasses attitudes and ideas about gender roles and representation, the appropriate male and female sexuality and behaviour, particular consciousness and subjectivity. The Italian way of life is first and foremost influenced by the centrality of the institutions of Church and family.

Italian Identity

Survey data shown in figures below suggest that the majority of Italian women living in England clearly feel different culturally, and the Italian community does distinguish itself from the rest. [1] The majority of women

[1] In this book, frequency and cross-tabulations tables are sample statistics which do not cover the entire Italian population. The measurements are therefore relative rather than absolute. All percentages are rounded up to the nearest figure.

in the sample exhibit a high degree of Italian identity, they keep their Italian citizenship, speak Italian, mostly socialize with other Italians, preserve their ethnic customs and show strong loyalty to the mother country (Figure 4.1). Most feel culturally different from the English (Figure 4.2). Frequency tables show that a fourth of Italian women believe there is discrimination against Italians in the job market and about a third opine Italians are discriminated against in British society (Tables 4.1 and 4.2).

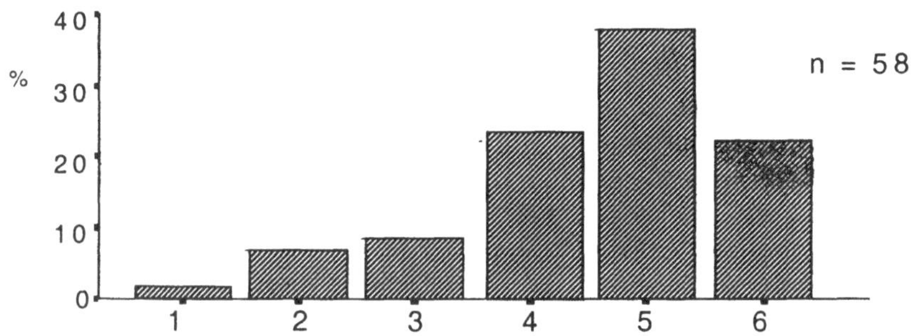

Figure 4.1 Italian identity

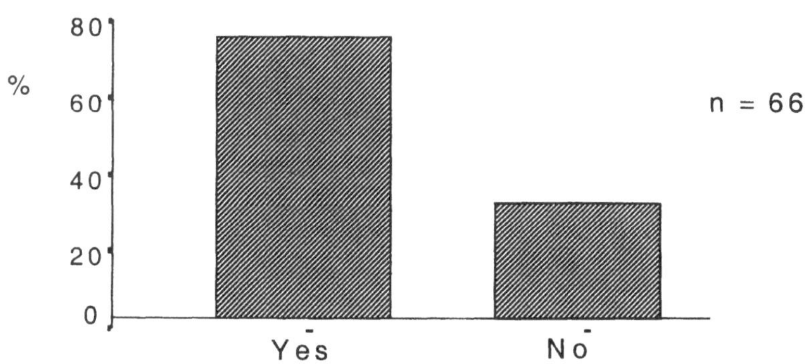

Figure 4.2 Italians' feelings of cultural difference

Table 4.1 Do you feel there is discrimination against Italians in employment?

Value Label	Value	Frequency	Percent	Valid %	Cum %
Yes	1	14	21.2	25.0	25.0
No	2	42	63.6	75.0	100.0
No answer	8	10	15.2	Missing	
Total		66	100.0	100.0	

Valid cases 56 Missing cases 10

Table 4.2 Do you think there is discrimination against Italians in English society?

Value Label	Value	Frequency	Percent	Valid %	Cum %
Yes	1	18	27.3	32.1	32.1
No	2	38	57.6	67.9	100.0
No answer	8	10	15.2	Missing	
Total		66	100.0	100.0	

Valid cases 56 Missing cases 10

The Italian community in Britain is strongly permeated by ethnic Italian culture. Most British Italians retain a strong Italian identity; they feel, and in many ways they are, different from the Anglo-Saxon majority. Some - a minority - feel discriminated against, in employment and in mainstream society. A different system of patriarchy applies to the Italian community with implications for the structures of patriarchy, the institutions they encompass, the form and degree of patriarchy and the main site of patriarchal oppression.

Differences Between the British and Italian Systems of Patriarchy

There is more than one system of patriarchy. Italian Patriarchy differs from British Patriarchy in 1) the range of its structures and the institutions these structures encompass, 2) the form of patriarchy in each structure, 3) the main site of patriarchy. Within the Italian community, the structures of employment, household production, culture, sexuality, violence and state enclose a range of institutions which distinguish them from the rest of British society. The form of patriarchy in each structure and the structure where women are most oppressed are also particular to the community.

Range of Structures and their Component Institutions

The six patriarchal structures as theorized by Walby (1990) do not apply comfortably to the Italian community. The Italians' cultural distinctiveness and their use of a mixture of Italian and British institutions distinguish the Italian patriarchal system. In other words, Italians are not strictly operating within British social structures, and as such do not exactly fit the same patriarchal structures which characterize the rest of British society. I recognize that British society is in fact quite differentiated in terms of its various ethnic communities (e.g. White Anglo-Saxon, African and Caribbean Blacks, Asian, Middle-Eastern, Greeks, Chinese, etc.). However, for comparison purposes I have used mainstream British culture and institutions as yardsticks. I have also assumed that all structures of mainstream British society are patriarchal, albeit to different degrees.

Employment

The pattern of patriarchal relations in the Italian structure of employment differs from that of the British society, in terms of: 1) place of employment, 2) employment status, 3) type of employment, 4) job category and 5) job satisfaction. Based on the women in the survey, the following figures and tables illustrate women's position in the Italian structures of employment, household, culture and sexuality. Italian and British statistics are subsequently compared.

Place of employment: on the evidence of frequency tables in the survey, half of the women are employed in Italian and the other half in non-Italian labour market.

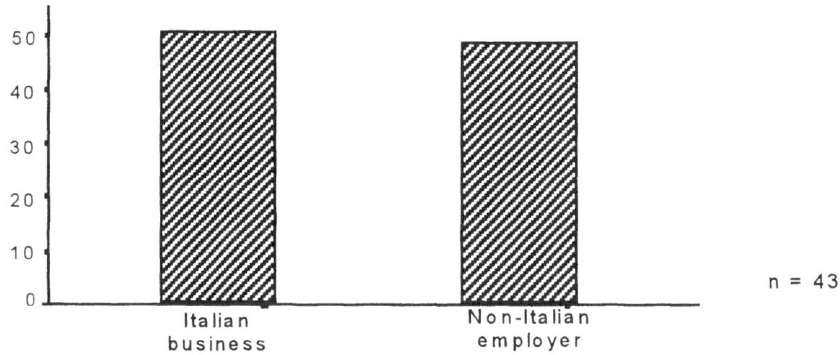

Figure 4.3 Place of employment

Employed women are almost evenly divided between Italian and non-Italian business. Italian women who immigrated after the the Second World War were mostly employed in family owned or Italian-owned, mainly catering businesses. In time they gradually moved to other careers, out of the strictly Italian employment niche (see Chapter 3).

Table 4.3 delineates the employment distribution according to age categories: from the younger generation sample (aged from less than 20 to 35) 9 are employed in mainstream British occupational market and 6 in the Italian niche. In the middle generation (36 to 55 years old) 9 work in non-Italian sector and 13 in Italian niche. From the older generation 5 to 75 years old), 3 worked in mainstream British market and 3 in the Italian niche. Despite the small size of the sample it can be observed from the table below that mostly younger Italians have broken out of the Italian employment niche.

Table 4.3 Employment distribution by age

Age	Italian business	Non-Italian business	Total	% total
Less than 20	1	1	2	4.7
20-25	1	2	3	7.0
26-35	4	6	10	23.3
36-45	8	5	13	30.2
46-55	5	4	9	20.9
56-65	2	3	5	11.6
66-75	1		1	2.3
Column total	22	21	43	100.0
% total	51.2	48.8	100	

Number of missing observations: 23

Employment status and type of employment: the majority of the women are employed in full-time jobs.

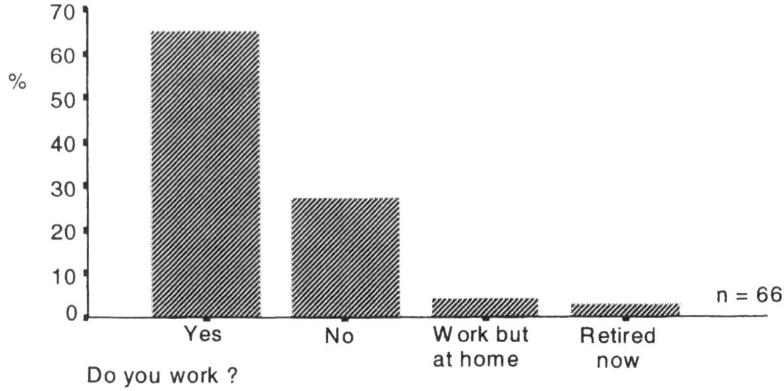

Figure 4.4 Employment status

Of the women surveyed, 65% are in paid employment, 5% work from home, 3% have retired and 27% are housewives or inactive. The majority are in paid employment. No recent employment statistics are available for the whole Italian community. In the United Kingdom, in 1996, a total of 66% of women aged between 16 and 59 were in paid employment, either full-time or part-time, 29% were inactive (Social Trends, 1997, p. 75). Thus there is no significant difference in the patterns of employment between Italian and British women - approximately the same percentage of women in both communities are engaged in paid employment.

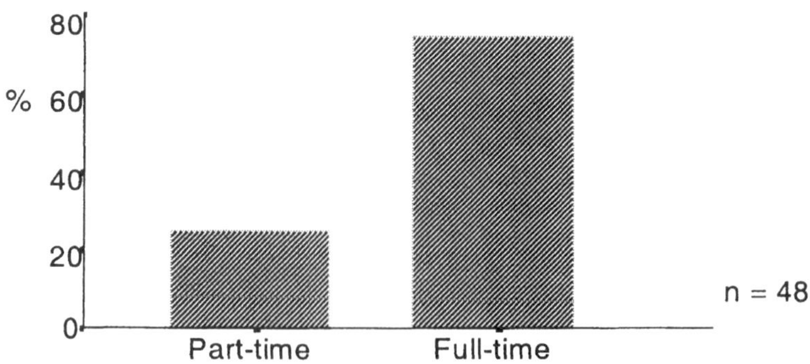

Figure 4.5 Type of employment

Three quarters of the working women in the survey are in full-time employment and only a quarter work part-time. In 1994 in Britain, 45% of all women in employment worked part-time (Social Focus on Women, 1995, p. 2). These results suggest that Italian women generally work more hours than British women. This is an interesting observation considering that Italian culture emphasizes the role of women as mothers and wives who are mainly responsible for housework. The burden of the double shift appears to be harder on Italian women, in comparison with British women.

Job category: most Italian jobs are categorized as lower middle class.

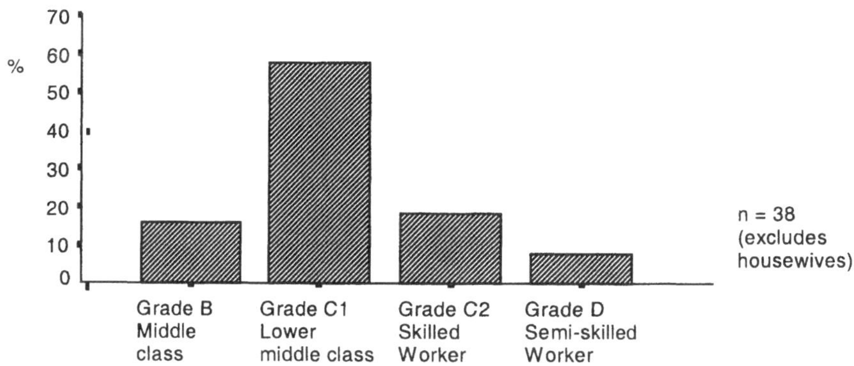

Figure 4.6 Profession

Only a minority of Italian women (16%) have middle-class jobs. The majority (58%) are employed in lower middle class jobs. 26% are categorized as skilled and semi-skilled workers. There is no cluster of upper middle class women in this survey. In the United Kingdom, in 1996, 30% of female working population were in professional, managerial and associate professional jobs (middle class), 54% in clerical, secretarial, sales and personal services (lower middle class). Only 4% worked as skilled manual and semi-skilled plant and machine operatives (Social Trends, 1997, p. 76). Comparing with the Italians, a larger percentage of British women are engaged in middle class professional jobs and a much lower percentage have skilled and semi-skilled jobs. Recent labour market analysis show that ethnic women are 'over-represented in areas of occupational decline and under-represented in the growth sectors, but they are also likely to be working longer hours, in poorer conditions for lower pay than white women' (Phizacklea and Wolkowitz, 1995, p. 7). Most British fully employed women are likely to be professional middle-classes:

85% of professional women are economically active as opposed to 68% of unskilled manual workers (Walby, 1997, pp. 60-61). By contrast, the majority of Italian women who are in employment (58%) are clustered in lower class categories.

Job satisfaction: Italian women claim to be satisfied with their jobs whether part-time, full-time, or low-paid. They seem resigned to the fact that they do not hold quality jobs and blame it on their lack of qualifications which is in turn either due to their own initial disinterest in pursuing higher education, or their families' opposition to it (see Chapter 5).

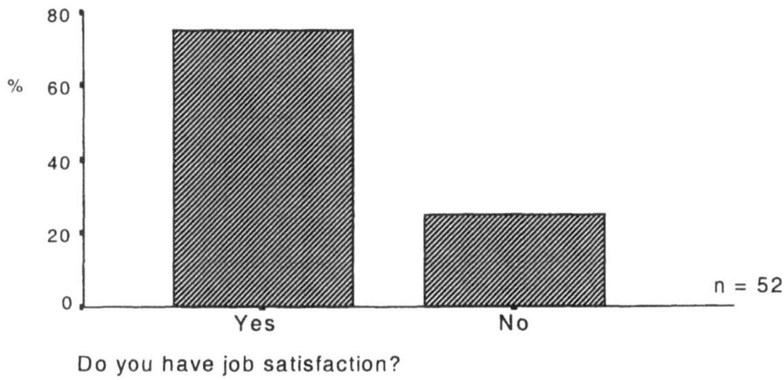

Figure 4.7 Job satisfaction

Despite the evidence that most working women in the survey have either lower middle class or skilled and semi-skilled jobs, the overwhelming majority (75%) claim they are satisfied with their jobs. Hakim (1991) has argued that the same contradiction, dubbed as the 'paradox of grateful slaves', exists within the British society. Women in the lowest grade, lowest skilled and lowest paid jobs report the highest levels of job satisfaction. Part-timers report higher job satisfaction levels than full-timers and the national job satisfaction rate for home workers who have low quality jobs is 90% (Hakim, 1991, p. 108). This paradox has been explained as 'women having different life aspirations'. In other words, they usually give priority to their roles as wives and mothers. They favour part-time, low paid jobs which allow them to fulfil their primary goals as homemakers. Less than 50% of adult women value paid employment as their primary goal in life (Hakim, 1991, p. 113). There is not much difference between Italian and British women in terms of job satisfaction. There is an ongoing debate in Britain with regard to women's perception of their roles in the household and aspirations in the employment market. Critics of Hakim (Crompton and Sanderson, 1990) contend that there is increasing evidence to show that women are determined to retain full-employment, even when their children are born. Phizacklea and Wolkowitz (1995) object to Hakim's arguments that women freely choose occupations which consolidate traditional gender roles because: 1) Men and women have differential access to employment features which enhance commitment and satisfaction; nevertheless there is evidence that there is an increase in younger women's employment aspirations. 2) Women apply different criteria in evaluating their careers and in expressing job satisfaction; these may differ with male criteria on what constitutes a good and satisfying job. Also many women, including some ethnic women, are in specific jobs not out of choice but because of limited employment alternatives, high male unemployment and lack of adequate state benefits. 3) High levels of job satisfaction in some surveys may be the result of inadequate questions and interpretations. Arber et al. (1996) further criticize Hakim's contentions by arguing that the documented increase in women's part-time employment indicates an increase in women's sense of identity, control of their own earnings and changing gender roles; being committed to their family needs does not preclude women's solid commitment to their part-time jobs. Arber et al. emphasize that it is the lack of full-time child care and old people's care facilities, women's scarce access to employment alternatives and week bargaining position which contribute to women's overwhelming presence in part-time, low paid jobs, not lack of commitment.

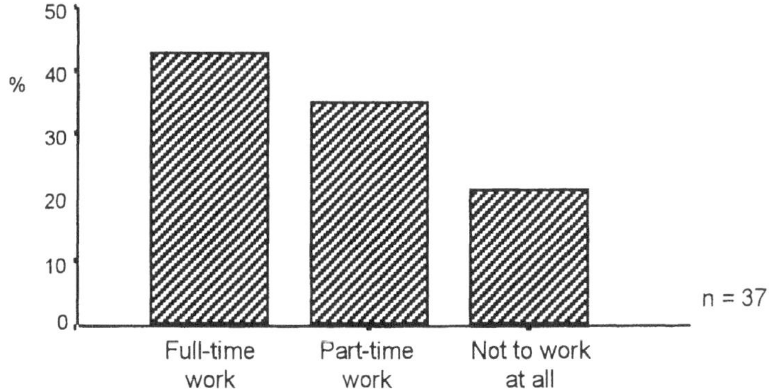

Figure 4.8 Employment preferences

Of the fully employed Italian women, 43% claim that even if they did not need to work they would still prefer to remain in full-employment. The rest would prefer to either work part-time or not work at all. The Labour Force Survey asked British women who were in part-time and temporary employment the reasons why they were not in full-time employment (e.g. could not find or did not want a full-time job). The Office for National Statistics who compile the Labour Force Survey have confirmed only women in part-time employment were asked about their job preferences (Correspondence with Mr. Neil Dube at ONS, October 1998). In Britain in 1996, eight in ten women (80%) in part-time jobs said they did not want to work full-time; this figure was raised to 90% among women who had a partner (Social Trends, 1997, pp. 76-77). Thus in comparison with Italians, a greater percentage of British women prefer part-time jobs.

Household

Over the years, there have been significant changes in the household composition and the domestic division of labour in Britain. There are differences with Italian households: in 1994, in Britain, 56% of the women were married (Social Focus on Women, p. 10). The Divorce Reform Act which came into force in 1971 has contributed significantly to the rates of divorce in the UK. In a 1994 European Union comparison, United Kingdom had the highest divorce rates, and Catholic Ireland and Italy, the lowest. In 1995, in England and Wales, the overall rate of divorce for the female population was 13.1 per 1,000 married couple (Social Trends, 1997, p. 46-48). In 1992-93, 18% of dependent children lived in a lone mother family (Social Focus on Women, p. 18). The overwhelming majority of the women in the survey are married and have children (85% and 75% respectively). Unmarried mothers are not looked favourably upon in the Italian Community (Figure 5.19) and most Italian households are headed by males. The majority of Italian women are religious (Figure 5.9); in the Roman Catholic Church, divorce is prohibited and consequently most have never been divorced (Figure 5.14).

In British society, some productive work previously done under relations of patriarchy, is now being carried out under capitalist relations of production or by the State: commercial household gadgets such as washing machines, dish-washers, microwaves, convenience foods, pre-cooked meals, state-run crèches and homes for the elderly have reduced some of the burden of housework on women (Gershuny et al., 1994). However, it is debatable whether Italian women do less housework nowadays. They are still likely to prepare elaborate dishes for their family instead of using convenience food and to personally take care of their elderly parents and relatives instead of confining them to state-run homes.

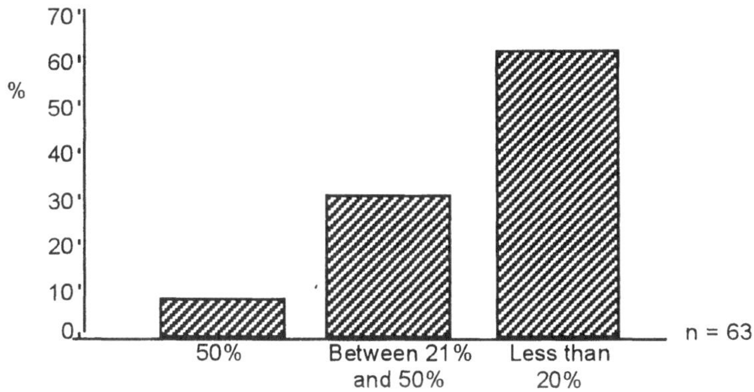

Figure 4.9 Percentage of household chores performed by men

62% of the Italian women surveyed admit that men in their households perform less than 20% of the housework. There is unequal sharing of household tasks in the Anglo-Saxon community, albeit to a lesser extent: in Britain, fathers spend 23 hours per week on household tasks (almost 30% of the housework) whereas mothers spend 62 hours doing the same (Social Trends, 1997, p. 215). The asymmetry between gender roles in ethnic Italian households, where fixed gender roles are entrenched in the culture, tends to be sharper than in the average British family (see Chapter 5).

Culture

The Italian and British patriarchal relations differ in the structure of culture: Italians have been widely exposed to British culture, especially British education and media, nevertheless they have preserved their ethnic Italian culture. As such, they are subject to a different set of patriarchal relations.

Italian children go to English schools since there are no full-time Italian schools in Britain. They are regularly exposed to the host country's language, social habits, religious beliefs, educational strategies. Nevertheless, Italian linguistic and cultural patrimony is perpetuated through the informal education the children receive at home and through the limited educational institutions of the community. Apart from a small elite, the majority of the Italians are not familiar with the Italian media such as film, theatre, art exhibitions, books, radio and television. They are more exposed to British media. While the institutions of Italian education and media play a marginal role within the structure of culture in the Italian community, religion i.e. Roman Catholicism is a solid pillar of the ethnic Italian community (see Chapters 2 and 6). The following figures illustrate the role of religion within the Italian community. Italian and British data have subsequently been compared:

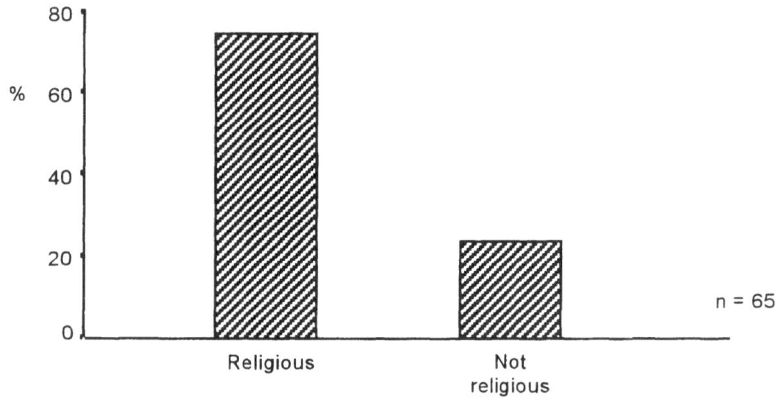

Figure 4.10 Degree of religiosity

The majority of the women in the sample (75%) say they are religious. Only a quarter are categorized as non-religious. In the United Kingdom, in 1995, only 21% of the population believed in the existence of God (Social Trends, 1997, p. 224).

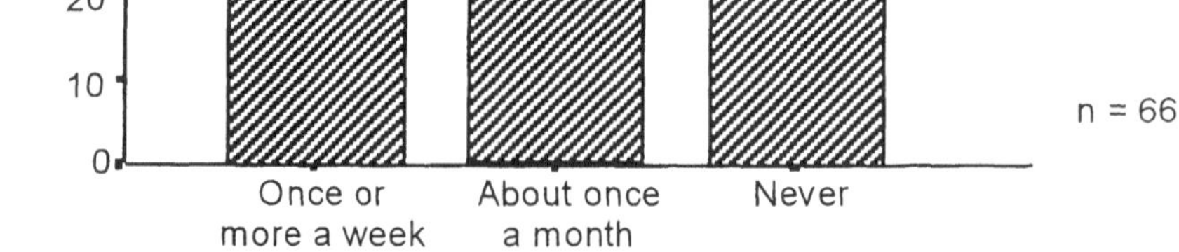

Figure 4.11 Church attendance

Almost half the women in the survey attend church about once a month,

32% attend once a week and only a minority (21%) never attend church service. In United Kingdom, in 1995, 50% of those with a religious affiliation said they had never attended church services. Only 11% said they attended at least once a week (British Social Attitudes Survey cited in Social Trends, 1997, pp. 224-225).

Figure 4.12 Type of wedding

The overwhelming majority of women in the survey (80%) married in church, only 20% did not have a religious wedding. In Great Britain, in 1993, 49% of marriage ceremonies were religious and 51% were civil (Social Trends, 1997, p. 47).

Figure 4.13 Children's baptism

96% of women in the survey who had children baptised them in church. 'Less than a quarter of all English babies are now being baptised into the

Church of England' (Madeleine Bunting cited in The Guardian, 7th February 1997).

Sexuality

There have been definite changes in the practice and perception of sexuality in 20th century Britain. British women have now a far more active sexuality due to technological advances in birth control (although the burden of birth control is still predominantly on women); divorce law has been reformed; pre-marital and extra-marital sex are on the rise and they do not entail harsh sanctions any more; there is greater tolerance for alternative sexual behaviours such as lesbianism.

Despite the liberalization of private forms of control over women's sexuality, many ethnic women in western societies still suffer from archaic forms of sexual oppression, thus becoming victims of both private and public patriarchy. Many ethnic Italian women are subject to traditional patriarchal attitudes in the structure of sexuality. The impact of Catholic sexual teachings underlie the particularity of the Italian structure of sexuality.

A contradiction may exist between what Italian women claim to believe and what their actual behaviour is (Hakim, 1991). They may believe that divorce, abortion, contraception, single motherhood, homosexuality and extra-marital affairs should be sanctioned by the Catholic Church. However, they may not be prepared to live their lives against the community norms and the 'divine' edicts of the Roman Catholic Church, risking both material and spiritual retribution: behaviour does not necessarily mirror belief. In the absence of similar risks of retribution, the disparity between British women's beliefs and behaviour might be smaller.

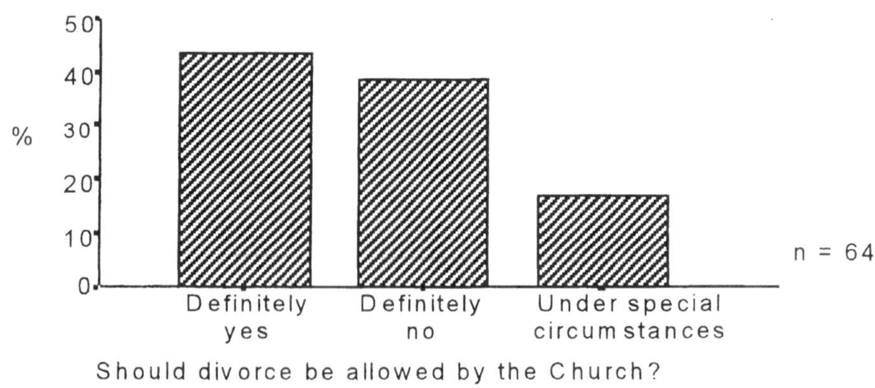

Figure 4.14 Opinions on divorce

44% of the women in the survey believe that church laws should allow divorce, 39% are adamant that it should not and a minority of 17% believe divorce should be allowed only under special circumstances (the wife is battered or marriage cannot be consummated). Fifty six % of the women do not favour divorce. This question is irrelevant in the case of British women for whom divorce became effectively possible in the 1920s and further facilitated by the 1969 Divorce Reform Act (Walby, 1990).

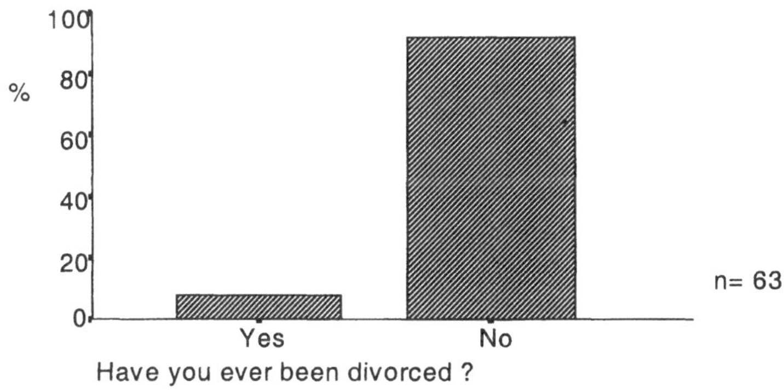

Figure 4.15 Frequency of divorce

The absolute majority of the women in the sample (92%) have never been divorced. In 1994, there were a total of 338,000 first marriages and remarriages in the UK and more than 15,0000 divorces (Social Trends, 1997, p. 46). This gives an approximate 44% rate of divorce in that year. Thus the rate of divorce in the Italian community is much lower than in mainstream British society.

The low rate of divorce amongst the Italian immigrants reflects that of Italy which has one of the lowest rates of divorce within the European community (Social Trends, 1997, pp. 46-47).

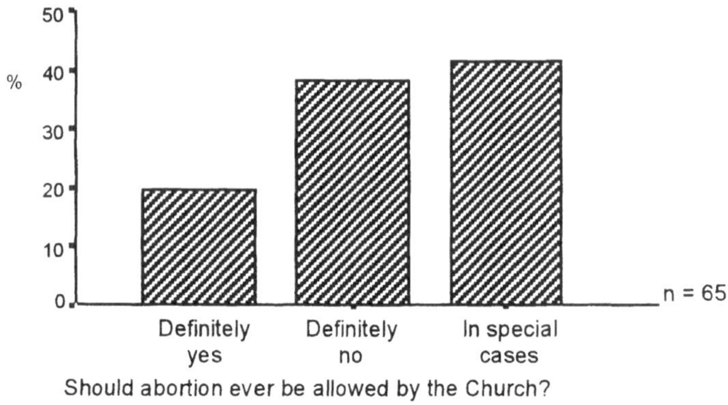

Figure 4.16 Position on abortion

Only a minority of the women in the survey (20%) are absolutely in favour of abortion. Thirty eight % are definitely against it and 42% think abortion should be allowed under special circumstances when the mother's life is endangered or the foetus has serious abnormalities. In a survey carried out by MORI in 1996 in Great Britain, over 80% of the respondents agreed that women should have the right to abortion. But over 50% stated that it was wrong for women to terminate pregnancy for non-medical reasons (Social Trends, 1997, p. 52). In comparison with the Italians, more British women are in favour of abortion.

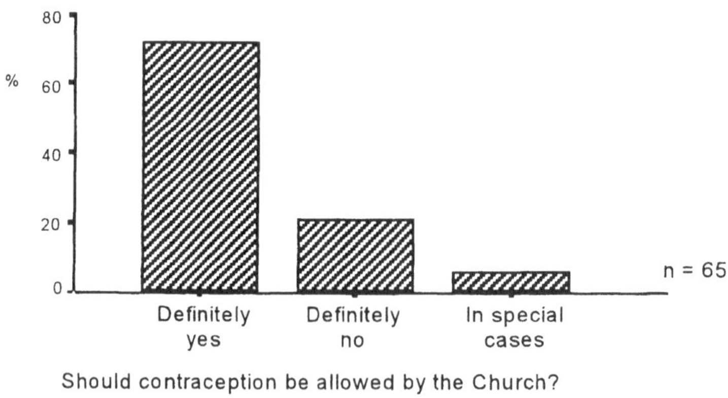

Figure 4.17 Position on contraception

The majority of women in the survey (72%) advocate the free use of contraception, 22% are definitely against it on religious grounds and 6%

favour contraception only under exceptional circumstances (e.g. health grounds). In Britain, amongst women aged 16 to 49, 72% use at least one method of contraception (Social Focus on Women, 1995, p. 19). As contraception is not a religious issue in mainstream British culture, it is not likely women would be asked in any survey whether they favour contraception or not. Therefore, the comparison between British and Italian women in this section is limited to the comparison of the Italians' views on contraception and the British frequency of use of contraception. The result is interesting and not anticipated. It appears that the percentage of Italian women who advocate free contraception is the same as British women who use it in one form or another.

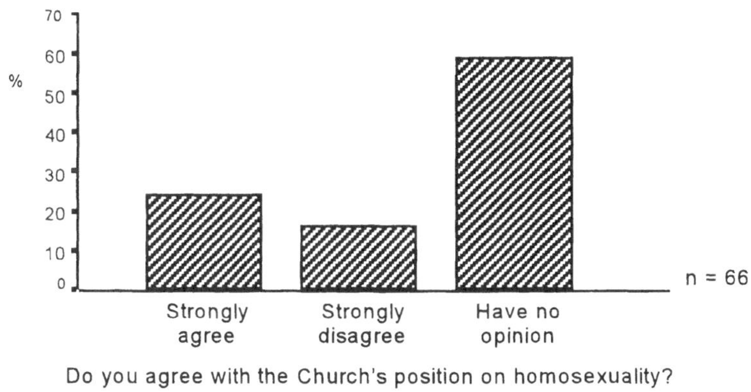

Figure 4.18 Opinions on the Church's attitude to homosexuality

Although the majority of women in the survey (70%) are aware that the Catholic Church condemns homosexuality, 59% are apathetic to the issue. Twenty four % strongly agree with the Church and only a minority of 17% condemn the position of the Church towards homosexuality. The British Social Attitudes Survey (1995, 13th Report, p.39) includes a 'sexual morality' question about homosexuality used here as a comparison index: fifty five % of those asked said homosexual sex is always wrong, 29% said it is rarely or not at all wrong. Comparing the Italians with the British on their attitudes to homosexuality is rather problematic: it is not clear whether the high percentage (59%) of Italians who are aware of the attitude of the Church towards homosexuality but have no opinion about it, actually condemn homosexuality or not. While 29% of the British do not find anything wrong with homosexuality, only 17% of Italians strongly condemn the attitude of the Church towards it. In comparison with the Italians, a larger percentage of the British appear to tolerate homosexuality.

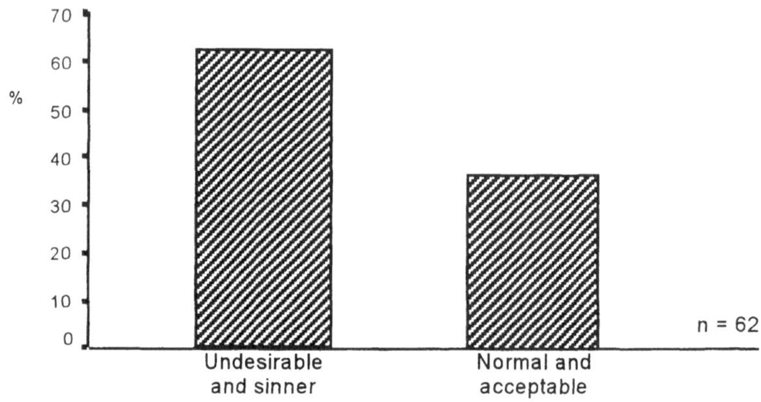

Figure 4.19 Single mothers' status in the Italian community

63% of women in the survey believe that in the Italian community single mothers are treated as undesirable and sinners. 37% believe their status is normal and they are accepted within the community. In 1995, in England and Wales, births outside marriage accounted for around 33% of all live births, with 5% being registered (Social Trends, 1997, p. 39). Lone parent families have steadily increased in the last three decades. Most are headed by single mothers. In 1994, single mother families constituted little more than 20% of all families with dependent children in the UK, almost three times the proportion in 1971 (Social Trends, 1997, p. 43). Compared with the above-mentioned Italian statistics which reveal only attitudes towards single motherhood, the steady increase in the number of British single mothers suggests that in Britain, single motherhood is relatively more tolerated. In 1989, in a British Social Attitudes Survey, people were asked whether they agreed with the statement: *'a single mother can bring up her child as well as a married couple'*. 45% of women disagreed and 35% agreed. Single, separated, divorced and widowed women were more likely to agree with the statement. Two thirds of women aged 55 and over disagreed with the statement; 60% of men disagreed as well (cited in Social Focus on Women, 1995, p. 18).

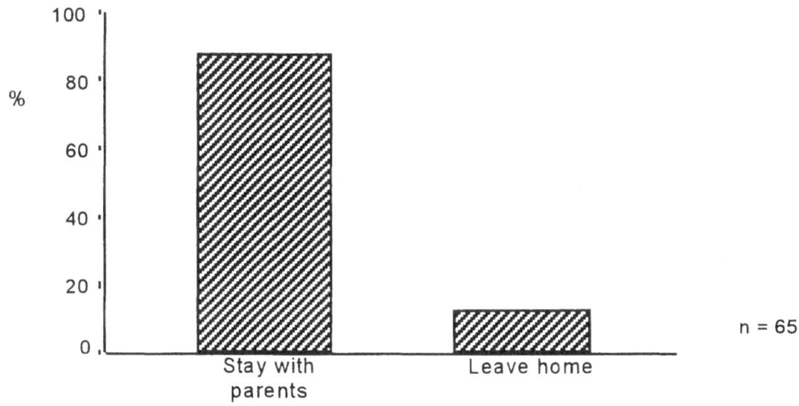

Figure 4.20 Unmarried Italian girls

88% of the women in the survey opine that within the Italian community unmarried girls stay at their parents' home until the time they marry. A minority of 12% claim young Italian girls leave home in their 20's. In 1995-1996, in England, just over a third of women in their early twenties lived with their parents. The rest had left parental homes (Social Trends, 1997, p. 43).

Male Violence

Male violence ranges from a continuum of rape, domestic rape, wife beating, child sexual abuse and sexual harassment at work or in public places. Domestic male violence has not been evaluated in this book. There are no known research or specific Italian statistics available on the subject. However, in reply to the question *'Is domestic violence prevalent within Italian households?'*, the overwhelming majority of women in the survey claimed there was none (Figure 4.21). Some interpretations of this result may be:

- Domestic violence truly does not exist within the Italian community: the machismo mentality not allowing the physical abuse of the 'weaker sex'. In much of the Latin speaking world 'The overpowering role of the mother who rules and nurtures a young boy's life and who consequently deserves a lifelong respect and trust that is assigned to no other woman is a contradiction to women's lack of public power' (Castleberg-Koulma cited in Redclift and Sinclair, 1991, p. 198).
- It is likely that the women surveyed did not reveal the extent of domestic violence because of personal or nationalist pride. In a

community firmly based on family ties and values, it would be hard for women to confess to any domestic rape, beating and child sexual abuse, especially to an unknown foreign researcher.

To determine the extent and distribution of male violence is extremely problematic at the national level as well. Evidence has often been highly speculative: official statistics reflect only a portion of male violence because not all the cases are reported; at the same time, there are no clear-cut legal guidelines on what constitutes violence, domestic violence, sexual abuse and rape (e.g. marital rape is not a criminal offence). The first British official crime survey in the 1980s unveiled much higher levels of rape and sexual assaults than hitherto recorded by the police (Mirrlees-Black, 1995).

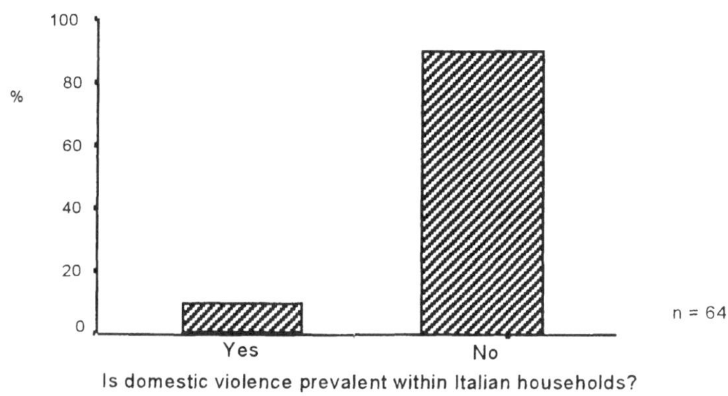

Figure 4.21 Domestic violence in the Italian community

91% of the Italian women in the sample claim there is no domestic violence within the Italian community. In 1993, in England and Wales, there were 837,000 incidents of domestic violence against women (Social Focus on Women, 1995, p. 51).

State

Ethnic Italians who live in Britain permanently are subject to the British State, its laws, its policing, its education and health care systems. However most still hold Italian citizenship and consider themselves to be primarily Italian, even when they have lived in Britain for decades or have been born here. The significance of this peculiarity is that ethnic Italians' political allegiance lies with Italy and the level of their political participation in Britain remains low.

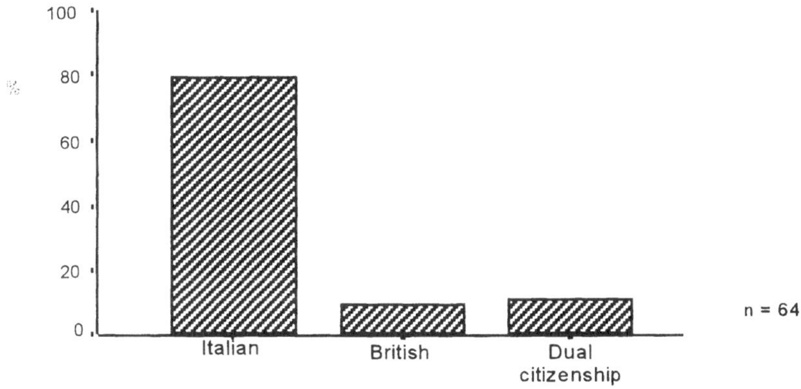

Figure 4.22 Italian citizenship

80% of women in the survey hold Italian citizenship, only 9% have British citizenship and 11% have dual citizenship.

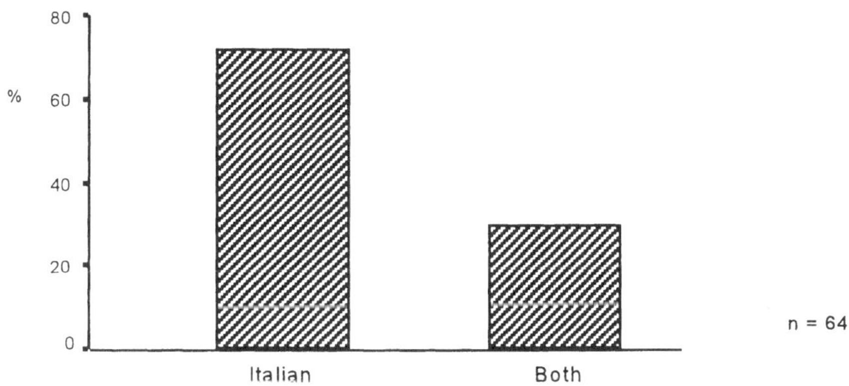

Figure 4.23 Respondents' reported national identity

72% of women in the survey feel completely Italian and only 28% feel they have both English and Italian identity. The overwhelming majority of the women identify themselves as Italian rather than British.

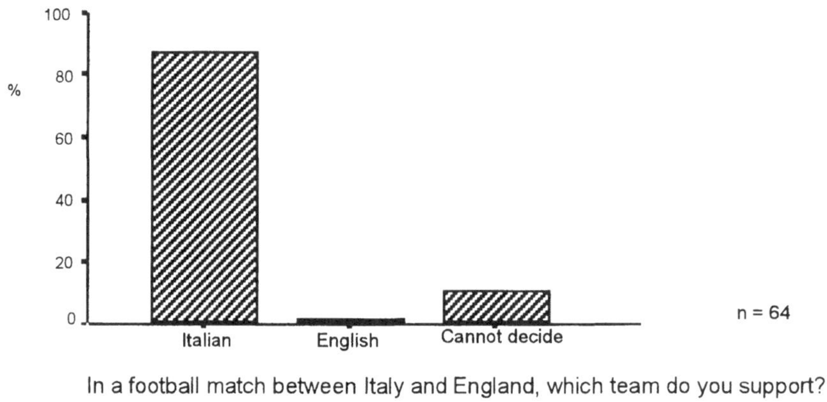

Figure 4.24 Preferred football team

Submerged ethnic sentiments can be given full expression in football stadiums and support for a team can be interpreted as support for a state, a nation, an ethnic community (Duke and Crolley, 1996). In a hypothetical football match between England and Italy, 88% of the sample root for Italy, 11% are undecided and only 1% back the English team. The results show that the Italians' loyalty lies primarily with Italy. They are important in that they reveal basic, impulsive emotional bonds with the mother culture and its symbol, the Italian State. Ethnic Italians live and work in Britain and are subject to British laws, yet they expect the Italian State to grant them the right to vote from abroad. Their allegiance to the State (whether British or Italian) is therefore ambiguous. On the eve of the Second World War, the Italian community sided almost en masse with Fascist Italy, mainly out of a sense of ethnic nationalism (Chapter 3).

Summary

Italian and British patriarchal structures are generally different, with similarities in some areas. In employment, both Italian and British women are consistently subordinated to men, are relatively excluded from higher grade jobs and remain satisfied with their low quality jobs. The burden of double shift still exists in both British and Italian households, although it seems Italians carry a heavier load. Italian women seem to be more controlled by the institution of religion which attempts to severely control their sexuality and curtail their sexual freedom. Anglo-Saxon religious institutions tend to have more liberal views on women's sexuality.

Assessment of the extent of domestic violence has proved most difficult both in Italian and Anglo-Saxon communities due to under-reporting of violence and its inadequate legal definitions. Italians have a complex relationship with the state in so far as they still feel strongly affiliated with Italy. This may have thwarted their social and political assimilation.

PART II: FORM OF PATRIARCHY IN THE ITALIAN COMMUNITY

Definitions of Private and Public Patriarchy

> Private patriarchy is based upon household production, with a patriarch controlling women individually and directly in the relatively private sphere of the home. Public patriarchy is based on structures other than the household, although this may still be a significant patriarchal site. Rather, institutions conventionally regarded as part of the public domain are central in the maintenance of patriarchy.......Public patriarchy is a form in which women have access to both public and private arenas. They are not barred from the public arenas, but are nonetheless subordinated within them. The expropriation of women is performed more collectively than by individual patriarchs. The household may remain a site of patriarchal oppression, but it is no longer the main place where women are present. In the private system of patriarchy the exploitation of women in the household is maintained by their non-admission to the public sphere. In a sense the term 'private' for this form of patriarchy might be misleading, in that it is the exclusion from the public which is the central causal mechanism. Patriarchal relations outside the household are crucial in shaping patriarchal relations within it. However, the effect is to make women's experience of patriarchy privatized, and the immediate beneficiaries are also located there. In the public form of patriarchy the exploitation of women takes place at all levels, but women are not formally excluded from any. In each institution women are disadvantaged (Walby, 1990, p. 178).

In Britain there was a move away from private patriarchy towards public patriarchy in the early decades of the 20th century, due to the combination of several economic and political factors: Capital's increasing demand for new supplies of labour, political victories of early feminists who secured women's citizenship rights such as the vote, access to education and the professions, property ownership and the right to divorce, led to women's mass entry in the labour market. The tension between patriarchy and capitalism over the exploitation of women's labour in the household and in paid employment has often led to women being segregated into lower grade, less remunerated jobs or excluded from the public sphere altogether. The choice or success of each strategy depends upon the relative strength of exclusionary patriarchy and inclusionary capital at a particular time, in a particular industry. These political and economic upheavals have inevitably led to the re-organization of the domestic, cultural, political and sexual mores. The number of divorces has steadily increased especially since the 1970s, non-marital relations or co-habitation have become less stigmatized, women have gained wide access to education and minor representation at the level of the state; however there have not been substantial changes in patriarchal relations of male violence. In short, in Britain the form of patriarchy has shifted from private to public and there have been a reduction in the degree of patriarchy in most structures due to feminist struggle (Walby, 1990, pp. 184-200). The ethnic Italian social structures have acquired different patriarchal forms.

Form of Patriarchy in the Italian Structure of Employment

> Participation in paid work will be taken as the best measure of the form of patriarchy in the area of paid work. High rates will be taken as evidence of the public form, and low rates as indicative of the private form (Walby, 1994a, p. 1345).

There is indication of public patriarchy in the Italian structure of employment: the majority of women are in paid employment, some are now retired and a small percentage work at home (Figure 4.4). Most have lower middle-class professions (Figure 4.6). Although the overwhelming majority is in full-time employment (Figure 4.5), Italian women are segregated in lower grade, less remunerated professions. More prestigious professions are likely to belong to men.

Form of Patriarchy in the Italian Structure of Household Production

By definition, the private system of patriarchy involves the exploitation of women in the household by their non-admission to the public sphere (Walby, 1990). Italian women have entered paid employment en masse and most work full-time jobs. Strictly speaking, the Italian institution of household production cannot be characterized by a private form of patriarchy any more. However, Italian women are still disadvantaged within the institution of the family (Chistolini, 1986; Colpi, 1991; also see

Chapter 5). Women still bear the burden of the double-shift. The rate of divorce is low and single motherhood is frowned upon within Catholic Italian community. The majority of households are headed by males who control women's way of life and sexuality. The Italian household is thus situated within a continuum where both private and public forms of patriarchy co-exist.

Form of Patriarchy in the Structure of Culture

The form of patriarchy has been assessed in the institution of religion which is the main constituent of Italian culture. Italian Education and media have very marginal effect on gender relations in the community.

The institution of religion is the source of beliefs which form the basis of an informal patriarchal education within the family: as illustrated earlier, all women in the survey are Catholics and most are religious. Their beliefs and behaviour closely reflect the teachings of the Church: most marry in church and have their children baptised. Few are divorced. Few believe that abortion should be allowed. Few care about the opposition of the Catholic Church to women's ordination or homosexuality. These attitudes reflect cultural patriarchy at the collective level: the institution of religion regulates women's lives and excludes them from the decision making processes related to religious affairs. It controls and subordinates women at the collective level, making the form of patriarchy in this structure public.

Form of Patriarchy in the Structure of Sexuality

The Italian structure of sexuality takes both the public and the private form: the institution of religion sets the rules at the collective level; the male-headed family internalizes them and accordingly regulates the conduct of the female members of the household. The sexual oppression thus extends to the whole community and women passively accept their submissive position.

The Italian structures of culture, sexuality and household production are closely interdependent through the nexus of religion. Catholicism regards women as being primarily homemakers, wives and mothers. It considers pre-- and extra-marital relations, abortion, contraception, divorce, ordination of women priests and homosexuality as cardinal sins. Religious edicts have considerable effect on Italian households. Although both sexes are obviously affected by the Church's 'divine' rules, it is women's sexual freedom which is ultimately curtailed. Italian men enjoy the sexual double standard (see Chapters 3 and 6).

Main Site of Patriarchy

The concept of patriarchy has been operationalized here in order to quantify the pattern and relative degree of institutional gender inequality within four patriarchal structures of the Italian community: employment, household production, culture and sexuality. Italian women appear to be most oppressed in the structure of sexuality which is identified as the main site of patriarchy. Results are interpreted as being relative rather than absolute, and are limited by the constrictions of the data file in this research. Patriarchy in the structure of violence has not been operationalized due to lack of national and ethnic data. Patriarchy in the structure of state has not been operationalized because Italian women do not really feel as integral subjects of the British State (Chapter 5).

Patriarchy in Employment

Patriarchy scores range from the lowest 0 to the highest 3.

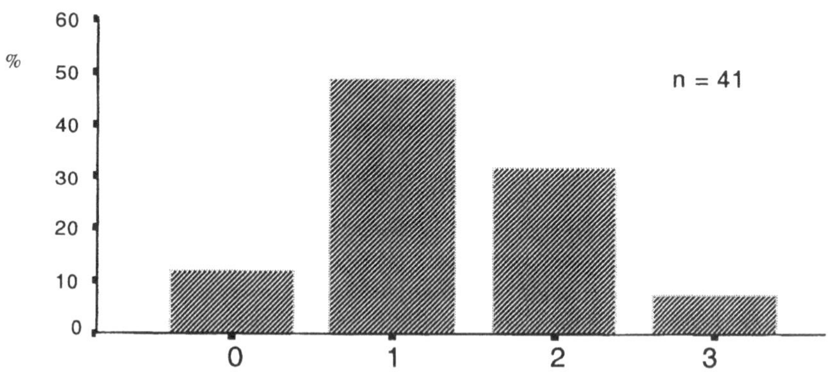

Figure 4.25 Patriarchy in employment

As illustrated in the above bar chart, 12% of the respondents scored 0, almost half of them scored 1, a third scored 2, 7% scored 3 and nobody scored the maximum 4. Thus in the structure of employment, the majority of the women are subject to average levels of patriarchy or they perceive that women in the Italian community are subject to an average level of patriarchy. Few women (only 12%) are in the very low category (score 0) and nobody falls within the high patriarchy category (score 4). The majority fall within the middle scores of oppression.

Patriarchy in the Household

The distribution of the patriarchy is denoted by amalgamated scores ranging from the lowest 0 to the highest 6.

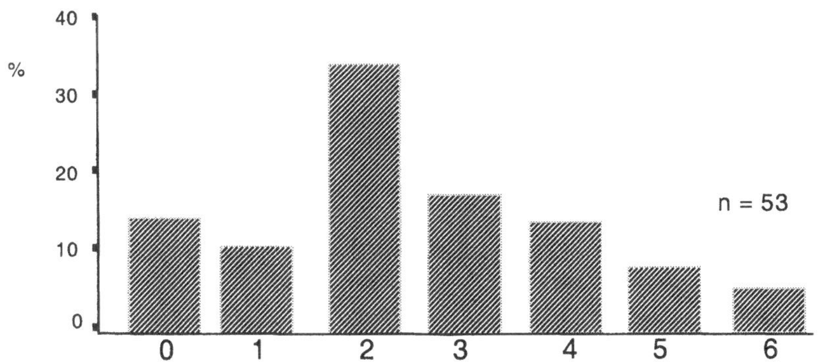

Figure 4.26 Patriarchy in the household

The bar chart indicates that less than a quarter of the respondents are in the very low category (scores 0 and 1). The single biggest majority (34%) comes under score 2. The great majority of the women (64%) come under the three middle range scores of 2, 3, and 4. Only 14% of the women in the sample fall within the highest scores 5 and 6. In the Italian community, the leading edge of patriarchal relations in the structure of household is within the middle range of patriarchy scores.

Patriarchy in Culture

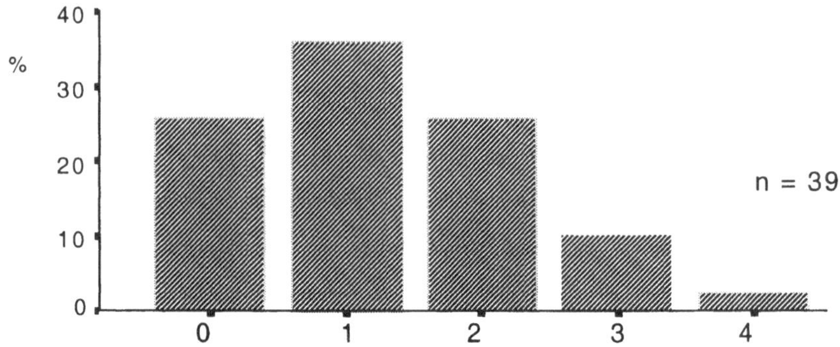

Figure 4.27 Patriarchy in culture

The above bar chart distribution illustrates that the majority of the women in the survey (62%) are concentrated within the lowest scores 0 and 1. Around one quarter of the women score the average 2 and a mere 13% come under the highest scores 3 and 4. It appears that in the structure of culture, as in the structures of employment and household production, the majority of women are concentrated in the lower categories of patriarchy.

Patriarchy in Sexuality

The bar chart illustrates the distribution of women in the survey, using amalgamated scores ranging from a minimum of zero to a maximum of 4.

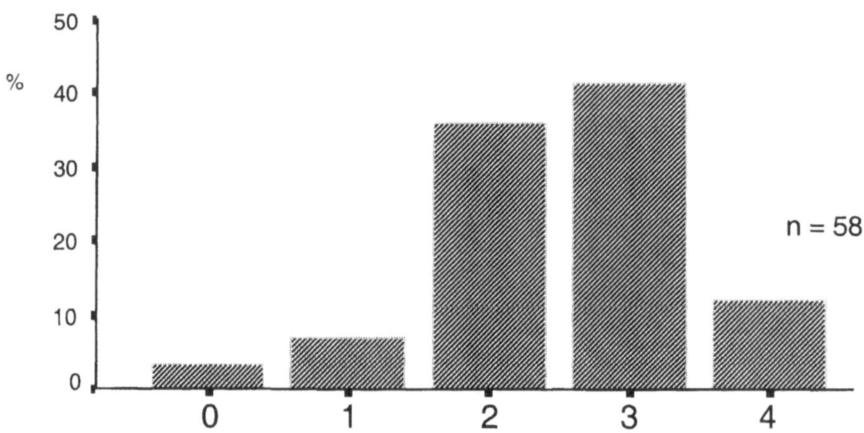

Figure 4.28 Patriarchy in sexuality

The chart demonstrates that the majority of women are clustered within the highest scores of 3 and 4. More than a third of the women come under the average score of 2 and only a minimum 10% are concentrated within the lowest scores 0 and 1. It is concluded that within the limits of the survey, most Italian women's sexuality is controlled by patriarchal institutions or by individual males.

Conclusions

Comparing the bar charts illustrating patriarchy in employment, household production, culture and sexuality, it becomes apparent that within the Italian community in Britain, the main site of patriarchy is the structure of sexuality.

Patriarchal relations prevail in all the ethnic structures examined. However, lower scores in the bar charts illustrate that Italian women do not perceive of unequal gender relations as being particularly oppressive within the structures of employment, household production and culture: most women have entered paid employment and work in mainly full-time jobs. Many are satisfied with their jobs and do not believe they are discriminated against because of their sex or ethnicity. They believe they are free to marry non-Italians, work, date, become single mothers and have access to higher education. The majority of the women in the survey believe the Italian and British media represent them in an equal fashion and they do not think Italian women are any less liberated than British women. In short, Italian women do not perceive of themselves as being overwhelmingly oppressed at work, at home or culturally. In contrast, within the structure of sexuality, the majority of women are concentrated within the high score range of patriarchal oppression. Patriarchal relations in this structure are shaped by the immutable teachings of the Catholic Church. These results are consistently corroborated in individual and focus group interviews (Chapter 5).

PART III: VARIATIONS IN PATTERNS OF PATRIARCHY WITHIN THE ITALIAN COMMUNITY

'Region of origin', 'degree of religiosity', 'age' and 'length of residence in England' are variables which are associated with changes in the configuration of patriarchal structures within the Italian community. The charts in the following sections depict the distribution of patriarchy in the social structures of the Italian Diaspora, according to these variables.

Region of Origin

British-Italians originate from all parts of Italy, North, Centre and South. Since the unification, various historical, political and economic factors have created cultural and socio-economic differences between the northern and southern Italian provinces. These differences have persisted into the 20th century and account for differentials in attitudes amongst Italian immigrants: the lengthy geographical layout of Italy is characterized by a lack of natural transport connections such as rivers and by a large proportion of non-arable mountainous land. Through the centuries, geographical differences have led to the development of diverse localized economies and regional cultural adjustments. Various parts of the country came under the rule of separate political regimes with varying degrees of competence, liberalism, despotism or corruption (Kemp, 1969). The Risorgimento (Italian unification) was achieved by a political manoeuvre, over the head of the masses, without any real economic or social reform; it involved administrative and political compromises with the old regional ruling classes who retained most of their power and influence. With a single tariff and currency, the underprivileged southern regions lost out in the competition with their more efficient northern neighbours which were geographically closer to the rapidly growing Western European market. The poor southern regions, with their traditional social structure, resisted change. Agriculture was neglected and southern landowners flocked to the towns; there was no incentive to invest in a poor region with no prospects of a flourishing market. Industrialization sharpened southern and northern differences (Kemp, 1969). Moreover, Roman Catholicism has always been stronger in southern Italy and throughout its rule, the Italian Christian Democratic government (1948-1992) drew most of its support from the southerners' votes (Villari, 1973; Ginsborg, 1990). There exists a closer economic and cultural similarity between northern and central regions of Italy, in contrast to the south. As a result, I have divided the variable 'region of origin' into two categories: 1) North and Centre, 2) South. In the following charts, patriarchy has been operationalized using low (0 and 1), medium (2) and high (3 and 4) scores.

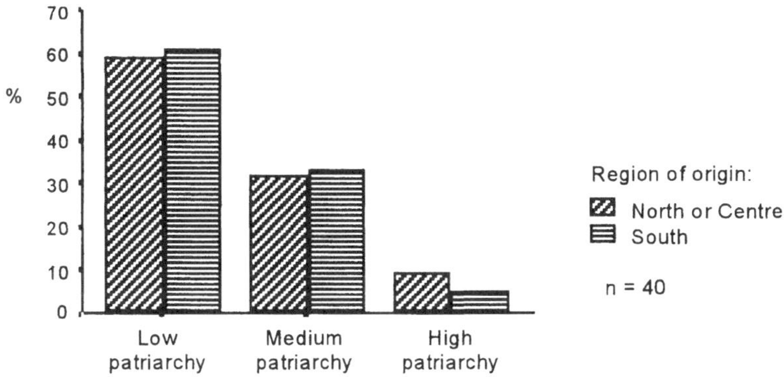

Figure 4.29 Region of origin by patriarchy in employment

Most Italian women come under the low patriarchy category and only a small minority is subject to high patriarchy. In all low, medium and high patriarchy categories, there is not much percentage difference (3%) between women who come from the South and those who come from the 'North and Centre'. It is concluded that in the structure of employment most women in the survey fall within the low patriarchy category and 'region of origin' does not make any significant difference in the distribution.

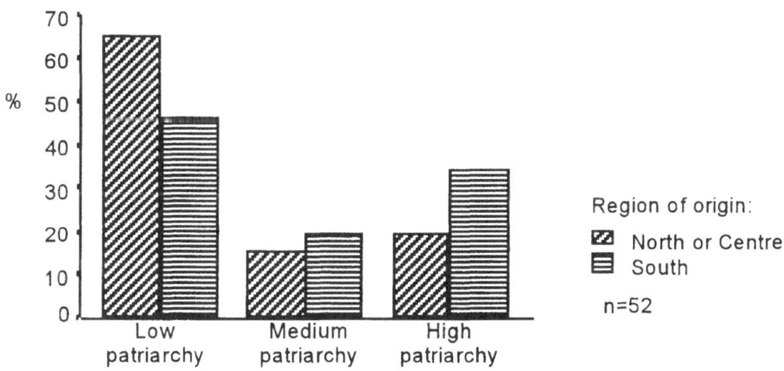

Figure 4.30 Region of origin by patriarchy in the household

In the structure of household production, most women in the survey fall within the low patriarchy category. However, a substantially larger number of women in the 'North and Centre' are subject to low patriarchy compared to southern women. Similarly, in the high patriarchy category, a greater percentage of women from the 'South' are subject to high patriarchy in the household. It is concluded that in the structure of household production, region of origin makes a significant difference in low and high categories of patriarchy. In other words, patriarchy seems to be more prevalent in households of southern origin.

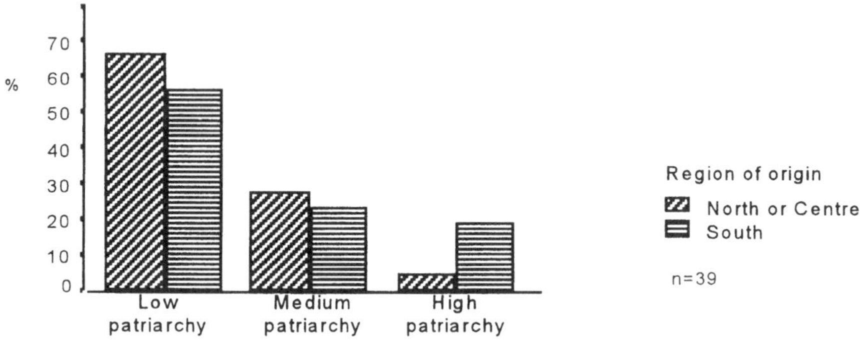

Figure 4.31 Region of origin by patriarchy in culture

In the structure of culture, the majority of the women come under the low patriarchy category. However, in the low patriarchy category the number of those from the 'North and Centre' exceeds that of the Southerners by 10%. In the medium patriarchy category, the number of 'Northern and Central' women exceeds that of the Southerners by 4%. In the high patriarchy category the situation is reversed: the southerners exceed those from the other regions by 13%. It is concluded that in the structure of culture there is a higher association between the southern region of origin and unequal gender relations.

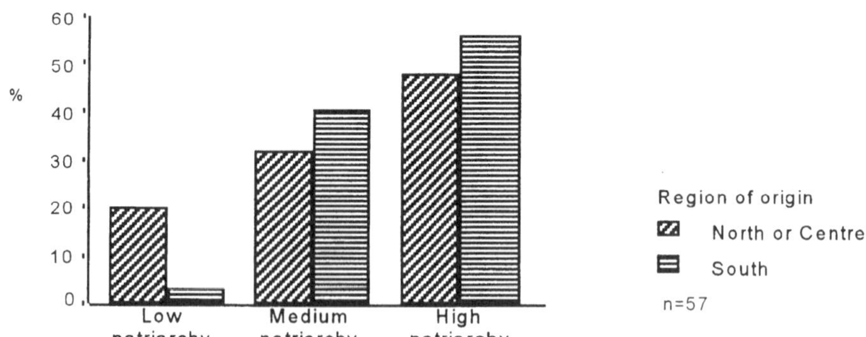

Figure 4.32 Region of origin by patriarchy in sexuality

In the structure of sexuality, most women in the survey are subject to high patriarchy. The majority of women from the 'North and Centre' and the 'South' fall within the high patriarchy category. A very low percentage of them are concentrated in the low patriarchy category. The difference is that in the 'South' even fewer women come under low patriarchy category. There is a strong positive association between high patriarchy and southern region of origin.

Degree of Religiosity

The edicts of Roman Catholicism uphold and reinforce unequal gender relations. A high degree of religiosity is associated with a high degree of patriarchy within the social structures of the Italian community.

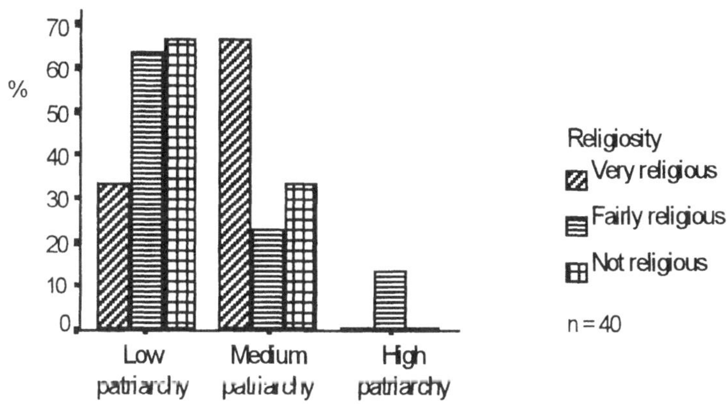

Figure 4.33 Religiosity by patriarchy in employment

Most 'very religious' women come under medium level of patriarchy and the rest under low patriarchy category. There is none under the category of high patriarchy. In the 'fairly religious' and 'not religious' categories, the trend is reversed and the majority are clustered under low patriarchy. In the low patriarchy category, the majority of women are almost equally divided between 'fairly religious' and 'not religious'; only a third are 'very religious'. Only 14% of the 'fairly religious' women within high patriarchy category. In the structure of employment, there is an association between non-religiosity and low patriarchy: 'non-religious' women are non-existent in the high patriarchy category but they fall in their majority (67%) within low patriarchy category.

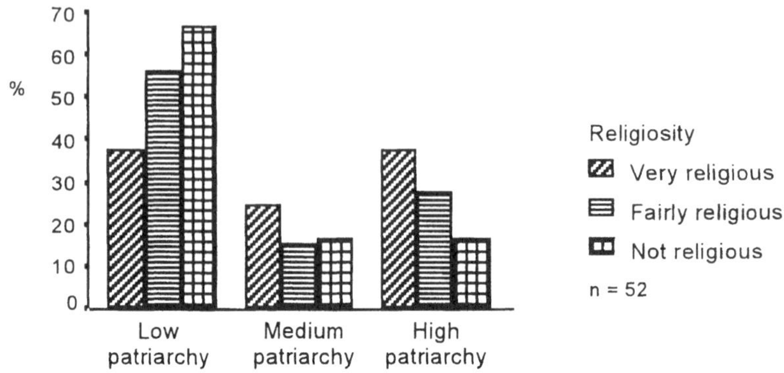

Figure 4.34 Religiosity by patriarchy in the household

In the structure of household production, the majority of the 'very religious' women are equally divided between low and high patriarchy categories. The 'fairly religious' and 'not religious' are mostly concentrated in the low patriarchy category. Highly religious women are equally divided between lower and higher categories of patriarchy. However, the largest percentage of women within the high patriarchy category is that of 'very religious' women. At the same time, most non-religious women are categorized as low patriarchy group.

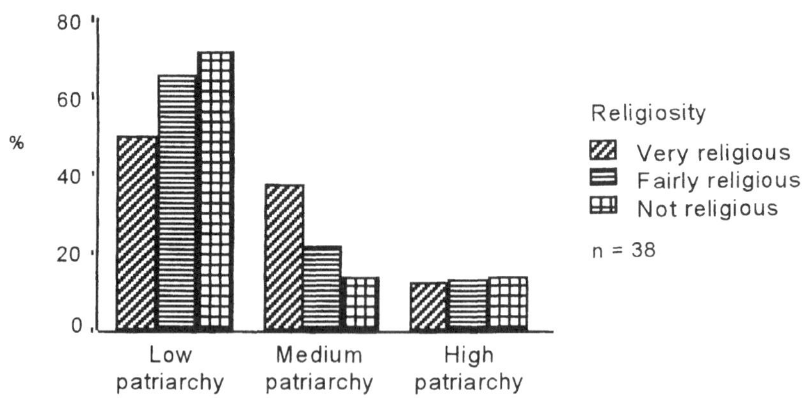

Figure 4.35 Religiosity by patriarchy in culture

71% of 'not religious' women, 65% of 'fairly religious' and 50% of 'very religious' women are in the low patriarchy category. In the medium patriarchy category, the largest percentage of the women are from 'very religious', 22% from 'fairly religious' and only 14% from the 'not religious' group. Only a minority of women are concentrated under the high patriarchy category and these are almost equally divided among 'very religious', 'fairly religious' and 'not religious'. It is concluded that non-religiosity is associated with low patriarchy in the Italian cultural institutions. At the same time, a high degree of patriarchy is not exclusively associated with a greater degree of religiosity.

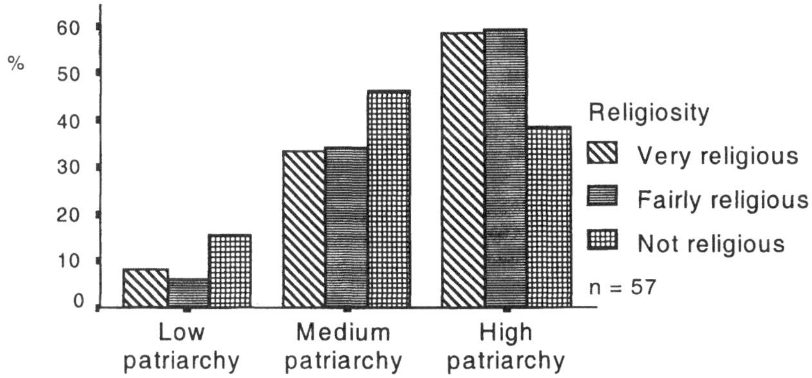

Figure 4.36 Religiosity by patriarchy in sexuality

In the 'very religious' and 'fairly religious' categories, the majority of women are subject to high patriarchy; only a minority, whether religious or non-religious, are in the low patriarchy category. In the 'not religious' category, the highest percentage falls within the medium patriarchy category. In the structure of sexuality, religiosity is positively associated with higher degrees of patriarchy. At the same time non-religiosity is associated with low patriarchy.

Age

Women in the survey belong to three age cohorts: the younger generation (less than twenty to thirty five years old); middle generation (thirty six to fifty five years old); older generation (fifty six to seventy five years old). Younger cohorts of immigrants are more readily integrated within the mainstream British institutions due to their wide exposure to the formal education system and media in the host country and peer group socialization. Thus lower patriarchy is associated with younger cohorts in the various social structures of the Italian community as shown below:

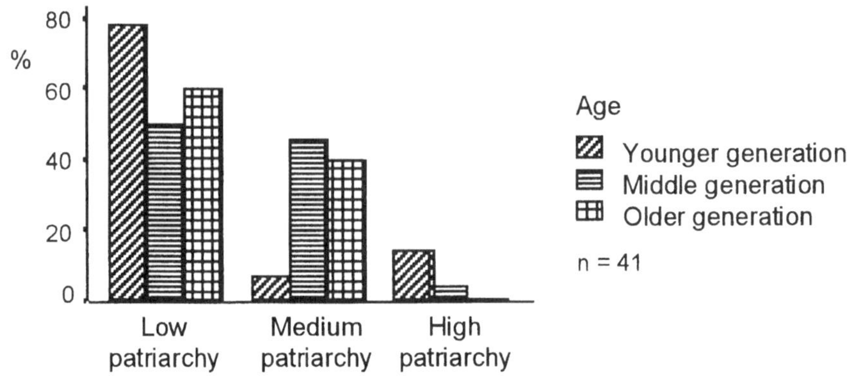

Figure 4.37 Age by patriarchy in employment

In all generational cohorts the overwhelming majority fall under low patriarchy. 79% of the younger generation, 50% of the middle generation and 60% of the older generation are concentrated in the low patriarchy category. Less than 10% of the younger generation fall under the medium patriarchy category and about 14% of the young are concentrated in the high patriarchy category. There are no older generation women in the high patriarchy category. Less than 5% of middle generation women are in the high patriarchy category. Thus 'age' makes a difference to the degree of patriarchy in the structure of employment: younger age is associated with lower patriarchy.

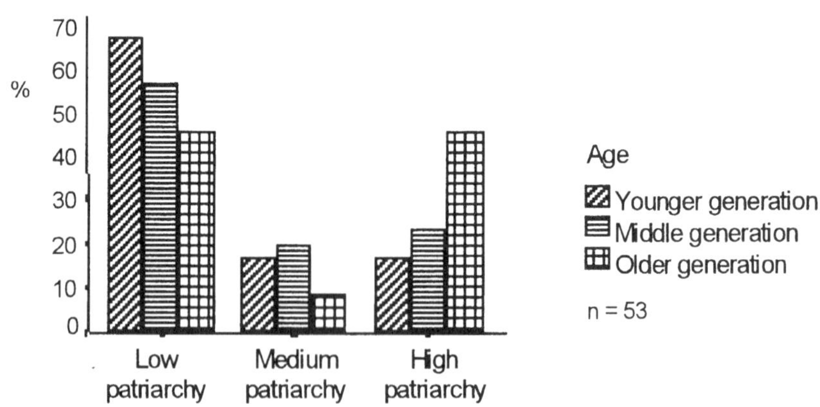

Figure 4.38 Age by patriarchy in the household

In the structure of household production, the young generation constitutes the greatest component in the low patriarchy category, followed by the middle and older generation respectively. The highest percentage of women in the high patriarchy category is that of the older generation (45%). The same percentage (45%) of older generation women are clustered under low patriarchy category, though this percentage is lower than that of the younger and middle generations. It is concluded that in the structure of household production, lower age is associated with low patriarchy and older age with high patriarchy.

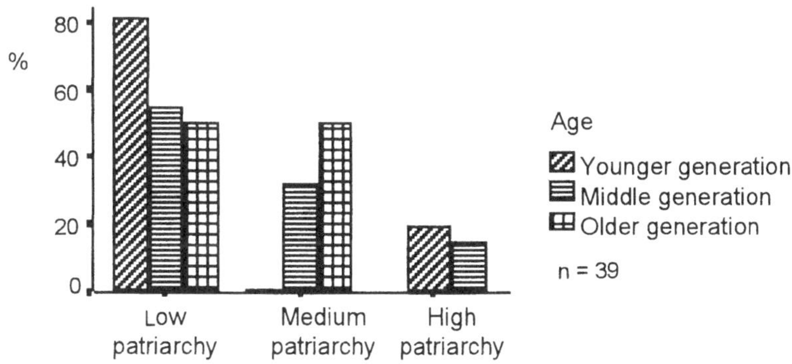

Figure 4.39 Age by patriarchy in culture

82% of younger generation women, 55% of middle generation and 50% of older generation women are in the low patriarchy category. Half of the older generation women and almost a third of the middle generation are in the medium patriarchy cluster. There are no younger generation women in this cluster. In the high patriarchy category, there are no older generation women and all are almost equally divided between the younger and middle generation. In the structure of culture, there is a definite association between younger age and low patriarchy. The surprising discovery is that within the high patriarchy category, there are no older generation while there are 18% of younger generation women.

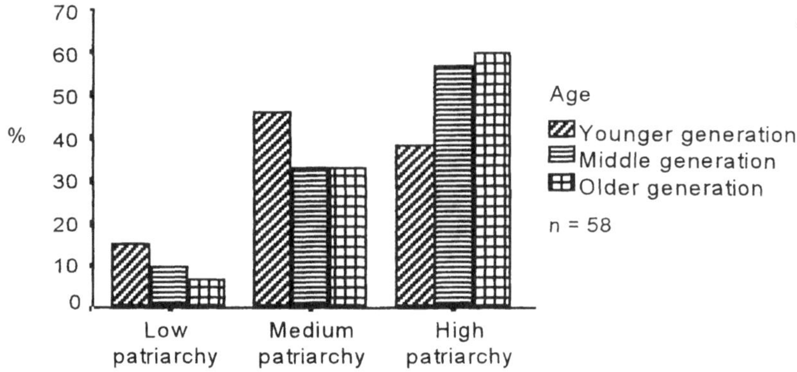

Figure 4.40 Age by patriarchy in sexuality

15% of the younger generation, 10% of the middle generation and 7% of the older generation fall within the low patriarchy group. Almost half of the younger generation and a third of both middle and older generation fall within the medium patriarchy category. 38% of the younger generation, 57% of the middle and 60% of the older generation fall within the high patriarchy category. The majority of women in middle and older generations are clustered under high and medium patriarchy categories. The majority of women subject to low patriarchy come from the younger generation. Also, although a minority from all generations come under low patriarchy, younger women are still the most numerous within this group; at the same time, the number of younger women who come under the high patriarchy category, is lower than the other two generations. Hence, in the Italian structure of sexuality, there is an association between younger age and low patriarchy and an association between older age and high patriarchy.

Length of Residence in Britain

British-Italians are heterogeneous in terms of their length of residence in Britain. The ethnic Italian women in this survey belong to four generational cohorts, according to their length of residence in Britain. Some women were born in Britain; some came as adults and have spent between eleven and twenty years here; others immigrated when they were very young and spent most of their lives i.e. twenty one to fifty years in the host country; and finally some Italians have come to Britain as adults in recent times and have spent only between one and ten years in Britain. Within the various

Italian generational cohorts, the length of residence in Britain affects patterns of unequal gender relations in the various social structures of the Italian community, differently.

Different Italian Generational Cohorts:

- Italians born in Britain have been exposed to British educational system, media and customs since birth. They have enjoyed an informal Italian education within the family and at the same time have absorbed many of mainstream British values.
- The Italians who have lived in Britain between 11 and 20 years could have been either youngsters or adults at the time of the migration. If very young, they are likely to have received a British education and been influenced by British cultural values. If already adult at the time of migration, they would not have had any formal British education and would have probably started to work upon arrival. They are thus most likely to have held on to their rural traditional cultural baggage, would be more resistant to assimilation and less flexible to positive changes in unequal gender relations. They might even have been temporary workers intending to return to Italy at some future point.
- Italian women who have lived in Britain between 21 to 50 years might have absorbed some of the British cultural values if they immigrated when they were very young. If they arrived in Britain as adults, it is likely they did not receive any formal British education, they are likely to have preserved their Italian cultural values.
- Women who have immigrated in the last ten years are mainly young adult students or young professionals (Colpi, 1991; Chapter Three).

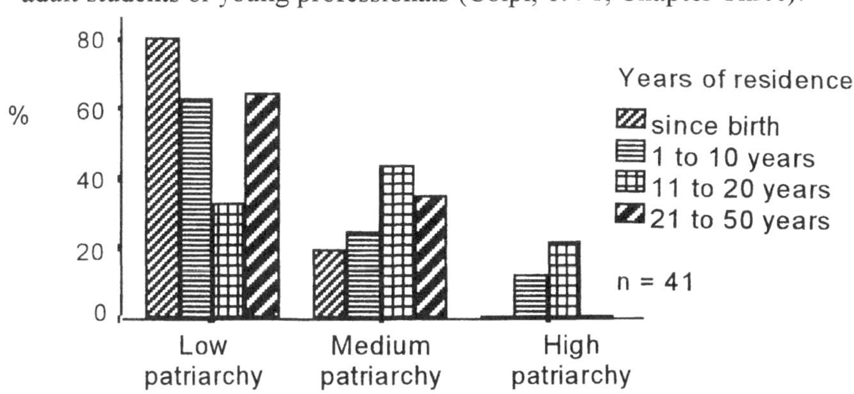

Figure 4.41 Residence in England by patriarchy in employment

The majority of women in the 'since birth', '1 to 10 years' and '21 to 50 years' categories fall within the low patriarchy group. Within the institutions of employment, the greatest percentage of women concentrated in low patriarchy belong to women who were born in England, followed respectively by those who have lived in England between '1 to 10 years', '21 to 50 years', '11 to 20 years'. Residence in Britain since birth is associated with lower patriarchy in employment. At the same time, those women who have recently arrived from Italy fall within the low patriarchy category, even though their length of residence in Britain is only between '1 to 10 years'. In other words the newly arrived Italians are concentrated in lower patriarchy categories and those who have lived in Britain between '11 and 50 years' are clustered in higher patriarchy categories. From the latter cohort only those who were very young when they first arrived in Britain fall within lower category patriarchy.

Figure 4.42 Residence in England by patriarchy in the household

The majority from most groups fall within the low patriarchy category. Most women who fall within the low patriarchy category are in the '1 to 10 years' group; this result reflects the social and cultural developments that have occurred in Italy within the last fifty years leading to a reduction in unequal gender relations (Chapter 6). Also the majority of women born in England fall within low patriarchy. The '21 to 50 years' group is almost equally divided between the low and high patriarchy categories. None of the women born in England fall within the high patriarchy category. Thus low patriarchy in the structure of household is definitely associated with recent emigration or with British-born migrants.

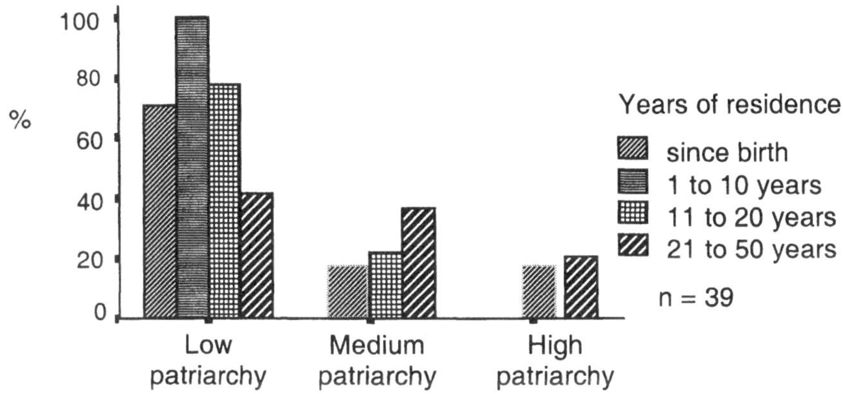

Figure 4.43 Residence in England by patriarchy in culture

All Italian women who have resided in England between '1 and 10 years', 78% of those who have resided in England between '11 to 20 years', 71% of those who have been born in England and 42% of those who have lived in England between '21 to 50 years' are in the low patriarchy category. 37% of the '1 to 50 years' group, 22% of the '11 to 20 years' group, 14% of those born in England are in the medium patriarchy category. There are no women from the '1 to 10 years' group. In the high patriarchy category there are only those born in England (14%) and those who have been in England between '21 to 50 years' (21%). Low patriarchy in the structure of culture is associated with recent and second generation migration.

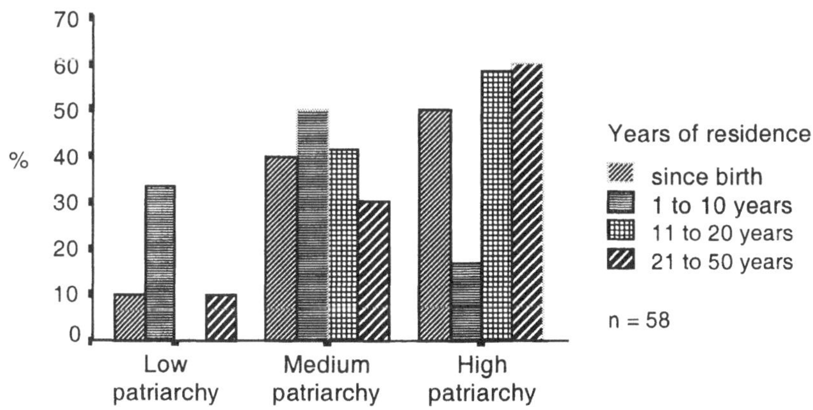

Figure 4.44 Residence in England by patriarchy in sexuality

Most women from all groups fall within the high and medium patriarchy categories. 60% of the '21 to 50 years' group, 58% of the '11 to 20 years', 50% of the 'since birth', but only 17% of the '1 to 10 years' group fall within the high patriarchy category. Thus, the largest percentage of women subject to high patriarchy consists of women who have lived in Britain between '21 to 50 years'. A third of the recent immigrants fall within the low patriarchy category. In the structure of sexuality there is an association between recent migration and low patriarchy.

Summary

Strong ethnic identity distinguishes Italians in Britain. They feel different from the Anglo-Saxon Protestant majority. The distinguishing features of the Italian community result in a different system of patriarchy, with different forms of patriarchal structures. Six patriarchal structures have been identified within the Italian Diaspora community. The Italian and British systems of patriarchy differ in the configuration of their structures and the institutions these structures encompass, the form of patriarchal structure and the main site of patriarchy: Italians do not operate strictly within British social structures. They work within both Italian and British employment niches; although at the beginning of the migration they were mostly employed in mainly Italian owned catering businesses, they have gradually spread into mainstream employment market. They are exposed to British culture at school, through the media, and in the public sphere; but they maintain their Italian customs, they speak Italian at home, they eat Italian food and attend Italian churches. They benefit from British education, healthcare and other social services offered by the British state; at the same time they take full advantage of all the social services provided in Britain by the Italian Church or the Italian state. Although well-integrated in Britain, they are not assimilated and maintain strong allegiance to Italy.

In the structure of employment, the majority of Italian women have entered full-time paid employment; however in comparison with British women, they work longer hours, they are involved more heavily in skilled and semi-skilled jobs and less in professional and managerial jobs. In the structure of household production, Italian women may differ from the rest of British women in the degree of the gendered asymmetry. Some Italians may consider their family, even when patriarchal, as a safe haven in the midst of an alien society and culture. In the structure of culture, the main difference between the British and the Italians stems from the institution of religion. The Roman Catholic Church is one of the most important pillars of the Italian community and it performs both pastoral and social functions. Religion plays a far more important role in the Italian community than in mainstream British society. The effect of Italian education and media on the community is limited and marginal.

The Italian structure of sexuality is deeply influenced by the edicts of the Roman Catholic Church which is strongly opposed to divorce, abortion, contraception, premarital sex, homosexuality, single motherhood and ordination of women priests. The church can control women's sexuality, thus consolidating unequal gender relations. The Italian and British structures of sexuality are different in the sense that the institution of religion does not control the sexual mores of the Anglo-Saxon community to the same extent: The Protestant Churches hold more liberal attitudes towards gender issues. To determine the extent of male violence amongst Italians has been problematic in the sense that Italian women in the survey have denied the existence of widespread domestic violence within the community. Measuring male violence is problematic within mainstream British society as well. This is due to the speculative nature of existing statistics and the lack of accurate legal guide-lines and definitions for male violence and domestic violence. The Italian women's position within the patriarchal structure of State is particular and subject to ambiguities: They live in Britain, are subject to British laws; they are beneficiaries of British education, healthcare, policing and other social services; however, most of them still hold Italian citizenship and consider themselves to be primarily Italian. Consequently their expectations from the British State remain low and their involvement in British political life which could have positive effects in reducing unequal gender relations, remain limited.

The form of patriarchy within the Italian structure of employment is public: based on the evidence of this survey, the overwhelming majority of Italian women are in full-time paid employment, yet they are mostly segregated in lower grade, less remunerated jobs.

In the Italian structure of household production, public and private forms of patriarchy co-exist: by definition, private patriarchy involves the non-admission of women to the public sphere and their exploitation within the household. Italian women have entered the public sphere en masse therefore strictly speaking they are not subject to private patriarchy. However, they are still disadvantaged within the household because they carry the burden of double-shift and their sexual lives are controlled by male heads of their families to some extent.

In the Italian patriarchal structure of culture, the institution of religion plays the crucial role, while the role of education and media is marginal.

The edicts of the Roman Catholic Church regulate women's sexual lives and exclude them from the decision making processes relating to religious affairs. The subordination of women is carried at the collective level making the form of patriarchy in this structure public.

In the Italian structure of sexuality patriarchy manifests itself in both public and private forms: The institution of religion sets gender regulations which are disadvantageous to women, at the collective level; at this stage patriarchy has a public form. Individual males internalize these patriarchal religious values and apply them at individual level to female members of their household thus controlling their sexual lives; at this stage patriarchy becomes private.

To determine the degree of patriarchy within the social structures of both the Italian community and the rest of British society is problematic due to the lack of adequate statistics and difficulties in quantification of abstract values such as exploitation, inequality, inclusion or exclusion from dominant institutions. However, I have operationalized the relative degree of institutional patriarchy within the Italian community and observed that amongst all patriarchal structures of the Italian community, the institution of sexuality is the main site of oppression.

Variables such as 'region of origin', 'degree of religiosity', 'age' and 'length of residence in England' influence patterns of unequal gender relations within the different social institutions of the Italian community.

Employment

The majority of women in the survey are concentrated in the low patriarchy category. The pattern does not alter significantly in any patriarchal category (low, medium, high) according to the region of origin whether North, Centre or the South. Most 'very religious' women fall into the medium patriarchy, about one third in the low and none in the high patriarchy category. On the other hand, the majority of 'not religious' women are concentrated in the low patriarchy category pointing to an association between non-religiosity and low patriarchy. A positive association exists between youth and low patriarchy. Almost 80% of the young generation are concentrated in the low patriarchy category. There are no women from the oldest cohort in the high patriarchy category. There is also an association between lower patriarchy and Italian women who were born in Britain, followed by those who have lived in England either between '1 to 10' years or from '21 to 50' years. Thus women who are not religious, are young and were born in Britain are concentrated in low patriarchy category. However, patterns of patriarchy do not alter according to region of origin.

Household Production

The majority of women in the low patriarchy category are from the 'North and Centre' region of origin. Also, the majority of 'not religious' women are concentrated in the low patriarchy category. There is a positive association between a higher degree of patriarchy and old age. The most interesting point to note is that of those who have lived between '1 and 10' years in England, the overwhelming majority are concentrated in the low patriarchy category as opposed to much lower percentages of those who have been born in Britain, or lived there between '11 and 50' years. This strengthens the assumption (see Chapter 6), that social and cultural upheavals which have helped reduce unequal gender relations in Italy have not reached the ethnic community in Britain to the same extent. Southern origin women, older women and those who were not born in Britain but lived here the longest are most likely to be categorized in the high patriarchy category.

Culture

The majority of women are subject to low patriarchy. However there is a positive association between higher degree of patriarchy and southern region of origin, high degree of religiosity and old age. In other words a greater number of older, very religious women, from the south, are subject to higher degrees of patriarchy.

Sexuality

In this structure there is a marked evidence of a positive association between high degree of patriarchy, southern region of origin, high degree of religiosity and a lengthy period of residence in England (between 21 and 50 years): there has historically been a cultural difference between the North and the South, with the Southerners being more conservative in their sexual attitudes and behaviour (Piccone Stella, 1979); Catholicism regulates and sets limitations to women's sexuality, therefore highly religious women are more restricted within sexual unequal relations; women who came to Britain as adults a long time ago (between 21 to 50 years ago) are more likely to carry the cultural baggage they came with from rural Italy, they are more conservative in their sexuality and sexual attitudes and are concentrated within high patriarchy categories.

In the Italian community, the three structures of household production, culture and sexuality are closely interconnected through the crucial role that the Catholic Church plays in the community. These three structures constitute the Italian Way of Life. Within this particular way of life, women perform most of the housework, they are prepared to sacrifice their life for their family, they are religious and they accept the patriarchal edicts and practices of the Catholic Church (see Chapter 6). They are subject to sexual double standard; their sexuality is regulated by the Church at the collective level and by the male head of the family at the individual level.

5 Italian Institutions in Britain

The Italian community in Britain is characterized by a range of distinct Italian institutions, which have helped the community flourish over the years and have kept it from being assimilated. Specifically these are the institutions of religion, education and media which constitute the Italian culture. Some aspects of these institutions and their development have played a significant role in the reproduction of a distinct system of patriarchal structures.

Religion (Italian Catholic Churches)

The strong standing of Catholic religion within the Italian community indicates that unequal gender relations are continually reproduced, especially within the structure of sexuality.

The function of ethnic churches within migrant societies is threefold: they perform 1) a religious and spiritual role; 2) a cultural role through organizing religious ceremonies in the ethnic language; 3) a social role by providing an array of social services for the community members.

> It is the ethnic church which more than any other institution preserves the culture of the Italians. It is the custodian of the language, and the religious artifacts symbolize a certain culture, tradition and way of life.......The fact is that social community and religion are closely related to, and reflected in, each other. Religion becomes a restatement on a mystical plane, where the most basic traits of social organization are made sacred and put beyond question.... The church of an ethnic group, threatened with the loss of its identity, serves more than any other institution to organize and maintain the group as a functioning community (Colpi, 1991, pp. 230-231).

From the inception of the Italian Diaspora community, the indigenous, highly Irish-influenced Catholic hierarchy in Britain tried desperately to integrate the Italian immigrants. Although English Catholics and the Italians do share the same religion, the cultural variations of their religious practice set them apart. English Catholics find the Italians' catholicism rather superficial, vague, even superstitious with an exaggerated devotion to the dead, the Madonna, the saints and their statues, a veneration bordering on idolatry:

> English people held a rather critical opinion about the Italians' religious convictions and practices. According to them, Italians did not go to mass every Sunday (which, for the English Catholic is central to his faith), during the ritual they used to talk and laugh and in any case participated with little attention and finally used to give little money for the collection (Bottignolo, 1985, p. 57).

In the long run, these cultural variations would have inevitably created rifts between the indigenous and immigrant Catholics. In addition, Italians had language difficulties in a Church that had begun to worship in the vernacular since 1964. Thus, there were sound justifications for the Italian migrants to create their own ethnic churches in England.

The main Italian Churches in England are:

- **St. Peter's Church in Clerkenwell,** London.
  Throughout the 19th and 20th century Clerkenwell was considered London's *Little Italy* and St. Peter's Church was founded in this neighbourhood as early as 1864 to cater to the needs of the Italian colony in London. It is run by the Pallotini Fathers whose activities in England are limited to London alone. St. Peter's publishes the monthly journal *Backhill, The Italian Community Magazine.*
- **Chiesa Cristo Redentore** at the Scalabrini Centre in Brixton, London.
  The Chiesa del Redentore is run by the Scalabrini Fathers and was founded in June 1969 to purvey religious and social services to Italians in South London and peripheral towns. The Scalabrini Centre has become one of the most important cultural centres for Italian immigrants. It was first opened in 1966 at a very modest address in Clapham Road, London S.W.9. The institution has been called Centre as opposed to Church or Parish, in order to reflect the global assistance offered to immigrants, which characterizes the Scalabrini denomination. In fact according to their Legge Fondamentale (Fundamental Law):

  > The apostolic finality of our mission leads us to promote the integral salvation of Man. Thus apart from the spiritual assistance, we offer our human, social and cultural help to the migrants (Centro Scalabrini di Londra 25 Anni di Servizio, 1993, p. 4).

  The Centre's headquarters were moved to a more spacious building in 1968. It consists of a Church, Social Centre, Club, Nursery School,

Youth Hostel and the offices of the newspaper *La Voce degli Italiani*. Italians could turn to the Centre for anything or any advice they need. The official inauguration of its Church took place in June 1969. It was named Chiesa Cristo Redentore (Church of Christ the Redeemer), with the view that such a title would embrace all Christians and would thus avoid the notion of *Foreigner* which is perhaps damaging to the sensibilities of the migrant's psyche. Also the mosaic picture of Christ on the facade of the Church holds a globe in his hand, emphasizing the Christian universality that characterizes the migrant's condition. The Crucifix on top of the altar (replaced by a fresco in 1993) was purposefully made of wood to represent the migrants' sufferings and hopes. In 1993 the celebrations for the 25th anniversary of the foundation of Scalabrini Centre coincided with the complete restoration of the Church. The funds for the restoration works were obtained through donations from the community members: within a year from the beginning of the solidarity campaign, more than £50,000 were collected.

- **San Giuseppe**, Peterborough, founded in 1962.
- **Santa Francesca Cabrini**, Bedford, founded in 1965.

These churches constitute the cornerstones of the Italian communities which have become consolidated in England. They are run by different Catholic denominations which cooperate with each other. Since the 1950s, numerous Italian missionary delegations have come into existence. The main ones are the Scalabrini Fathers (London), the Pallotini Fathers (London), the Stigmatini Fathers (London) and the Consolata Fathers (Enfield). The denominations are all financed through contributions, some from Italian congregations and some from the Italian State. If in need, funds are requested from the Mother Denomination in the Vatican. There are no contributions from the British government. There are seventeen Italian priests and sixteen nuns serving the community. The priests regularly organize Italian Masses for their congregations at local Catholic churches as well as in Italian churches. The priests cater to the spiritual and religious needs of Italians and the nuns' main function is to provide catechism lessons and visit the elderly and the ill. The missions are based in Enfield, Bedford, Bradford, Birmingham, Nottingham, Peterborough, Shenley and Woking.

The number of baptisms and marriages have been quite stable, with no great variations throughout the years since the late 1960s and early 1970s. In the diocese of Southwark, Mass attendance has been stable, around an average of 300, except for the peak year of 1983 when it was 782. In the diocese of Westminster, Mass attendance has kept at a high level of generally more than 1,000, since the 1960s until 1991 when it started to decrease. One reason for the decrease may be that Italians have now dispersed, they are not concentrated in 'little Italies' any more and are encouraged by the Italian churches themselves to integrate in their local Catholic churches. Women and older people tend to attend Mass more often and more regularly (see Tables A.1 and A.2 in the Appendix).

Notwithstanding variations in Mass attendance, Italian churches still play an important spiritual role within the community. Italians regularly use them for baptisms, confirmations and marriages and hundreds celebrate Mass in Italian. This, despite the fact that the Italian population is now geographically dispersed and the active policy of the Italian clergy is to encourage integration.

In June 1996, the Catholic Mission in Enfield published the final report of a research on the Italian Immigrants in Britain. A sample of fifty adult couples and fifty young single Italians, from 26 British regions were interviewed using questionnaires. Forty seven couples declared they attended only Italian Mass and 14 individuals said they attended the English Catholic Mass. Forty four couples said they encouraged their children to attend Sunday Mass and Catechism classes. The majority of the Italian families expressed their preference to use Italian churches because Mass is conducted in Italian, they know the priests and they get an opportunity to meet with friends and relatives.

Italian churches are very active in providing social services to the Italian community. Since the beginning of the immigration, missionaries and priests have acted as interpreters, translators, estate agents, therapists and dispensers of solace. To this day, they still provide space and accommodation for the various regional associations, Italian language courses, nursery schools, youth hostels, youth clubs, women's club, home for the elderly. They publish Italian language newspapers. All the social institutions affiliated to and run by the Italian churches are self-financed. Ritualized life-cycle events such as baptisms, communions, weddings and funerals constitute appropriate occasions for members of the Italian community to reunite with friends and extended family. Such occasions also provide the best opportunity for the young members of the community to socialize and maybe chose their future partners, thus ensuring the perpetuation of Italian culture. Although to a lesser extent than the older generation, young Italians still constitute a large share of the faithful and seek assistance from Italian churches to a considerable extent; they use their various social services such as hostels and clubs, social gatherings, language courses and free dinners. Young Italians, including a number of unemployed and drug-addicts, spend entire days at St. Peter's, where free dinner and lunch are served every Tuesday and Friday, and where they can stay around, until late at night, watching television.

In summertime, Italian churches organize various religious processions. An example is the annual *Madonna del Carmine* procession followed by extensive festive activities. The institution started in 1883 and was the first of its kind since the Reformation in Britain under the reign of Henry VIII: not until 1829 had British Law allowed Catholics to have civil rights such as the right to vote, to enter Parliament and to occupy public office. It has been suggested (Umberto Marin, 1975; Terri Colpi, 1991) that the pioneering St. Peters Church helped de-stigmatise local Catholicism through the festive and colourful traditions of this religious procession. Other important religious processions in the Italian community are Madonna del Rosario in Manchester, Festa of the Patron Saints in Bedford and Sant'Antonio procession in Peterborough.

Numerous social institutions are organized and run by Italian churches:

- **Club Italia,** inaugurated in 1969, organizes social evenings, theatre, concerts, Italian language and culture courses, card game competitions, dinner dances, sport events. Italians of all ages and from all over London enjoy these activities.
- **Italian Nursery School**, managed by Dorotee di Cemmo Sisters was inaugurated in April 1969 and accepts both Italian and non-Italian children. The purpose of this bilingual day-nursery is to preserve the Italian language and culture while preparing children for their future English education. Here children receive their first preparatory religious education. There are other two Italian nursery schools in Bedford (run by Operaie della S. Casa Sisters), and in Cheshunt (run by Canossian Sisters).
- **Hostel for Italian boys and girls,** founded in 1969, gives assistance to numerous Italian boys and girls who come to London to study, to work or merely as tourists.
- **Women's Club,** founded in 1984 by a group of women, organizes recreational and socio-cultural activities such as films, conferences, fashion shows, cookery classes, first-aid classes, exhibitions. Only women can attend. The club is also involved in fund-raising for the elderly, the babies and the youth.

In 1954, the Scalabrinis founded their mission in Bedford where there is another large concentration of Italians. It is complete with the previously mentioned Santa Francesca Cabrini Church, a nursery and a spacious site for social activities. Similarly, in 1957 an Italian mission was inaugurated in Peterborough. In 1971, the Scalabrini Fathers expanded their activities and the Woking Mission was founded to serve the Italian residents of Arundel and Brighton diocese. Thanks to the initiatives of The Italian Women's Club, Villa Scalabrini, a home for elderly Italian people in Shenley was inaugurated in 1986. The Enfield Italian Catholic Mission has been active since 1975. It is run by two nuns and two Diocesan priests. The sisters arrange prayer groups, teach catechism, singing, embroidery and crochet to Italian children. They organize monthly parents' meetings with the priests. There are also monthly meetings with the elderly. The sisters visit Italian families and very often their task is to deal with family disputes. Second generation children have sometimes ambivalent attitudes towards their parents' culture and this can create generational conflicts which the nuns try to resolve.

The institution of the Italian Catholic Church has changed in the sense that Italians are not heavily concentrated in specific areas (such as Clerkenwell and Soho in London) any more; many tend to use their local Catholic churches, often with the active encouragement of the Italian clergy themselves. Today, some Italians may gravitate towards British social services, rather than rely entirely on the Italian Church. Nevertheless, Italian Catholic churches are central to the life of the Italian community and the majority of Italian families still prefer to use their services. The fact that so many church affiliated institutions are still solvent and fully functional, solely through immigrants' financial contributions, points towards the solid ties which link the Church and the community.

In stark contrast to the significance of the Italian Catholic Church within the community, latest figures have demonstrated that there is a sharp decline in church attendance, number of baptisms and confirmations in the Church of England:

> Official figures show that average attendance in 1995 is now close to the psychologically significant million mark at 1,045,000, a fall of 36,000 on 1994. Baptisms have dropped by 9,000, confirmations continue to decline at the rate of 4,000 fewer every year. Even attendance at Christmas and Easter shows a dramatic decline over the year in the number of worshippers -1,00000 and 35,000 respectively, reversing small recent gains (Madeleine Bunting in The Guardian, 7th Feb.1997).

Education

Italian education has a minimal impact on patriarchal relations within the community because both adults and children are exposed to it marginally.

The Italian Ministry of Foreign Affairs has followed an active policy in promoting Italian culture in Britain through the Italian consular network. Apart from purveying administrative services, various Italian consular offices throughout Britain have educational departments which organize and finance Italian courses. Education offices in London, Bedford, Manchester, Birmingham and Nottingham indicate the geographical location and concentration of Italians and the changing social character of the community. The consular network of educational services is backed by COASIT (Committee for the Assistance to Italian Schools). In conjunction, there are a number of voluntary parents organizations which work closely with the consular authorities. Although Italian administrative officials find a controlled integration of the Italians in mainstream British society desirable, they emphasize it should not be at the expense of losing their cultural heritage. Local integration and preservation of the Italian cultural patrimony are considered as perfectly reconcilable, with education playing a prominent role in the process:

- There is a high demand for educational facilities amongst Italians. They consider language courses as highly indispensable in order to reproduce their cultural heritage. With the help of the Italian government, the community strives to make adequate educational facilities available to all Italian immigrants and their British-born children. Although there are various Italian courses on offer throughout Britain, there are no full-time Italian schools. The number of Italian courses for Italian children of school-age is approximately 820: 487 in the London and Bedford area, 163 in the Manchester and Liverpool area and 170 in Scotland (Letter 2732 from the Italian Embassy in London, dated 31st July 1995). The F.A.S.F.A (Federation of the School and Family Associations and Committees) with 59 adherent sub-committees all over England, oversees the organization of Italian courses and parents/teachers relations. Children, between six and eighteen years old, constitute the majority who use Italian language and culture courses. Sometimes, first-generation Italian adults who came to this country with a basic educational formation and who are now mainly engaged in manual labour use the courses made available by ENAIP (an organ of Professional Instruction). ACLI (Association of Christian Italian Workers) and ENAIP offer courses on Import/Export and Computer to help adult immigrants, some of them unemployed, acquire professional training. There are both evening and daytime integrated

Italian courses (GCSE and A-Level). The integrated system is supposed to promote the Italian language and culture within mainstream British society. However, many Italian parents prefer evening courses to the integrated ones, where all students are of Italian origin and the course can be conducted at a more accelerated pace. The courses are given 4 hours per week and consist of general culture, reading, writing, Italian language, geography and history. The Italian ministry of Education, specifically the 'Collegio di Docenti', sets the curriculum but there is always a leeway for every teacher to modify the teaching program. Both parents and teachers admit the quality of the courses is not adequate and they mainly blame it on lack of funds. The Italian government funds the courses, but lately because of financial difficulties, parents have started up associations to organize new courses.

- **The Dante Alighieri Society**, founded in Rome in 1889 as a non-profit organization which promotes Italian language and culture all over the world, has a branch in London and offers courses against fees, upwards of £200. The Association aims to promote Italian culture through lectures, conferences, international meetings, concerts, tours of Italy and scholarships. However, due to the relatively high cost of the courses, the main beneficiaries tend to be British enthusiasts of the Italian culture and not the mass of Italian migrants.
- **The Italian Institute of Culture** was founded in London in 1950; it has mainly served to promote Italian culture amongst non-Italians in Britain, through lectures, art exhibitions, musical events and language courses. The language courses cost between £160 to £210 and are mainly attended by non-Italians. There has been little contact between the Institute and the immigrant masses.

Media

Presently the Italian media has a minimal effect on the cultural development of Italian immigrants. Any benefit reaped from the media and high culture in terms of changing unequal gender relations is marginal.

The main Italian language newspapers and magazines, printed in England, are:

- **La Voce degli Italiani**, a fortnightly newspaper published by the Scalabrini Centre, was founded in 1948 and has a UK circulation of 6,000 copies. It is a Christian inspired newspaper which debates Italian immigrants' main social problems. At the same time, it is a venue for Italians in Britain to advertise their products and services. Considering the size of the Italian community (estimated at 220,000), a mere 3% of the Italians read the leading British based Italian newspaper *La Voce degli Italiani*.

- **Backhill Magazine** covers a wide range of religious, cultural, social and ethnic issues. It was founded in 1977, has a distribution of about 1,000 in London and the South East. It is published ten times per year.
- **Londra Sera** is a bilingual newspaper printed in London. Founded in 1976, it provides cultural and commercial information about the community.
- **Il Messagero Italiano** is a bilingual newspaper printed in Manchester. It was founded in 1993.
- **Spectrum Radio International** is printed by the Italian sector of Spectrum Radio in London.

Italian immigrants do not have extensive access to Italian cultural activities such as books, film, theatre and art exhibitions. The Italian Bookshop, the European Bookstore and Grant and Cutler bookshop are the main book stores which stock Italian books in London. However their clientele consists mainly of elite, highly educated Italian and British people and not the mass of Italian immigrants. On the other hand, light Italian magazines such as Oggi and Gente, imported from Italy, have a wide readership in the community.

The high cultural functions of the Italian Institute of Culture target mainly the British public. Due to limited resources, the activities of the Institute do not extend much to the Italian community at large. Some officers at the Institute opine that cultural organizations such as the Italian Institute of Culture and the Accademia Italiana (founded in 1987 in London, as a private charity to promote Italian art and culture) are elitist institutions and their patrons are therefore mostly people of a certain cultural level. In the last fifteen years, due to a notable degree of internationalization and Europeanization of major industrial, economic and governmental Italian institutions, there has been a new wave of highly educated, professional, elite Italian emigrants. This is the group most likely to take advantage of cultural events organized by the Accademia Italiana and the Italian Institute of Culture.

Culture has changed and developed in Italy but not to the same extent within the community in Britain. There have been even changes in the Italian language: the *National Commission of Parity between Men and Women* has come up with suggestions to strip the Italian language of its patriarchal syntax (see Chapter 6). However, Italian women in Britain are not likely to be exposed to such ideological debates and practices. One reason for the relative lack of interest in high cultural activities within the community, is that those who immigrated did so mainly out of dire economic straits. They came from the poorest and most socially and culturally deprived segments of Italian rural society. They came to Britain to work, and that is exactly what they did in order to build an easier life for their children. They had neither the time nor the desire to get involved in cultural or social events.

Spectrum Radio International is a commercial radio station which boasts an Italian audience of 100,000 in England. It was founded by Wolfgang Bucci as a pirate station but succeeded to obtain a licence in 1989. It broadcasts from 4 to 6 p.m., every week day and 3 hours on Saturdays. Italian football is broadcast live every Sunday from 2 to 5 p.m. Commercials and contributions from community members fund the station. There are no subsidies from the Italian State. The radio program ranges from sport, light entertainment and music to political and social debates.

The Italian media has a limited influence on the community members, because a dominant media is almost non-existent. There are no intellectual debates in the existing British-Italian media. Only a minority of the immigrants have Cable T.V. or satellite, therefore their access to Italian television channels is scant. The main Italian newspapers printed in England are *La Voce degli Italiani* and *Backhill*; they are both affiliated to the church, have an exclusively religious orientation and therefore a limited scope for wider intellectual discourses. The Italian immigrants listen to the radio with greater ease than they spend time on reading. Spectrum which is aware of this reality, broadcasts from time to time programs which argue for the preservation of the Italian culture and its traditional values, advocate the Italian unity and urge fellow countrymen to resist values of consumerism. Mr. Bucci, the radio's director, maintains that the radio often sends out feminist messages through its social and political debates. In his opinion, Italian immigrants came to this country to work, involved their whole family in their business and consequently had very little time or interest for high culture, be it Italian or English. That is, he says, one reason why feminist emancipationist ideas prevalent in the wider British society, did not really reach the core of the Italian community.

I organized a focus group interview with ten Italian women in order to investigate their opinion on Italian gender relations: The women (aged between fifty to sixty years old) interviewed during the focus group session in Enfield, have resided in Britain between 31 to 40 years. They have worked full-time all their lives. They had all been employed in semi-skilled jobs in English factories. Most are retired now. They said they have never been to school: 'we are here to work not to study'. They have never applied for British citizenship out of patriotic feeling and said that their British-born children had also Italian citizenship. They all considered themselves completely different from the British but added that they had a better life in Britain and respected the British. They were unanimous in stressing that the family is at the centre of the Italian way of life and that the mother willingly sacrifices herself for the children. They considered the English mother as very different and more selfish. Some of the quotes were as follows:

'The family is everything'.
'We sacrifice everything for our children'.
'It is a disaster when an Italian man marries an English woman'.
'An English mother is capable of leaving her children to go off with another man. I do not say it does not happen within our community; but if it happens 10% of the time with the Italians, it is 50% with the English'.
'English mothers do not have hearts like ours'.
'Our hearts are made of flesh, English women's hearts are made of bronze'.

One woman protested and said that she has a wonderful English daughter-in-law who has learnt Italian and is very kind, maybe kinder than Italians. All women stressed that their children stay at home until they get married and they find it a source of pride and joy. Should they want to leave, it would be a cause of deep pain and offence to them:

'English mothers cannot wait to get rid of their children'.
'English parents make their children pay when they stay on at home'.

All women said that they have always done full-time paid work and taken care of all the housework. Upon my enquiry that it appears that Italian women carry the burden of the double-shift, their various responses were:

'We like to work'.
'We would have worked even if we did not need to economically'.
'We prefer to work full-time'.
'Italian women work hard, much harder than English women, that is why they hate us'.
'An English woman used to ask me for help in the factory, then stand there idle and look at me'.

'We take pride in our beautiful houses, even though our husbands help, we have to do everything ourselves'.
'Men do not know how to do housework properly anyway'.

All the women said that they felt deeply religious and agreed with the opposition of the Catholic Church to divorce, abortion, contraception, ordination of women, homosexuality. Various comments were as follows:

'The Church is right in everything'.
'We are Catholics and do what the Church tells us'.
'All our children get married in the Italian Catholic Church'.
'We consider a single mother a sinner but we are Christians, we take pity on her and treat her well; times have changed now, we just say she has been very unfortunate'.
'There is divorce amongst the community, but not too many'.
'We do not like women priests'.
'I would be shocked if we had women priests'.
'If Jesus wanted women priests, he would have made Mary one'.
'I would never accept women priests; I know the English do but we don't'.
'We do not like homosexuals' (everyone agreed).
'We are probably different from Italians in Italy, because we have conserved our customs since we immigrated; they have changed'.

Most women agreed that although their children and even some grand-children speak Italian, the new generations have absorbed many British cultural traits and in future, an increasing rate of inter-marriage will mean an increase in integration.

At the end of the interview, I summarized saying: *'it appears that Italian women sacrifice their lives for their family, work very hard both in paid employment and at home without much help from their husbands. Their sexuality is controlled by the edicts of the Catholic Church'*. They all agreed. I then asked whether they felt in any way oppressed and exploited. They all said '*No*' in protest and exclaimed that nobody obliges them to live the way they live, that is what they want themselves. This contradictory statement demonstrates that while women are subordinated within the different social structures of the community, they embrace their lot and discount claims of oppression and exploitation.

Way of Life

The *Italian Way of Life,* of which culture is a constituent, is to a significant extent independent from the underlying economic structure. Thus, although the Italian immigrants have greatly improved their economic status since the early days, their distinctive Italian-ness has not altered to a great extent.

The various people interviewed in the course of this research concorded with the argument that the institutions of religion, family and school reinforce a distinct Italian way of life which encompasses the use of language, dialect, ethnic traditions, culinary habits, characteristic social life and gender relations values. The Italian way of life is distinct from that of mainstream British society. It is undeniably a function of factors such as age, region of origin (North-South divide), profession and consequently economic position, but this is only to a limited extent and always within an Italian framework. Italians have undoubtedly contributed immensely to British society and in turn have been influenced by it. They are well integrated but they have not gone through the processes of acculturation, identification and amalgamation in order to become fully assimilated (see Chapter 2). In the Italian community the institutions of religion and family are closely inter-related and they reinforce each other. Within the family there are definite gender roles and attributes which underlie unequal gender relations (sexual double standard, the sacrificing role of the mother symbolized by the Madonna, women's double shift). Gender inequalities are most prevalent in the structure of sexuality, making it the main site of patriarchy within the Italian community.

6 Structural Changes in Italy

In early twentieth century Britain, there was a move away from private patriarchy towards public patriarchy, due to a series of socio-economic and political factors. The transformation followed women's mass entry into the labour market and their access to the vote, education, professions, right to divorce and property ownership. Equally, since the late nineteenth century, the articulation of a series of sociological, historical and economic milestones has transformed patriarchal gender relations in Italy. In comparison with both mainstream Britain and Italy, gender relations within the Italian Diaspora have not undergone major dynamic transformations. Generally, the greatest changes in gender relations within the community are most perceptible amongst the younger generational cohorts and those who have recently emigrated from Italy.

The condition of women in Italy has evolved since the 19th century, through the Unification, the two World Wars, the Fascist period and the post-war years. A number of historical, political and socio-economic factors (e.g. Risorgimento, wars, Feminist Movement, Economic Miracle, migrations, events of 1968) have steadily eroded the power of the Church and made a tremendous impact on gender relations. The relationship between this cultural change and women's emancipation has been dialectical: women have been both active agents and objects in this transformation.

The Catholic Church

Since Emperor Constantine made Christianity the official religion of the Roman Empire in AD 313, the Catholic Church has had a significant political role in Italy, whose capital, Rome, is the site of the martyrdom of St. Peter and the home of Papacy. Moreover, since the 16th century and with the exception of the present Pope who is of Polish origin, all the Popes have been Italian and as such have demonstrated particular interest in Italian political affairs. During the Fascist period, the influence of the Church was all embracing and extended to all areas of socialization. Separate Catholic organizations for men, women, young men, young women, children, students (all branches of Catholic Action, an organization of lay Catholics under the direct orders of the Vatican) enjoyed the full support of the Fascist regime. The latter had signed the Lateran Pacts with the Pope, giving the Church immense social power. By the time of the Liberation, Catholic culture was nationally hegemonic and could control dissident or unorthodox Catholic intellectual expression by the threat or actual measures of excommunication. At the end of the Second World War, some 95% of Italians were baptized as Catholics and around 60% of the population counted as actively religious. This latter figure has been reduced to circa 30% in recent times (Baranski and Lumley, 1990, p. 80).

Italian society has become rapidly secularized since the 1950s. Alternative cultural traditions such as Communism have emerged, thus giving force to Gramsci's contention that the use of plural is appropriate when discussing culture.

The basic principles of the Catholic culture can be summarized as follows: the virtue of private property, the family, rural values; the belief in the subordinate position of women and the acceptance of one's social station; the virtue of obedience; the punishment of revolutionaries and sinners. Numerous Catholic institutions propagated this culture: the Catholic Action and its dependent organizations; the Trade Union Confederation; ACLI (the labourers' organization); the Christian Democratic Party; the Catholic Press including the most popular 'Famiglia Cristiana'; and finally cultural apparatus such as state schools, radio and television controlled by the Christian Democratic government (Caldwell, 1978).

With the advent of the 'Economic Miracle' and the rapid economic, social and demographic changes that it entailed, the credibility and appeal of traditional Catholic culture was seriously undermined. Urbanization, by itself, had a dramatic role in the decline of the influence of the Church. Falling Church attendance in the northern industrialized cities was partly due to the fact that southern migrants missed their local customs, patron saints and religious festivals and did not appreciate the barren and cold feel of northern churches. In October 1962, Pope John XXIII called the Second Vatican Council in order to reconcile the realities of the emerging social values with the doctrine of the Church. The major notions springing from the Council were identification with poverty and liberation, peace, the liturgy in the vernacular and pluralism i.e. dialogue with dissenting social and ideological forces. The Second Vatican Council marked a significant change of outlook and cultural orientation within the Catholic Church. In April 1963, the Pope issued Pacem in Terris (Peace on Earth), his last and most famous encyclical (Baranski and Lumley, 1990). It stressed the need for profound social and economic changes within the international community, for cooperation between peoples of different ideological and religious beliefs. The encyclical further called for increased social and economic development of the working classes and support for the anti-imperialist struggles in the Third World; it also argued in favour of women's entry into public life. The new position of the Church was very different from the time when it had forbidden Catholics to participate in Italian politics (The 'Non expedit'of 1871).

There followed the emergence of a whole series of spontaneous religious groups, which inevitably led to an organizational and cultural fragmentation of the hitherto monolithic Catholic movement. The Church lost major credibility and the crisis reached its peak with the successful Divorce referendum of 1974. The relentless campaigning of the Women's Movement should not be underestimated in the crisis of the Catholic culture in Italy. Women's social and legal gains in the late 1960s and the 1970s were almost all obtained at the expense of the hegemonic Catholic culture. Since the renewal of the Lateran Pact between the Vatican and the government of Bettino Craxi in 1983, religious teaching is no longer compulsory in Italian schools (Caldwell, 1978; Ginsborg, 1990; Forgacs, 1990; Kaplan, 1992).

On the 5th October 1993, Pope John Paul II published his encyclical 'Veritatis Splendor', which includes what is considered absolute moral truths as taught by the Catholic Church. He warned against idolizing 'Freedom' at the expense of 'Truth' and urged Catholics throughout the world to obey the moral codes of the Church which are valid, he said, for everyone at all times (see Corriere della Sera, 6th October 1993).

The Risorgimento

The economic and social crises that have plagued Italy for the last century are a direct result of the way in which the country was unified in 1861 and transformed from the 'geographical expression' -in the words of Metternich-, into a modern nation state. The Risorgimento (unification) was a political compromise imposed by Cavour's diplomacy (Acquaviva and Santuccio, 1976). It created the historical alliance between northern capital and southern land. Having won the leadership of the movement for unification, the Piedmontese bourgeoisie succeeded in imposing their economic policy on the new nation, thus eliminating all obstacles to the free movement of people, capital and goods between different regions, and expecting beneficial effects alike, for backward and advanced economic sectors of the newly unified nation. National credit policies were concentrated on the industrialization of the North while the South had to be content with occasional public works programs and temporary forms of assistance. All this was accomplished with the tacit agreement of the southern gentry who were then left free to enjoy their local political and economic privileges. Through a system of patronage (clientalism), they busied themselves in sustaining national, mainly Christian Democratic governments, with the necessary parliamentary majorities. The result of this political compromise is the persisting characteristics of development and underdevelopment, creating crisis at every social and economic level in Italy (Allum, 1973; Acquaviva and Santuccio, 1976).

On the 20th September 1870, Italian troops entered Rome, which was the last vestige of the papal Principality, and the territorial unification of the Italian peninsula was thus completed. At the same time, this was the beginning of a conflict between the Church and the Italian State which was to last for sixty years. The Pope's temporal powers were drastically curtailed and he was left with the possession of the Vatican, the Lateran palaces and the summer residence of Castelgandolfo. Pius IX, the incumbent Pope, withdrew from public life in protest at the usurpation of his temporal power by the Italian State, and forbid Catholics to take part in Italian political and public life. The conflict would finally be resolved by the 1929 Lateran Pacts negotiated between Cardinal Gasparri and Benito Mussolini (Villari, 1973).

Position of Women within the Newly Formed Nation-State

Women's movements in Italy started in the second half of the 19th century, lagging behind English, French and American movements (Bono and Kemp, 1991; Kaplan, 1992). The ideological influences can be traced back to the rationalist ideals of Diderot and Condorcet, the French Revolution, the American women's movements already active since 1848, and the utopian ideas of Fourier. The most prominent Italian 'feminist' figure of this period was Anna Maria Mozzoni, who would be categorized as 'liberal feminist' in today's terminology. She fought for women's right to education, which in 19th century Italy, would at best reach and benefit middle-class and aristocratic women and not the masses of Italian women who were mainly peasants, labourers in textile factories or domestic servants in the cities. These were living at such a subsistence level that obtaining the right to education would not have made any difference to them. However, in the late 19th century Italy, women accomplished some isolated cultural and social activities (Kaplan, 1992):

- Beccari founded the journal 'La Donna' devoted to social and political matters concerning women.
- De Sanctis founded two institutions of higher education for girls training as primary school teachers.
- Textile women workers founded the Union of Sisters of Work to claim better working conditions, in 1889.

Despite all these, the impact of women on the Risorgimento and their role in public life appears to have been mainly as exalted wives and mothers of patriotic heroes, Garibaldi's wife, Anita, being the most noted. However, with the gradual industrialization of the country's northern triangle, the composition of the family started to change and the extended family structure began to disintegrate. Peasant women were recruited into factories. Within the aristocratic and middle-class families, the position of women was exalted as mothers directly responsible for the nurturing and education of their children, as opposed to using wet-nurses and nannies.

The following statistics (David Forgacs, 1990, p. 19) illustrate the general literacy rate in Italy:

Table 6.1 Literacy rates in Italy between 1861 and 1951

Number of illiterate people aged 6 upwards per 100 according to national censuses, 1861-1951:

1861	1881	1911	1931	1951
75	62	38	26	14

(Source: ISTAT, Annuario Statistico Italiano, various years)

After unification the number of illiterate women remained consistently higher than that of men, with wider gaps in the South than in the North.

The following table (Forgacs, 1990, p. 19), from a 1911 population census, illustrates the number of illiterate males and females per 100, aged 6 upwards, in eight regions in that year:

Table 6.2 Regional illiteracy rates in Italy in 1911

	Males	Females
Piedmont	9	13
Lombardy	13	14
Veneto	20	29
Tuscany	32	42
Abruzzi-Molise	46	67
Basilicata	56	73
Calabria	59	78
Sardinia	52	64

The First World War

With the advent of the First World War, a rapid process of feminization of industrial employment came about because men were engaged in fighting at the front. There was compulsory conscription for women, similar to the British 'National Register' in 1915. Many women seized the opportunity to enter public life, accepting lower salaries than their male colleagues. At the end of the war, there was a brusque contraction of the female labour market and the level of employment fell almost to that at the beginning of the century. However, this time there was a tremendous modification in the composition of female occupations. Numbers increased in the tertiary sector and there was a drastic drop in the number of domestic servants. In addition, at least in the newly industrializing North, political ideologies of the Left had begun gaining credence among an exploited working class. Under the leadership of Antonio Gramsci, a truly practical and theoretical workers' culture began to emerge and women formed an active part in this culture.

Fascism and the Second World War, 1922-1943

Fascist gender ideology incorporated complex and contradictory aspects (Forman, 1974; Weiss, 1967; Baranski and Vinall, 1991). Just like the Nazi policy of 'Küche, Kinder, Kirche' (kitchen, children, church), it exalted the maternal role of women, restored male authority within the family, embarked on a policy of complete repression of female sexuality and tried to restrict and segregate women's education through a series of legislation and very aggressive propaganda tactics (Koonz, 1987). In their implementation, the Fascist leader Benito Mussolini had not to fear any resistance from the Catholic Church, the monarchy or the military (Kaplan, 1992):

- In 1923 it was forbidden for women to be promoted to the position of school principals, by decree of the monarch.
- In 1924 Mussolini proclaimed the use of contraception and any other form of birth control legally punishable.
- Adultery was punishable for women but not for men; women's physical chastisement was permitted by law; women could not leave the domicile against the husband's will.
- In 1929 the Fascist state signed the Lateran Concordat with the Vatican, thus giving pre-eminence to Canon Law in Italy. The consequences of this were going to be dire for women in view of the attitude of the Church towards them: Pope Leo XIII had declared in 1880 that *'a man rules a woman as Christ rules his Church'* (Kaplan, 1992, p. 234).

According to the Roman Catholic Church, a woman's role in life was limited to reproduction, preservation of family traditions and self-effaced devotion to members of the family. Paid employment outside the home was considered seriously detrimental to the well being of the family and, therefore, strongly discouraged. The Vatican's encyclical 'Quadragesimo Anno' (1931) reconfirmed women's place as being at home, thus reinforcing a series of Mussolini's decrees limiting women's participation in public life. In 1930 the State declared that abortion would carry severe imprisonment penalties. The Vatican regained control over marriage, divorce, the use of contraception and abortion.

The marriage of convenience between the Fascist dictatorship and the Catholic Church, was possibly more virulent and damaging to women than the notorious misogyny of the Nazi regime: it is far easier to overcome a dictatorship than to psychologically exorcise, individually or collectively, the dictates of God transmitted through an infallible Pope! Fascist state imperialism had its parallel in family imperialism, where women were completely subordinated. Their role was exalted as producers of soldiers and heroes for Italy (Baranski and Vinall, 1991; Kaplan, 1992).

Apart from the anti-emancipationist policies of the Fascist State, the contraction of the female job market in this era was also linked to the overall national and international economic crises of the 1920s and early 1930s. With the abolition of trade unions and all democratic parties, proletarian women took the impact of the class violence to which the whole working class was subjected. Women became the double victims of sexism and class relations. Hardest hit during this crisis were female agricultural labourers, especially those in the South, and the lower middle class women in the cities. Paradoxically, these women had traditionally formed the backbone of consensus for the Fascist regime. The latter, having barred or restricted women from the productive sector, was busy recruiting them, through propaganda and even compulsory measures, into female Fascist organizations of an aid/support nature. The contradiction of misogynist Fascism lied in the fact that while excluding women from public life, it was trying desperately to use their political consensus to its own advantage.

The Italian Communist Party founded in 1921, was not only conceived as the main democratic counter-force to Fascism but, under its protective umbrella, the feminist movement stayed alive and continued to grow. Antonio Gramsci, one of the founders of the Italian Communist Party and editor of the famous communist newspaper 'L'Ordine Nuovo', launched 'Tribuna delle Donne' a newspaper covering exclusively women's issues; it was renamed 'Compagna' in 1922. Togliatti, the General Secretary of the Italian Communist Party (1926-1964) firmly believed in the intimate relationship between the women's question and the materialization of true democratic socialism (Kaplan, 1992).

The Resistance

In September 1943, Italy was practically divided in two: in the South there were the King and the 'liberating' forces of the Allies; the North and the Centre were invaded by the German Army. Sections of the peasantry, members of the working classes, ordinary patriotic citizens and the partisans in the North and Centre soon became united in their cause to rid their country of the foreign invaders. The CLN (the Committee for National Liberation) was founded on the 9th September 1943 in Rome and invited the Italian population to join the Resistance and liberate their nation from the yoke of Nazism. The Resistance movement remained limited to the Northern and Central regions of Italy because the South, though in the grips of severe deprivation and social injustice, had no foreign enemy to fight against. The Italian Resistance numbered probably 100,000 active men and women (Ginsborg, 1990, p. 70). Other estimates have mentioned a total of 200,000 partisans, of which 70,000 were women (Kaplan, 1992, p. 238). At a time when the Italians were widely discredited throughout the international community for their support of Mussolini's fascist regime, the sacrifices of the partisans did much to salvage the tarnished image of Italy and to give some measure of self-respect back to the Italians. The Resistance movement further succeeded in creating an anti-Fascist legacy which was to persist into the 1960s and 1970s (Ginsborg, 1990). It constituted one of the most important elements in revolutionizing the traditional Italian culture: until then women's place was in the matrimonial home and not alongside men fighting, commanding, taking initiatives, manipulating arms and risking their lives in the struggle for liberation. The massive participation of Italian women in the Resistance movement was partly the result of the contradictions inherent in the Fascist gender ideology: inciting or forcing women to remain at home and dragging them into the labour market when the war economy was in crisis. When the hardships and miseries of the war reached the peak, when their sons and husbands were being deported to Germany or looking for hiding places, Italian women from every class and age did exactly what they had been taught by the Fascist regime: they undertook to protect and assist their men, but this time against the Fascists. They participated at every level, with a minority taking part even in armed struggle. Many anti-Fascist women's organizations emerged and credit goes to the communist party for creating the initial ones. By 1945, women had acquired a great sense of pride and confidence, they felt they had proved their worth to their countrymen and became political in their demands for an egalitarian society.

The Reconstruction

In June 1945, Ferruccio Parri, a much loved partisan, became Prime Minister and for a while it appeared as if the leftist oriented Resistance had come to power. But, in reality, there was the gradual development of two opposing fronts within the Italian society: the Capitalists, the Christian Democrats and the United States on the one side and the working class movement, the Communists and Soviet Union on the other. In the referendum of June 1946, Italy emerged as a Republic and the Christian Democrats by far the most powerful political party (Ginsborg, 1990). The American-backed capitalist, Christian Democratic party was clearly winning.

The United States of America had an important role in the post-war recovery of the Italian State and economy. At the end of the war, it swiftly filled the power vacuum left in the Mediterranean after the waning of British influence. Harry Truman, the incumbent American President, had long nurtured a desire to block Russian expansionism. Thus, following a policy of containment that became known as the Truman Doctrine, the

United States was to intervene militarily, diplomatically and economically, on a global level, anywhere the Russian threat became evident.

In 1947, George Marshall, the US Secretary of State, announced the birth of the European Recovery Program (ERP), widely known as the Marshall Plan. The ERP was to last four years and provide 29 billion US dollars in American assistance to Europe (Ginsborg, 1990, p. 78). The reasons behind the creation of the Marshall Plan were not purely ideological. The United States was also aiming to reconstruct Europe and to create a market of immense dimensions within the international capitalist trading structure. Failing that, the United States would risk returning to the gloomy conditions of the Great Depression. 176 million US dollars were thus designated to Italy in the first months of 1948 as 'Interim Aid', and after that the Marshall Plan entered into full operation (Ginsborg, 1990, p. 115).

The American aid to Italy consolidated the Christian Democrats and the capitalist classes of the country. George Marshall had warned that, in the event of a Communist victory in the 1948 Italian elections, all help to Italy would cease immediately.

Before the elections of 1948, the Vatican had succeeded in including the Concordat (or Lateran Pact) signed in 1929 between Mussolini and the Church, unchanged, in the new Italian Constitution. The Pact made religious education compulsory in state schools and proclaimed Catholicism the official religion of the country. The Church permeated the Italian society profoundly through its various welfare and educational institutions such as hospitals, nursing homes, nursery schools, libraries and monthly bulletins.

The right to vote in 1945 was the first concession of the new democratic government to women. The Italian Communist and Socialist parties were instrumental in drafting a new constitution which gave women the right to vote and endorsed the concept of gender equality. However, the right to vote was conceived more as a prize to thank women for their sacrifices in the Resistance than their actual right. For example, a special clause excluded prostitutes from voting, making it clear that the system functioned on the basis of women's merit rather than rights. It was not until 1958 that this clause was abrogated. The subsequent years brought more disillusions to women who saw that many articles of the new constitution regarding women's rights either did not get the support of parliamentary enforceable laws, or became practically useless due to the persistence of patriarchal culture or the intransigence of the Church. Thus, in the immediate post-war years, official feminist activities started gaining ground in Italy in order to preserve and put into practice such rights as women had gained for themselves. The Italian Women's Union (Unione Donne Italiane - UDI) although founded, financed and run by the Italian Communist Party, accepted women from all political parties. Its membership reached one million and its official newspaper -NOI DONNE (We Women)- was selling 200,000 copies, by 1949 (Kaplan, 1992, p. 240). UDI was the first women's organization that openly discussed, in print, the issue of abortion. One year after the foundation of UDI, in 1948, a conservative Catholic women's organization, 'Centro Italiano Femminile' was formed. It attracted a large membership and constituted a rival force against the more radical leftist-oriented UDI. In the late 1950s, UDI's political agenda began to falter gradually under the onslaught of the nascent Italian capitalist 'Economic Miracle'. By then, Italian society had split into Marxist and Capitalist Catholic blocs and the government became characterized by a notorious political continuity, dominated by the Christian Democrats. UDI's activities became increasingly focused on aid and support rather than political activities.

The Economic Miracle

Until the mid 1950s, Italy was still mainly an agricultural country, and in many ways still an underdeveloped country:

> In 1951 the elementary combination of electricity, drinking water and inside lavatory could be found in only 7.4 % of Italian households (Ginsborg, 1990, p. 210).

The growth of international trade, Fordism and consumerism brought unprecedented levels of economic prosperity to the Western World and:

> in the twenty years from 1950 to 1970 per capita income in Italy grew more rapidly than in any other European country: from a base of 100 in 1950 to 234.1 in 1970, compared to France's increase from 100 to 136 in the same period, and Britain's 100 to 132. By 1970 Italian per capita income, which in 1945 had lagged far behind that of the northern European countries, had reached 60 % of that in France and 82 % of that in Britain (Ginsborg, 1990, p. 239).

Italy achieved such a major economic expansion because:

- The end of Italy's trade protectionism propelled the country to the forefront of European economic integration and its industrial sector, although of modest proportions, withstood the forces of competition and challenge from other European counterparts. There were great technological advances in the steel, petrochemical, fertilizer and synthetic rubber industries. At the same time, Marshall Aid from the United States of America played an important role in the introduction of new machinery and technological expertise.

- Infrastructural construction such as highways linking all corners of the country, non-taxation of business interests, favourable lending rates by the Bank of Italy, and monetary stability served the private sector to a great extent and created favourable conditions for the accumulation of capital and its subsequent investment in industry. The exploitation of Italy's phenomenal unemployment rates and consequent low wage rates in the 1950s, combined with the absence of effective trade union power in the post-war years, played no minor role in this economic boom.

> Between 1953 and 1960, while industrial production rose from a base of 100 to 189, and workers' productivity from 100 to 162, real wages in industry fell very slightly from 100 to 99.4. With labour costs as low as these, Italian firms were highly competitive on international markets (Ginsborg, 1990, p. 214).

However, the 'Economic Miracle' exacerbated the pre-existing social and economic structural imbalances in the country and created new ones which were to plague the country for the decades to come. Export-oriented economic growth was not matched by any corresponding development in internal public expenditure i.e. low-cost housing, schools, hospitals, public transport. It exacerbated the dualism between the dynamic, rationalized, technologically advanced sector and the traditional, labour intensive, low productivity sector which constituted an enormous section of the Italian economy. The 'Miracle' was essentially a northern phenomenon. It further deepened the existing social and economic rifts between the North and South of the country and drew huge migratory waves from the rural South. It was in fact the migration which involved the southerners in the 'Miracle'.

The 'Economic Miracle' entailed an extraordinary process of transformation in every aspect of Italian culture: lifestyle, family life, gender relations, social and sexual mores, consumption habits, leisure activities, even the spoken language (Ginsborg, 1990). Italians experienced rapid per capita income rise, which, together with an aggressive advertisement campaign, turned their society into an unprecedented consumerist one, similar to the American model. The greatest cultural upheaval was caused by the introduction of television in 1954. A state monopoly, it was controlled by the Christian Democrats and therefore heavily influenced by the policies of the Catholic Church. Its programs were appropriately censored so that they would be in line with the sacrosanct Catholic conception of family values. Advertising took an original form in Italian television: advertisements were grouped together and shown for half an hour at peak time, just before the nine o'clock news. The name of the product was mentioned for a few seconds in each spot and the rest of its time allowance was devoted to fairy tales or cartoons for children. This half-hour mini-program called 'Carosello' became extremely popular with children all over Italy. Parents became accustomed to send children to bed just after the 'Carosello'. By 1960 it had become the most popular television program in Italy! The astuteness of this novel and uniquely Italian advertising policy was that it succeeded in capturing the attentions of a whole generation of children and introduced them to the delights of consumerism. On the other hand, 'Carosello's consumerist message turned out to be inconsonant with the teachings of the Catholic Church. In the words of Pier Paolo Pasolini:

> The Vatican never understood what it should or should not have censored. For example, it should have censored 'Carosello' because it is in the all-powerful 'Carosello' that the new type of life which the Italians 'must' lead explodes on to our screens with absolute, peremptory clarity. And nobody can tell me we're talking about a way of life in which religion counts very much. On the other hand, the purely religious broadcasts are so tedious and so repressive in spirit that the Vatican would have done well to have censored the lot (cited in Ginsborg, 1990, p. 241).

With the advent of the television as a necessary feature in every Italian household, cinema-going declined to some extent but not altogether. The Italian film industry was brilliant in this period, with directors such as Fellini who exposed the corrupt lifestyle of the Roman nouveaux-riches in *La Dolce Vita*, and Visconti whose unforgettable *Rocco and his Brothers* portrayed the dramatic account of life for a family of southerners in Milan.

The paperback boom began in 1965, the year the publishers Mondadori launched their Oscar series. There was a marked increase in sales of women's magazines (Amica, Annabella and Grazia) which covered traditional women's subjects such as fashion, beauty, cookery, home decoration.

The expansion of the media and their ability to reach all corners of the country, coupled with the new mobility of Italian families, many of whom had acquired FIAT 500s and were hurtling along the newly built highways throughout the peninsula, helped to homogenize Italy culturally.

These social upheavals also transformed the family and gender relations: family sizes began declining, most markedly in the urban industrialized North-West. In Italy as a whole, the size of the family shrank from 4 members in 1951 to 3.3 in 1971 (Ginsborg, 1990, p. 243). Families were becoming smaller privatized units and, although they were less open to community life and some may have suffered from it, the privacy afforded by these new urban structures relieved the majority of people, especially the young, from the scrutiny of their fellow rural countrymen.

In the 1960s, at the peak of the 'Economic Miracle' and the consumerist age, it became common for women to be full-time housewives, to take full responsibility for their children's education and to take care of the husbands who, especially in the industrialized North, were working very long hours. The media in this period never stopped to exalt this new figure of the Italian woman, encouraging her to enjoy the fruits of a prosperous economic age. Piecework at home was common amongst married women. For younger, unmarried women, there was undoubtedly greater autonomy from their patriarchal traditional families. Sexual attitudes and taboos changed very slowly everywhere in Italy, but slower in the South. The sexual double-standard and codes of honour persisted well into the 1960s, although by then a few popular magazines had already ventured timidly to discuss pre-marital sex, adultery and other sexual matters. It was not until another decade had passed that major transformations occurred in the sexual mores of the Italians (Ginsborg, 1990).

Migration

> In all, between 1955 and 1971, some 9,140,000 Italians were involved in inter-regional migration..... In the five years of the 'miracle'(1958-63) more than 900,000 southerners changed their places of residence from the South to the other regions of Italy..... So great and persistent was the flow from the South that by the end of the sixties Turin had become the third largest 'southern' city in Italy, after Naples and Palermo (Ginsborg, 1990, pp. 219-220).

Young, intrepid, unmarried men were the ones who left their rural villages first, later to be followed by other members of their families. As a general informal rule, married women did not work outside their homes but took up some piecework jobs at home. For the first time some young southern women took up jobs in factories. They enjoyed and appreciated their new-found freedom although their wages were approximately half those of their male counterparts and working conditions were hard, unsafe and unstable. Some southern women ended up in prostitution. By the late 1960s, the difficult period of adjustment to the uprooting and transition was slowly drawing to an end and a more prosperous life for the immigrants was beginning.

The South and those who did not migrate fared differently in the 'Economic Miracle'. By the mid 1960s there were profound transformations in the South as well due to massive public investment by the Cassa del Mezzogiorno (Fund for the South), money sent back home by the emigrants and the designation of special southern zones as new poles of industrial development. However, these developments were of limited nature and apparently the result of successful clientalistic pressures and lobbying rather than sound rational economic planning with multiplier effects. The investments were nearly all capital-intensive rather than labour-intensive and thus failed to resolve the age-old problem of southern unemployment. Such monumental investments were later sarcastically referred to as *'Cathedrals in the Desert'*.

The Events of 1968

The centre-left governments had failed to keep pace with the multiple demands of a rapidly modernizing Italy. In 1968, the lethargy of the ruling classes finally gave rise to a shake-up from the grass roots. During this extraordinary period of social ferment, which spread from schools and universities into factories, the organization of Italian society was profoundly challenged at most levels.

The 1968 protest movement had both material and ideological bases. Absentee professors, traditional curricula, shortage of classrooms and textbooks, gloomy prospects of employment, high cost of university courses constituted the material base of university students' dissatisfaction. At the same time an ideological reaction to the then prevailing principles of individualism, consumerism and a series of international events such as the Vietnam War, the death of Che Guevara, the Chinese Cultural Revolution and the May 1968 events in France, concocted a potent cocktail of dissatisfaction which culminated in student riots in major cities of the North. Very soon they linked up with worker protest movements in the factories and, although to a lesser extent, reached the sleepiest corners of the Centre and the South.

The spontaneous 1968 protest movement in Italy, though Marxist in nature, was anti-authoritarian and iconoclastic and did not have a coherent political agenda. One of the most obvious targets of the movement was the family. It denounced the inadequacies of the nuclear family, its authoritarianism and absolute values. The movement was libertarian with regard to all relations including sexual relations. Young women, although subordinate to males within the movement, experienced fervent political commitment along with sexual freedom, as never before. The movement lost its intense momentum within a year. However it constituted a prime mover behind social and political reforms and left a lasting effect on modern Italian society. There was to be more open attitudes towards authority and gender relations (Ginsborg, 1990). Nevertheless, Italian Law still contained the oppressive and degrading Fascist family laws. Women were still barred from legal and diplomatic careers, they occupied a very low percentage of jobs in the public service and there were large salary differences for work performed by men and women.

> In 1871, 48% of the total workforce had been women. Exactly one hundred years later, the participation rate of women in the workforce had declined to 17%. In 1971, 5% of Italian women were illiterate, 27% had not completed primary school and a further 44% had no education beyond elementary level, that is, seven in ten Italian women had just the minimum exposure to formal education (Kaplan, 1992, p. 243).

Thus the 1970s mark the beginning of the intense activities of the Italian Feminist Movement which set out to determine the country's political agenda that had so far failed to keep pace with Italy's momentous economic, social and cultural transformation.

The Italian Feminist Movement

The particularities of Italian feminism make it distinct from British and American feminisms: gender studies have not been institutionalized within Italian universities and although there have not been mass demonstrations in the last few years, women's debates have traditionally been taken to the streets. There is a multitude of women's cultural centres, bookshops and publishing houses specializing in gender issues. Italian feminism has a strong political character. Women have been active in the Resistance movement, in the 1968 movement, in the Communist Party where they significantly changed the position of the Party on the abortion law. Italian feminism is separatist, in the sense that it advocates relating first and foremost to other women (Hellman, 1987; Bono and Kemp, 1991). Italian feminist political practice designates women as the primary reference. This does not exclude women's conflicts and differences amongst themselves, only that they should not lose sight of their own value as 'women'.

Until the late 1960s Italian feminism had been active within the restrictive political context of the parties of the Left and in that context, women's oppression had been conceptualized as the 'Questione Femminile' (the feminine question). In the early 1970s, Italian women began organizing into radical, independent, politically oriented feminist groupings. They were disenchanted by the lukewarm actions of the leftist parties and trade unions vis-à-vis women's concerns such as abortion and the antiquated Fascist family laws. Women had gained a much deserved self-confidence, thousands had become war widows, were left behind by migrant husbands to raise families single-handedly, had witnessed the events of the 1968 and had become politicized. The movement involved women from diverse social strata and professions and they were not willing to be treated as a marginal group with marginal problems any more.

Four strands have been broadly identified within the Italian Feminist Movement of the 1970s (Hellman, 1987; Kaplan, 1992):

- The Women's Liberation Movement (Movimento di Liberazione della Donna - MLD) which was founded in Rome in 1970 and was affiliated to the radical party.
- A group led by UDI (Unione Donne Italiane) affiliated to the Communist party.
- An autonomous branch, constituting the backbone of the extra-parliamentary opposition.
- A group developed out of the New Left, resolutely anti-institutional, proclaiming the inalienable value of 'difference' and hostile to the abstraction of the Law.

The movement continued to produce numerous small groups with their own independent agenda and political programs. Many of the small groups have now either disappeared or merged into larger ones (e.g. Demau, Via Cherubini, Rivolta Femminile).

> Italian feminist ideology was never one set of ideas, adopted by women everywhere in the country, but many different conceptions and activities that gave rise to new conceptions in different places. It was not one ideology but many, and it was not even one feminism but many 'feminisms', each shaped by the specific political, economic and social features of the setting in which it grew. In short, there was no single body of feminist thought or practice; there were many feminist thoughts and many different practices (Hellman, 1987, pp. 53-54).

However, the issue of abortion helped create cohesion and solidarity amongst various feminist groups. Civil divorce was legalized in 1974 through parliamentary channels and without much input from the feminists. In October 1965, Loris Fortuna, a Socialist deputy, first introduced his divorce bill. Although very moderate in content, its progress was blocked by the dominant Christian Democrats. They were backed by the hierarchy of the Catholic Church in their vociferous attacks on the bill. By 1969, public opinion supported by LID (The Italian League for the Institution of Divorce) and the Communists, along with further complementary proposals from the liberal MP Antonio Bislini, lent momentum to the call for legalizing divorce. It passed into law on 1st December 1970. Various Catholic organizations swiftly gathered the necessary signatures and decided to call a referendum on the issue. The referendum took place on the 12th May 1974 and the divorce law was consolidated, much to the surprise of all political parties (Ginsborg, 1990, p. 328).

While the feminist movement became very vocal and active on the issue of abortion, the Pope, backed by the State, fiercely maintained his anti-abortionist stance. There were violent clashes between the police and the feminists during mass demonstrations. The problem with the abortion issue was that even the progressive parties of the left were reluctant to endorse it for fear of alienating masses of Catholic voters. Finally, after numerous demonstrations and due to the feminists' relentless persistence, a restrictive abortion bill passed through parliament in 1978. According to this law, the minimum age for abortion was to be 18 years, and the maximum period during which abortion was allowed was 90 days; however, any doctor could refuse to perform the operation on grounds of conscientious objection. The abortion bill, however restrictive, constituted a cultural revolution against the powerful Church and a major success for feminists (Kaplan, 1992). The abortion law was challenged twice in later years and each time huge mass rallies were organized to safeguard it.

In the 1970s, feminist issues were widely publicized through a proliferation of women's writings, newspapers, magazines and journals. *Noi Donne, Quotidiano Donna, Donnawomanfemme, Differenze* and *Memoria* are just some of these publications. Italian feminists had their own radio and television programs, and a multitude of cultural associations and activities. The new-wave feminist movement was indeed a national movement. Feminist groups sprang up in the smallest towns, from the most remote corners of the Deep South to the industrialized North. Feminist collectives were formed in schools, suburbs and city quarters. The ability to swiftly organize and mobilize large numbers of women, on a national scale, was unprecedented and unmatched in Western Europe (Hellman, 1987).

The late 1970s witnessed a period of high social unrest and terrorism unleashed by both ultra-right and left political groups. The state reprisals against terrorism caught feminists in the crossfire. Many were arrested, amongst them Maria Rosa Dalla Costa, who had championed the idea of wages for housework. Feminists and women in general became the target of ordinary males' violence. It has been suggested that the terrorist activities of the 1970s, while directed at the state, were carried out against the people, with a particular vengeance for those recalcitrant women who were doggedly determined to rise against the machismo pervading the Italian culture (Kaplan, 1992). The 1970s thus witnessed an extraordinary, hitherto unprecedented spectacle of gender warfare. Violence against women found its public expression in the number of recorded rapes. There were 16,000 recorded rapes per year in Italy in the early 1970s the heyday of the new women's movement, compared to 7,000 in West Germany (Kaplan, 1992, p. 250). Italian law had no provisions against sexual violence. It was not until 1982, that due to extensive lobbying by feminists, rape became a punishable crime through an amendment of the criminal code. Before that, social custom prescribed that after dark no woman should venture out unaccompanied by a male; therefore were a lone woman raped at night on the streets, she had no one to blame but herself for having ignored the social rule of *'accompagnamento'* (to be always accompanied by a male). Obviously, such traditional rural custom had not reckoned with working night shifts in factories or attending classes after dark or just plain socializing in a modern urban society. However, thanks primarily to the relentless activities of the feminist movement and to a lesser extent the support of the traditional parties of the left and the forces of the New Left, the 1970s and 1980s witnessed some very advanced legislation concerning women's condition:

- The Divorce law, enacted in 1970, was upheld in the 1974 popular referendum (Ginsborg, 1990, p. 328).
- The maternity law of 1971 secured jobs for one year after the birth of the child; 80% of the last salary is paid for the first five months of the maternity leave; a further half year can be taken off with 30% of the last salary; men have a right to some paternal leave as well, but in practice very few men take advantage of it (Kaplan, 1992, p. 255).
- In 1971 the laws forbidding the sale of contraceptives and the dissemination of birth control information were repealed (Kaplan, 1992, p. 265).
- The new Family Law, signed in 1975, overturned a Fascist code which had stripped women of many socio-economic rights. According to that

family code, women required their husbands' permission in order to travel or seek a job; they had no say in determining the place of domicile. The new Family Law corrected these anomalous legal features (Kaplan, 1992, p. 252).

- 1975 witnessed the decriminalization of therapeutic abortion, and 1978 the enactment of the abortion law (Kaplan, 1992, p. 252).
- The 1977 Law for the Equality of Treatment abolished a number of discriminatory policies. At present, the National Commission for Equal Opportunity, which has its headquarters in the Prime Minister's palace, is responsible for a great many activities aimed at eradicating discriminatory practices (Kaplan, 1992, p. 252).
- Since 1982, rape has been punishable by between 3 to 8 years imprisonment, with harsher treatment for gang rapes. Domestic rape is not considered as 'rape' (Kaplan, 1992, p. 253).

The power of the Church was thus seriously undermined but not broken:

> Indeed, between the encroaching secularization and the general population's deep-seated religiosity, also present amongst feminists, a new compromise was struck. Religion in Italy has gradually shifted from signifying catholicism to being an expression of personal conscience as 'believers' (credente). In any case, the Concordat now means much less than it once did, because the introduction of civil divorce, of contraceptives and abortion rights cut deeply into catholic dogma and effectively overruled or sidestepped, canon law (Kaplan, 1992, p. 257).

The Italian feminist movement has lost its initial revolutionary fervour and in the 1980s has increasingly shifted the ground of activities from the street to theoretical work. It is now characterized by a kind of unease towards women's social position: in 1979, Italian sociologist Laura Balbo first introduced the concept of 'double presence' which has since generated a vast amount of research. Balbo defined 'double presence' as the condition of a growing number of women in advanced capitalistic countries, who think and act transversally within different worlds: public/private, family/work, personal/political. The concept of 'double presence' differs from 'double shift'. Whereas 'double shift' implies a stressful situation where the woman suffers the double burden of both productive and unremunerated reproduction work, 'double presence' tends to introduce the possibility to practice a life-project by an ever growing number of women - transversally within diverse material and symbolic worlds i.e. family, community, the services, places of collective action. 'Double Presence' is both descriptive and interpretative. It designates a practical and mental female space adaptable to individual ties and conditions but also a generator of new social and political mutations. 'Double presence' goes beyond 'double shift', the subordination of women at work and their marginality in politics, and analyses the active presence of women's strategy in these diverse contexts, not on the basis of parity or protection, but on the basis of 'difference' It is stressed that women live, think and act differently within the public life; this diversity of presence has to be valued and the organization of public life itself should be altered.

The concept of 'double presence' has generated a large number of studies by Italian feminists (Balbo 1978, 1991; Zanuso, 1978; Bianchi, 1980). These emphasize gender difference and claim that the policies of 'parity' and 'equality' have not been able to modify the organization of either production or reproduction. In this unchanged masculine context, a minority of women have been pushed into production work, thus suffering the 'double shift' instead of enjoying the 'double presence' with its ambitious and optimistic connotations. On the other hand, large masses of women, who are either excluded from the labour market or marginal in it, are suffering a new type of unease: whereas before, having a career was one possible action as opposed to taking on a family role, now, self-affirmation in public life has become an imperative. From that, has resulted the de-legitimization of life choices of large masses of women (Bianchi, 1980).

The feminist movement has had an overwhelming impact on the rigid, chauvinistic code of ethics which prevailed in Italy, especially in the South. The media, although still guilty of representing women as the inferior sex or simply as sexual objects, has been instrumental in homogenizing the Italian culture on a national level. It has undermined the all embracing influence of the Catholic Church. Women have the freedom to abort, to use contraceptives and to obtain a divorce; rape (but not domestic rape) has become punishable by law. The relationship between the State and women has been transformed from confrontational in the turbulent 1970s, to one where women try to improve their position from within the political system. However, women's success at entering the highest ranks of government has not been spectacular: in the first Italian state legislature (1948-53), 7.8% of the MPs and 0.9% of the senators were female. In the (1983-88) legislature, 7.9% of the MPs and 4.9% of the senators were female (Kaplan, 1990, p. 256).

Transformation of the Italian Language

The culturalists have emphasized the importance of language as a pervasive vehicle of women's subordination and marginality in social, economic, political and cultural life (Alexander and Seidman, 1991).

The National Commission for the Realization of Parity between Man and Woman has set out to eliminate sexism from the Italian language through a series of Recommendations to the media, educational book editors and the general public: 'everything that is conserved in language is mortal, including patriarchal hegemony' (Camboni, cited in Kemp and Bono, 1993, p. 91). The Commission, while recognizing that the elimination of linguistic sexism does not automatically lead to an ideal cultural and social modification, believes nevertheless that the linguistic universe has been organized around 'man', with 'woman' remaining a derivative and presented as marginal and subaltern. Such a universe, argues the Commission, does not reflect the social dynamics of gender relations.

In short, the Risorgimento, the two World Wars, the Resistance, the Economic Miracle, migrations, the events of 1968, the Feminist Movement have all been instrumental in shaping the Italian culture and way of life; they have redefined the role of the Catholic Church in civil society and established new patterns of gender relations.

On the other hand, the Diaspora community has not been subject to the same socio-economic and political catalysts which helped curb the power of the Church and reduce the intensity of unequal gender relations in Italy. Ethnic Italian way of life has been preserved partly as a reaction to actual or perceived threats from the dominant Anglo-Saxon culture. In the absence of a powerful homogenizing Italian media and educational system, many immigrants still speak in their original dialect and are not familiar with standard Italian language. Most have not been assimilated in mainstream British community. They arrived in this country with a rural-traditional culture which they have tried to preserve. While that culture has undergone great transformations in Italy, the immigrant culture, by contrast, has firmly retained many of its patriarchal features. A great number of the immigrant Italians still hold Italian citizenship, consider themselves to be Italian and do not actively participate in British politics or feminist struggles to influence gender relations. The Italian Catholic Church has become the spiritual and social focus of the Diaspora community and has been consequential in reproducing traditional patterns of gender relations. However, some change is noticeable within the younger generational cohorts, those born in Britain and those who have migrated most recently from Italy.

7 Conclusion

Any analysis of patriarchal relations in contemporary multicultural Britain has to take ethnicity into consideration. In the western industrialized world, it has been traditionally assumed that ethnic collectivities are non-white. Thus most ethnic sociological investigations have been carried out amongst racialized minorities, those who display visible differences with white people. But although Italians, the subjects of this book, are white, European and Christian, they nevertheless constitute an ethnic minority in Britain. They live in Britain but they are differently situated within the various social structures and as such their respective patriarchal structures are distinct. Italian gender relations acquire specific forms on a continuum between private and public patriarchy within each social structure. Italians are mostly Catholic and the institution of religion plays a paramount role in constructing and reinforcing unequal gender relations within their community; moreover, the interplay of religion and ethnicity reinforces the importance of the Church and reproduces women's subordination. Female oppression is most felt in the Italian structure of sexuality. In short, structural theories of patriarchy cannot be applied universally and should be ethnically specific.

There are differences amongst women of the Italian community which are directly reflected in gender relations: Italians originate from various northern, central and southern parts of Italy; they are of different ages; some were born in Britain, some have lived in this country for most of their life, others are more recent immigrants; some are more religious than others. Thus independent variables such as region of origin, age, degree of religiosity and length of residence in Britain introduce variations in the pattern of Italian patriarchal relations, and dynamics of change are noticeable in all Italian social structures. However, in comparison with Italy where tremendous social, cultural and political changes have led to a reduction in gender inequality, patriarchal structures within the older Italian community in Britain have undergone slower transformation. Future generations that form new social and cultural combinations will perhaps introduce a swifter pace of change.

Theoretical Context

A major preoccupation of feminist literature lies in identifying the reasons for women's oppression, the location of oppression, the differences of oppression and possibilities of change and liberation. According to liberal feminists, women are oppressed because of their unequal access to civil and political rights. However, liberal feminism has been mainly the voice of white, bourgeois feminists and tended to neglect the economic, racial and sexual facets of womanhood. Marxist feminism has often theorized gender oppression in terms of the material social structure, stressing the nature and function of women's work as the basis for unequal gender relations. While contributing to the understanding of relations between capital and the family, much of Marxist feminism tends to neglect issues of sexuality, racism and ethnicity. Recently, some Marxist feminists have acknowledged the relative importance of such issues. Radical feminism identifies patriarchy as being universal and the most comprehensive form of women's exploitation. It sometimes overlooks issues of ethnicity, class, civil rights, power relations. Much of radical feminist theorization is informed by issues of sexuality. In doing so, radical feminists have frequently posed the right questions and tackled issues hitherto neglected by other schools of feminist thought. However, they have often come up with essentialist, reductionist, Eurocentric theorization even though they define patriarchy as all encompassing and universal. Socialist feminism theorizes women's oppression according to their role in both production and reproduction. Within socialist feminism, the dual-systems theorists have combined traditional Marxist analysis of capitalism with an analysis of patriarchy. Some dual-systems theorists (Walby, 1990) have used a full range of patriarchal structures (paid employment, housework, sexuality, culture, violence and the state) in order to analyze unequal gender relations. The theory has been criticized for being universalist and essentialist with no dynamics of change; for not being flexible enough to deal with temporal and spatial gender inequality. Psychoanalytic feminism theorizes women's subordination using some aspects of the Freudian theory of human sexuality. Psychological determinants, motherhood, traditional arrangements for child rearing are identified as crucial causes of women's subordination. Psychoanalytic feminism is Eurocentric and has overlooked issues of ethnicity, culture and class. Existentialist feminism explains unequal gender relations in terms of Sartre's existentialist theory according to which Man is the 'Essential' and Woman is the 'Other'. This theory has ignored ethnicity and the material aspects to women's subordination. Postmodern feminism theorizes sexuality and the body not as biological and essentialist but as social constructions produced by power relations within specific discourses. As such feminine subjectivities are not fixed but fluid and changing. Postmodern feminists theorize that the causes of women's oppression are fixed, phallologocentric assumptions about 'truth', patriarchal language, disregard of the positive aspects of female 'Otherness', the neglect of difference and the variety of women's life experiences. Postmodern feminism has overlooked the role of such patriarchal institutions as the economy, the state and religion. Moreover, the postmodernist concern with the concept of 'difference' may lead to analytical chaos and anarchy, to a state where anything different is accepted as cultural relativism and where issues of value of difference, inequality and power remain unresolved.

Whereas most theoretical analyses leave out some aspects of womanhood (class, sexuality, ethnicity, reproduction, state, religion, customs variations), Walby's six patriarchal structures encompass all aspects of women's lives from private to public, and evaluate the articulation and friction between material and cultural systems of oppression. Although Walby's theory has not sufficiently developed issues of ethnic diversity, it is flexible enough to be adapted to any ethnic configuration including the Italian ethnic community and to accommodate as many variables introducing difference, as need be.

In contemporary western industrialized countries, in particular Britain, women have entered en masse into the labour market and the exclusionary practices of 19th century patriarchy have in the 20th century given way to the segregating practices of public patriarchy (Walby, 1990). Women are thus concentrated in part-time, low grade, low paid jobs and they are subordinated to men. The position of women within the household and the composition of the household itself have undergone significant changes since the Second World War. People marry and have children later in life; the rates of co-habitation and divorce have steadily increased; fewer households are composed of the typical male breadwinner and the female home-maker; the number of single mothers heading households is on the increase as is that of impoverished divorced mothers. Although due to the existence of technologically advanced household gadgets, convenience food, etc., women do comparatively less housework, men have not moved significantly towards sharing domestic chores with their working wives. Within culture, there have been significant changes in the formation of gendered subjectivities. The family, the State, the educational system and the media have all been instrumental in implementing changes within the process of gender socialization. Women have now generally an active sexuality, due to scientific advances in birth control and the liberalization of divorce and abortion laws. Pre-marital and extra-marital sex do not entail severe legal and social punishments any more and alternative sexual behaviours are tolerated. However, the sexual double standard still persists and there has been an expansion of pornography based on sexual hatred and abuse of women. It is extremely difficult to assess the extent of male violence towards women, both in its range and in magnitude. There are no definite legal guidelines on what exactly constitutes domestic and public male violence and such acts remain hugely under-reported. The State has so far been inefficient in reducing or eliminating violence. Although it has introduced some policy changes regarding gender relations, the relative absence of women from positions of power within the economic and political establishment, the low levels of state benefits for impoverished divorced female heads of families and the relaxation of censorship regulations which permit circulation of hard-core pornography, still point to the oppression of women. Patterns of unequal gender relations within the Italian community are different from those of mainstream British society. Ethnicity matters.

Nature of Ethnicity within the Italian Collectivity

The array of varying definitions and uses of the term 'ethnic' has given rise to a degree of confusion within social sciences. An ethnic group has been variously defined as: a collectivity with shared racial, linguistic and national identity; a group of people with no exclusive religion, language or culture but who believe in their membership of a certain community and thus set arbitrary ethnic boundaries; a group which has a culturally distinct awareness and maintains a minimum of contact with others; an informal interest group or political entity which operates through the medium of shared customs.

I define an ethnic group as a group of people to whom most of the following conditions apply: they share the same cultural and historical origin; as part of their common culture, they speak the same language, practice the same religion and have the same customs; they believe in their common historical origin, assume that they have the same fate and that they are distinctive from other groups; their loyalty and solidarity is usually directed towards the members of their own group, specifically in times of crisis.

Italians, as a non-racialized, white, European and predominantly Christian group may not be automatically categorized as an ethnic group. This is because traditionally the notion of ethnicity has been equated with non-European, coloured immigrant groups, thus confusing it with the concept of race. However, the Italians' characteristics as a group, are consistent with the above definition of ethnicity: Italian language is widely used within the community; Italians are proud of their common cultural heritage and are eager to maintain and perpetuate their traditional social customs; the majority are Roman Catholics; although socially well integrated into British life, they have a slow rate of assimilation; at times of crisis, such as the Fascist period during the Second World War, they have shown allegiance to their mother country. Italians do constitute an ethnic group, albeit a non-racialized one which has at times been described as an 'invisible ethnic group'. As such, they have not endured traumatic racial experiences suffered by coloured, non-European and non-Christian collectivities. Italians often are and usually feel different from the rest of British society. Their community is pervaded by solid elements of Italian ethnic identity. Strong family ties, Italian culinary customs, music, fashion, type of entertainment, religious traditions and distinct gender roles and attributes distinguish most Italian families in Britain. Sexual double standard reinforced by the teachings of the Church, the symbolic self-sacrificing mother and the women's double-shift reproduce unequal gender relations. Women are not confined to the household any more; the majority have entered paid employment. However, they remain disadvantaged within the household in terms of the amount of housework they perform and the way their sexuality is controlled and regulated. A particular aspect of the Italian community is that many women regard this as normal rather than oppressive. This is perhaps because they do not have access to alternative systems of belief. The Italian way of life is thus created at the intersection of three structures of household production, culture and sexuality and it encompasses attitudes and ideas about gender roles and representation. This will introduce an ethnically specific system of patriarchy, structures and site of oppression.

Assimilation has been slow within the Italian community. According to assimilationist theories (Yinger, 1994), assimilation in the host country is hastened when immigrant groups are small, are residentially scattered, their return to the homeland is difficult, they share the language and culture of their host country, their visible attributes are the same or very similar to the dominant group, they experience little discrimination, their average level of education is high and they are heterogeneous in class and occupation. In the case of the Italians some of the above conditions apply but most do not: Italian immigrant groups are not small and since the Second World War their numbers have gradually increased to the present 220,000. In the early days they were concentrated in specific areas of the large British cities and not scattered around (Chapter 3). It was only much later that they started to move out of specifically Italian neighbourhoods. Except for the early stages of migration when poor immigrants could not afford to travel, access to the mother country has not been very difficult and Italians regularly commute to Italy for business, to visit relatives, to chose partners. Italians do not share a common language nor a common religion and customs with the dominant groups in the host country. Italian language, Catholicism, elaborate Italian social customs, family kinship and primordial loyalties to their collectivity and mother country constitute the signifiers of the boundary between them and the rest of the British people. Italians' visible attributes are not identical but generally similar to the dominant group; as such they do not experience as much discrimination as racialized minorities normally would and many have had the possibility to climb up the social ladder. On the other hand, during the Second World War, Italians were targeted as the fifth column in Britain and many (amongst them complete innocents) were interned in concentration camps. The latter incidents constitute a setback for assimilation as older Italians have never forgotten the crisis. Early Italian collectivities were not heterogeneous in terms of class and occupation (Chapter 3). Immigrants had generally low levels of education and occupied low grade, low paid jobs, mainly in an Italian employment niche. However in time, new generations of ethnic Italians have acquired higher levels of education, moved up the occupational ladder and entered the mainstream employment market.

Younger generations of Italians may have adopted a 'hybrid' consciousness as they are bilingual and have been widely exposed to British education, culture, customs and media. However, the concept of 'hybridity' does not fully account for the fluid nature of identity, especially in sub-dominant groups. In other words, in changing social and political circumstances, similar to the events of the Second World War when the Italians were interned, 'hybrid' Italians may reject the British part of their consciousness and revert to being totally 'Italian'.

Although the cultural interchange does not occur on an equal footing, the minority Italian community has in turn had its impact on the British majority: Italian food, music, fashion and art have made their indelible mark on British culture.

Role of Religion and its Interplay with Ethnicity

The Italian Catholic Church fulfils a crucial ethnic role within the Diaspora collectivity. From the inception of the community, the Italian Church has catered to the spiritual and social needs of the migrants who faced personal and social problems in an alien, potentially hostile environment. Although Italians share the same religion with the Irish and the English Catholics, it became obvious from the early stages of the immigration that they needed their own Church. They had difficulty understanding Mass in the vernacular and the cultural variations of their religious practice set them apart from the other Catholics. Many Italian churches and missionary delegations came into existence across the country. Apart from pastoral duties such as Mass in Italian, marriage, baptism, confirmation and confession, Italian churches have been actively involved in providing social services such as preparing food for the homeless and poor, counselling couples in difficulty, visiting the sick at home, organizing regular social gatherings; and they have created Italian institutions such as language schools, nursery schools, youth hostels, women's clubs, home for the elderly, newspapers (Chapter 5).

Within the Italian community, there has always been constant articulation between ethnicity and religion. It is true that today many Italians have gravitated towards British public institutions which dispense social services; but the Italian Church has created an array of organizations which are still widely used. The community members' financial contributions to many Church-affiliated social organizations keep them solvent and fully functional. They are proof of the solid ties which link the community and the Church.

For the dominant majority community, religion may not have the same significance as for ethnic minorities. Mainstream communities in secular industrialized countries are well established, have elaborate kinship systems, control power networks, have the necessary know-how to use the various social services available, feel at home, do not suffer discrimination or racism; social services are organized and offered by the secular State and not by the Church. Ethnic immigrants on the other hand arrive in the host country generally from poor backgrounds, feel isolated and lonely in their new environment, do not initially have broad based kinship systems, are not in socio-political power positions, feel alienated, do not know how to use the available social services efficiently, may suffer discrimination and racial slurs, often speak a different language, practice different social customs and have a different religion. An institution such as religion may assume a crucial role in the lives of immigrants by catering to their psychological, cultural and material needs. In so doing, the Church strengthens the boundaries of the ethnic community and the ethnic community becomes increasingly tied up to the institution of religion. The two reinforce each other. In the ethnic Italian community, the interplay of ethnicity and religion has conferred an importance upon the role of the Church which it might not have had on its own. The consequences of this interplay for Italian gender relations are manifold: masculinity is valued more than femininity in the ethnic Italian popular culture. Roman Catholicism opposes divorce, contraception, abortion, pre-marital sex, single motherhood, homosexuality and ordination of women priests. The edicts of the Church set sexual and social regulations which are disadvantageous to women and reinforce unequal gender relations within both private and public spheres. The institution of religion strongly links the three structures of culture, household production and sexuality which constitute the Italian way of life. The interplay of Italian ethnicity and Roman Catholicism which strengthens both institutions, reinforces unequal gender relations at the same time.

In the Italian community the three structures of household production, culture and sexuality are closely interdependent through the influence of religion. In comparison, the same structures within mainstream Protestant British community are more independent of each other. This is because Protestant Churches are not only more liberal on social issues, they also exert less influence on their followers.

Difference between Italian and British Patriarchal Structures

Six patriarchal structures have been identified within the Italian community. While most British people may be categorized in fully British structures, ethnic Italians float in and out of both British and Italian social structures. Due to the ethnic dimension of the collectivity, I have used a different configuration of the six structures (Walby, 1990) in order to analyze Italian unequal gender relations. I have grouped some of them and yet split another. The structure of culture is here defined by the institutions of religion, education and media. In this structure I have separated religion from the other two cultural components because of the crucial role the Church plays within the Italian community in contrast to the marginal function of the institutions of education and media. Also, Italian children are widely exposed to British education and media; and in terms of their effect on gender relations, Catholic religion and British education and media pull in different directions.

Within the Italian community, the Italian Church performs both pastoral and social roles. It provides an array of social services which allow many Italians to remain within the institutions of the community instead of becoming completely assimilated into mainstream British society (Chapter

5). The institution of religion constitutes a solid pillar of the ethnic community. In comparison, there are no fully developed, established systems of Italian education and media within the community. Italian children go to English schools and receive full English education. Many take Italian language supplementary courses in special language schools or as part of integrated courses in English day schools. However neither the quality nor the extent of the Italian education children receive, warrants the analysis of education as a major contributor to the Italian structure of culture. Equally, Italian media has not a profound cultural effect on the collectivity. The few newspapers issued from within the community are published by the Church and have relatively low circulation. Some but not all Italians read newspapers published in Italy or regularly watch Italian cable T.V. The community has also a radio station with limited broadcasting hours. Only the social elite in the community attend cultural events (films, conferences, concerts) regularly held at the Italian Institutes of Culture in Britain. In short, Italians are exposed to the Italian media to a limited extent. Instead they are widely exposed to British media. Thus education and media are marginal parameters of ethnic Italian culture.

The three structures of household production, culture and sexuality are highly inter-related and form the Italian *Way of Life,* and the institution which underscores and maintains the nexus amongst the three structures is the Italian Catholic Church. The opposition of the Catholic Church to divorce, abortion, pre-marital sex, contraception, ordination of women, single motherhood, alternative sexual behaviours, does not remain limited to the spiritual domain and spills over into the everyday life of Italians; it regulates their sexual behaviour and reinforces unequal gender relations.

Italian and British systems of patriarchy differ in the range of their structures, the configuration and form of patriarchal structures and the main site of oppression. Italians live within both British and Italian social structures.

In the structure of employment most Italian women are in paid employment, to the same extent as British women, though in contrast to British women, the majority work full-time. Also, in comparison with British women, Italians are employed more heavily in skilled and semi-skilled jobs and less in professional and managerial jobs. They have gradually moved away from a totally Italian employment niche, and half of them are now employed by non-Italians. Patterns of female subordination are similar to the Anglo-Saxon community in that most women are in paid employment, they are segregated into lower grade, less remunerated jobs, and the majority express satisfaction with their jobs, however low grade or badly remunerated. In comparison with British women, Italian women work more hours, in both public and private spheres. Walby (1990) argues that in Britain the expropriation of women's labour by individual patriarchs has been replaced by a more collective appropriation within the structure of employment. I would argue that paid employment has transformed the Italian family to the extent that Italian women are not solely confined to the household any more; their labour power is expropriated collectively by the capitalist system; however, collective expropriation has not totally supplanted individual patriarchal expropriation and at least not to the extent it has happened in mainstream British structures of employment and household production. Italian women's labour power continues to be expropriated at home, just as it has always been. Perhaps Italian women's jobs have not been of a high enough grade for employment to have a similar effect in the Italian community as in dominant British community, or the impact of culture (religion) on the family has been too strong to transform traditional gender relations within the Italian household.

The family lies at the centre of the Italian structure of household production. Most women marry, have children and have males as heads of their families. In addition to their paid work, Italian women are responsible for and perform most of the housework. They are prepared to sacrifice their own well being for the sake of their family and consider this state of affairs as normative and part of their culture. Although fully integrated within the institutions of mainstream British society, Italians have resisted assimilation on a large scale. This may be due to a number of reasons: 1) Historically, the Italians' assimilation process suffered a huge setback when during the Second World War, they became targeted as enemies of Great Britain. 2) Their religion is different from that of the Establishment and their Church has been actively involved in catering to their ethnically specific needs. 3) As a non-racialized ethnic group, they do not generally suffer racism, are proud of their cultural heritage and see no need to assimilate. Thus, even when patriarchal, the Italian family is valued by community members as a unit where their culture can thrive, a haven against the onslaught of discrimination, isolation and assimilation by the dominant culture. Italian and British structures of household production are similar in that in both structures women are the ones who perform most of the household chores, even when they hold outside employment. The difference may be the degree of this gender asymmetry: Italian women may work more hours within the household than British women. This is because they go to great lengths preparing non-convenience food for their families, they prefer to take care of their elderly and sick themselves rather than use social services. As minority women they may attach a higher value to the sanctuary of the family. In Italian households divorce rates and rates of single motherhood are lower than in Anglo-Saxon Protestant British families.

Within the Italian structure of culture, the Italian Catholic Church exerts the crucial influence, while the role of education and media is marginal. Italians use British educational institutions and are exposed mainly to British media. They use Italian educational and media institutions only to a limited extent. The Italian and British structures of culture are different in that religion plays a far greater role in the Italian community than in mainstream British society; also while the British exist solely within the British structure of culture, Italians live their cultural lives within both Italian and British structures.

Catholicism regulates Italian women's life and sexuality through its edicts and practices such as opposition to divorce, abortion, contraception, pre-marital sex, single motherhood, homosexuality and ordination of women priests. Within mainstream British society, Protestant Churches tend to hold more liberal views towards these issues. While Protestant churches have gradually lost their grip on the population, traditional Roman Catholic religious tenets and ecclesiastical authority have proved more resilient. While the Vatican has consolidated both the papal authority and patriarchy by periodically issuing encyclicals on social concerns (e.g. Rerum Novarum of 1891 which exulted the powers of the father), enlightened forces such as Marxism and feminism began appearing in bureaucratic, secular Protestant milieux (Therborn, 1995). In Italy itself the influence of the Church has been gradually reduced since the Second World War. However in immigrant communities, the ethnic feature of religion has enhanced the latter's pivotal role even further: the primary role of the Catholic Church has not been that of promoting the Italian culture overseas; but in ethnic communities, notably the Italian community in Britain, the Church has successfully merged its pastoral and cultural duties and catered efficiently to the social needs of the immigrants. The indirect effect of such social services has been the strengthening of the position of the Church within the community and the preservation of the Italian culture and way of life. The Italian and British structures of sexuality are different in the sense that religion does not control sexual mores in mainstream British society to the same extent as in Italian ethnic community.

The assessment of male violence in both ethnic and mainstream communities is problematic and very difficult to measure; this is due to the lack of clear-cut legal guidelines on what constitutes violence, and inadequate statistics since many cases go unreported.

Although Italians are engaged in many ways with the British State, their political allegiance still resides largely with Italy. Traditionally, most have kept their Italian citizenship, have not assimilated and consequently have not become politically involved in Britain. Gender relations in the Italian structure of the state have possibly suffered from this handicap, since women's active political participation in feminist movements could have been instrumental in the decrease of patriarchy within the Diaspora community. Italians have an ambivalent relationship with the structure of state, that is they are both inside and outside it, a situation which is inimical to the creation of equal gender relations. Italian women do not benefit from the legal, social and culturally progressive upheavals in Italy; they do not participate in Italian political life, yet they expect the Italian State to assume major responsibilities for them. On the other hand, they remain disadvantaged because they do not feel integrally British and thus fail to fight for their cause or contribute to the feminist struggles in Britain. The Italian and British structures of state are different in that mainstream Britons remain solely under the jurisprudence of the British State. Ethnic Italians on the other hand live their lives under the jurisprudence of both British and Italian States.

Form of Patriarchy within the Community

Public patriarchy has been defined as a system of patriarchy where the exploitation of women takes place at a collective level. In private patriarchy women are subordinated by individual patriarchs. British patriarchal relations have moved from an intense form of private patriarchy in the 19th century towards public patriarchy in the 20th century (Walby, 1990). In the context of Capital's demand for increased supplies of labour and feminist victories to gain citizenship rights, women gained en masse access to paid employment where they again became subordinated. The development of capitalism in the 20th century created new sites of power in the public sphere from which women were debarred.

The form of patriarchy in the Italian structure of *employment* is public since the majority of women are in full-time paid employment, yet they are mostly segregated in low grade, low paid jobs. Italian women who immigrated to Britain came in search of work and a better economic life. They easily entered the paid employment market in the context of capitalist development and demand for cheap labour in Britain.

The form of patriarchy in the structure of *household production* is situated on a continuum between private and public. The majority of Italian women are not excluded from the public sphere and confined to the household under the orders of a patriarch. They have entered en masse into paid employment where they hold the lower grade, least remunerated jobs. In this way patterns of Italian and British patriarchy are similar. Yet Italian women still carry the burden of double shift and still suffer from sexual double standard. In other words, Italian women are not subjected to absolute private patriarchy any more because they can now freely enter paid employment and they are not confined to the household; however, within the household they are still disadvantaged, they perform most of the housework and their sexual lives are handicapped by sexual double standard. Italian women are possibly more disadvantaged than British women at home. This is because they consider much of the unequal relations within the home as normative and cultural rather than oppressive, and they shoulder more housework. It is fair to suggest that within the Italian household, patriarchy is situated on a continuum between private and public patriarchy, perhaps closer to private patriarchy. In contrast, in the British structure of household production, patriarchy is situated closer to public patriarchy.

In the Italian structure of *culture* the form of patriarchy is public: the Italian structure of culture has been split for analytic purposes into the institutions of religion, education and media. Through its religious edicts and their influence on social customs, especially in an ethnic community, the Roman Catholic Church reinforces gender inequalities at a collective level and the all-male priesthood is exclusionary of women. Italian women possibly perceive a lesser degree of patriarchy within the structures of their community because the hegemonic influence of the Catholic Church legitimates much of unequal gender relations and patriarchal oppression as cultural heritage. Education and media have a larger impact on mainstream British culture than religion. Protestantism is generally more liberal than Catholicism and has less significance within the structure of culture. While religion reinforces Italian unequal gender relations, Italian education and media have a marginal effect on patriarchal relations. At the same time Italians are widely exposed to British education and media which have helped reduce traditional patriarchal values at least amongst the younger generations and those who have been born in Britain, at a collective level. There arises a contradiction: whereas one component of culture i.e. religion reinforces unequal gender relations in the structures of household production and sexuality, the other two components of culture i.e. education and media may help to reduce patriarchy, at least in some sections of the ethnic community.

In the Italian structure of *sexuality* patriarchy is manifested in both public and private forms: the Roman Catholic Church sets the patriarchal rules at the collective, public level. The Church tries to privatize women's sexuality but not women's labour. It exalts the family as the most sacred social unit. The family internalizes the oppressive religious edicts and sexual oppression of women takes place by individual patriarchs at household level. Thus the sexual subjugation of women gradually extends to the whole community. In mainstream British society, Protestantism holds more liberal views of sexuality than the Catholic Church. Moreover, the Church of England does not have the same moral authority in order to set stringent regulations which seriously affect people's sexual lives.

Degree of Patriarchy within the Community

To determine the degree of unequal gender relations is problematic in all the structures and in any system of patriarchy. This is due to the lack of adequate statistics. In the Italian community, the highest degree of unequal gender relations is found in the Italian structure of sexuality (Chapter 4).

For 'hybrid' future generations, there would possibly be a reduction in the degree of private patriarchy within the structures of household production and sexuality. This is because younger generations may form new social combinations within mainstream British society with less traditional household and sexual inequalities.

Main Site of Oppression within the Italian Community

Italian women are not excluded from the public sphere by a patriarch. Although segregated in low grade, low paid jobs, most are now engaged in full-time paid employment and are satisfied with their jobs. Most agree with the conservative position of the Church regarding sexuality and everyday life. The majority claim that there is no domestic violence within the community. These observations all point to the direction that most Italian women are, or perceive themselves to be, concentrated in the lower patriarchy categories. It is however within the institution of sexuality that higher degrees of unequal gender relations are most prevalent. That is the structure where Italian women feel the injustice of the double standard. They become stigmatized within their community for having abortion, divorce, pre- or extra-marital affairs, for being single mothers or homosexual, for co-habitation without formal marriage. Thus, whereas the patriarchal structures of employment and the State are the main sites and causes of patriarchy in mainstream British community, sexuality constitutes the most oppressive structure for Italian women, and the Roman Catholic

Church is the institution which constructs and reinforces unequal gender relations within this structure.

Variations in Italian Patriarchal Relations

The concept of structure is flexible enough to cope with ethnic diversity and can be useful in analyzing social change. Within the Italian community in Britain, different Italians experience different types of patriarchy and differences such as region of origin, degree of religiosity, age and length of residence in Britain introduce variations in the degree of unequal gender relations within all the social structures. In all Italian social structures, there is a positive association between degree of patriarchy and southern region of origin, older age, high religiosity. However, the association is most perceptible in the structure of sexuality. In other words, Italian women who originate from the Southern regions of Italy, who are older and who are more religious, tend to be subject to a greater degree of patriarchy, especially in the structure of sexuality. Length of residence in Britain has some bearing on the degree of patriarchy. Predictably, in most cases, those who have lived in Britain between 1 and 10 years form the group which is the least patriarchal, followed by those who have been born in Britain. The most patriarchal group is in most cases formed by women who have lived here the longest but were not born in Britain.

Different Trajectories: Ethnic Italians in Britain Compared to Italians in the Mother Country

In Italy culture has undergone major transformations, with notable consequences for gender relations, resulting in a model of patriarchy which is more similar to mainstream British patriarchal paradigm. In comparison, Catholic culture has remained relatively unchanged within the Italian Diaspora and consequently ethnic Italian gender relations have not changed to the same extent. In Italy, a combination of historical, cultural, economic and political events (the two World Wars, Fascism, the Resistance, the Migration, the Economic Miracle, the 1968 student uprisings, the Feminist Movement, the Media revolution) have led to a gradual loss of power of the Catholic Church and dealt a serious blow to the hegemonic Catholic culture and to unequal gender relations. Religion, education and media have undergone major transformations in Italy since 1945. The Catholic Church has lost much of its legal and political power. Education, which had previously been the realm of Catholic teaching, has become secularized and reached the masses (Chapter 6). Finally the Media has been driven to reflect these social transformations through the press, television, films, literature and even language structure. Since 1945, culture and gender relations have undergone a profound and dramatic transformation in Italy.

These economic and cultural upheavals did not take place within the Italian community in Britain. Contrary to the mother country where social transformations curtailed the influence and power of the Catholic Church, the ethnicity of the immigrant community has been reinforced by the pastoral and social functions of the Italian Church. The Church has thus come to be seen as a haven against assimilation, discrimination, isolation and its position has in turn been reinforced within the ethnic collectivity. Instead of rebelling against the institution of religion, the Italian community has cocooned and protected its values. As emigrants, Italians have not reaped the social and political benefits that the Resistance, the 1968 student movement and the feminist movement brought for their fellow citizens in Italy. The energy which could have gone into struggling against unequal gender relations, has gone instead into preserving Italian identity, culture and customs in a foreign land. In short, as a result of the symbiotic interplay of religion and ethnicity, changes in unequal gender relations have been more limited within the ethnic Italian community in Britain, than in Italy itself. However different generational cohorts are situated differently with respect to ethnic gender relations: Italians born in Britain have been exposed to the British educational system, peer group pressure and media; thus they are likely to be concentrated within low patriarchy categories. Italians who have lived in England between 10 and 50 years arrived in the host country either as children or adults. If they arrived when they were children, they most probably benefited from British educational system and were exposed to British media. Therefore, like British-born Italians mentioned earlier, they are likely to be in low patriarchy categories. If they arrived when they were already adults, they are likely to have carried over their traditional rural cultural baggage. They are religious and hold conservative patriarchal values towards sexuality. They are thus expected to be concentrated in high patriarchy categories. The most recent immigrants are those most likely to have benefited from improving gender relations in Italy. They tend to be less religious, less traditional and have more liberal values towards sexuality. The differentials amongst the cohorts are further complicated by the region of origin. The most recent immigrants, whether of Southern or North/Centre origin tend to be more emancipated. Amongst those who have been born in Britain and older cohorts, southern origin is associated with more patriarchal attitudes.

At the beginning of the immigration regionalism and the divisions it created within the community itself were clearly demarcated; however with the passing of time regional origin has gradually become less of a dividing factor within the community and is likely to continue to do so in the future.

Appendix

Table A.1 Diocese of Westminster data

The following table exhibits data compiled by the 'Westminster Year Book' since the 1960s, regarding Mass attendance, number of infant baptisms and marriages in St. Peter's Italian Church in the Diocese of Westminster:

Year	Mass attendance	Infant baptisms	Marriages
1968	1450	305	122
1970	1250	226	96
1972	800	216	69
1974			
1975		130	152
1976			
1977			
1978	900	142	64
1979	900	139	82
1980			
1981			
1982	850	121	96
1983	950	145	71
1984	1000	140	95
1985	1000	142	79
1986	1500	150	102
1987	1500	175	102
1988	1600	213	97
1989	1650	191	89
1990	1700	266	67
1991	800	192	89
1992	573	193	87
1993	476	189	71

Table A.2 Southwark Diocese data

This table exhibits data compiled by Southwark Catholic Directory, since the 1970s, regarding the number of infant baptisms, confirmations, marriages and Mass attendance at the Italian Mission in Brixton, in the Metropolitan See of Southwark:

Year	Mass attendance	Infant baptisms	Confirmations	Marriages
1974	312	18		
1975	283	29		7
1976	420	35		6
1977	253	22		5
1978	247	35	59	12
1979	238	26		9
1980	243	21	45	4
1981	260	29		4
1982	280	34	45	5
1983	782	25		6
1984	300	29	30	5
1985	360	24		5
1986	315	32	37	4
1987	300	25		2
1988	350	26		3
1989	380	26	49	5
1990	320	20	20	3
1991	280	24		
1992	280	13	15	1
1993	200	10	8	3
1994		19	8	3

Bibliography

Abbot Pamela and Wallace Claire (1990), 'An Introduction to Sociology - Feminist Perspectives', London, Routledge

Abbot Pamela and Wallace Claire (1991), 'Gender, Power and Sexuality', London, Macmillan Academic and Professional

Abercrombie A., Warde A., Soothill K., Urry J., Walby S. (1988), 'Contemporary British Society', Cambridge, Polity Press

Acker Joan (1989), 'The Problem with Patriarchy', in 'Sociology', volume 23, No.2, pp. 235-240

Acquaviva S.S. and Santuccio M. (1976), 'Social Structure in Italy', London, Martin Robertson and Co.

Adler Alfred (1927), 'Understanding Human Nature', New York, Greenberg

Adler-Hellman Judith (1987), 'Journeys among Women', Cambridge, Polity Press

Afshar Haleh and Maynard Mary eds. (1994), 'The Dynamics of Race and Gender', London, Taylor and Francis

Agrawal Bina ed. (1988), 'Structures of Patriarchy', London, Zed Books

Alexander Jeffrey and Seidman Steven (1991), 'Culture and Society', Cambridge, Cambridge University Press

Allum P.A. (1973), 'Italy - Republic Without Government', New York, W.W. Norton and Company Inc.

Althusser Louis (1971), 'Lenin and Philosophy and Other Essays', London, New Left

Altorki Soraya (1986), 'Women in Saudi Arabia', New York, Columbia University

Amir Menachem (1971), 'Patterns in Forcible Rape', Chicago, Chicago University

Amos Valerie and Parmar Pratkha (1981), 'Resistance and Responses: the experiences of black girls in Britain', in McRobbie A. and McCabe T. eds. 'Feminism for Girls: An adventure story', London, Routledge

Anglim Mgr. Peter ed. (1992), 'Westminster Year Book', Manchester, Gabriel Communications by Authority

Anthias Floya and Yuval-Davis Nira (1992), 'Racialized Boundaries', London, Routledge

Arber Sara and Gilbert Nigel eds. (1992), 'Women and Working Lives, Divisions and Change', London, Macmillan

Arber Sara et al. (1996), 'Feminist Fallacies: a reply to Hakim on women's employment', in 'British Journal of Sociology', volume 47, No.1, pp. 167-174

Archer John and Lloyd Barbara (1982), 'Sex and Gender', Harmondsworth, Penguin

Ashley David and Orenstein David M. (1995), 'Sociological Theory', Boston, Allyn and Bacon

Backhill, The Italian Community Magazine (1994), February issue

Balbo Laura (1978), 'La Doppia Presenza', in 'Inchiesta', No.32, pp. 3-6

Balbo Laura (1991), 'Tempi di Vita', Milano, Feltrinelli

Baker Adrienne (1993), 'The Jewish Woman in Contemporary Society', London, Macmillan Press

Bammer Angelika (1991), 'Partial Visions', London, Routledge

Banks Olive (1981), 'Faces of Feminism', Oxford, Martin Robertson

Banton Michael (1967), 'Race Relations', London, Tavistock

Baranski Zygmunt G. and Lumley Robert eds. (1990), 'Culture and Conflict in Postwar Italy', London, Macmillan Press

Baranski Zygmunt G. and Vinall S.W. (1991), 'Women and Italy', London, Macmillan Academic and Professional

Barot Rohit ed. (1993), 'Religion and Ethnicity: Minorities and Social Change in the Metropolis', Kampen, Kok Pharos Publishing House

Barot Rohit (1994), 'Hinduism and Hindus in Europe', in Gill Sean, D'Costa Gavin and King Ursula eds., 'Religion in Europe', Kampen, Kok Pharos Publishing

Barr-Hamilton Margarita (1996), Personal Communication, July, London

Barrett Michele (1980, 1988), 'Women's Oppression Today', London, Verso

Barrett Michele and Phillips Anne eds. (1992), 'Destabilizing Theory', Cambridge, Polity Press

Beechy Veronica (1978), 'Women and Production: A Critical Analysis of Some Sociological Theories of Women's Work', in Kuhn and Wolpe eds., 'Feminism and Materialism: Women and Modes of Production', London, Routledge and Kegan Paul

Beechey Veronica and Perkins Tessa (1987), 'A Matter of Hours: Women, Part-time Work and the Labour Market', Cambridge, Polity Press

Belotti Elena Gianini (1975), 'Little Girls', London, Writers and Readers Publication Cooperative

Ben-Tovim Gideon et al., (1986), 'The Local Politics of Race', London, Macmillan

Bertram J.C. and Grunebaum H.U. (1981), 'Mothers, Grandmothers and Daughters Personality and Childcare in Three-Generation Families', New York, John Wiley and Sons

Best Steven and Kellner Douglas (1991), 'Postmodern Theory, Critical Interrogations', New York, Guilford Press

Bianchi Marina (1978), 'Oltre il Doppio Lavoro' in 'Inchiesta', No.32, pp. 7-11

Bianchi Marina (1980), 'Le 150 Ore Delle Donne: Spazio Intellettuale e Identita Collettiva', Convegno Nazionale FLM, Milan

Billington Rosamund et al (1991), 'Culture and Society', London, Macmillan

Bilton Tony et al. (1987), 'Introductory Sociology', London, Macmillan

Bono Paola and Kemp Sandra (1991), 'Italian Feminist Thought', Oxford, Basil Blackwell

Bottignolo Bruno (1985), 'Without a Bell Tower', Rome, Centro Studi Emigrazione

Braidotti Rosi (1997), 'Comment on Felski's The Doxa of Difference: Working Through Sexual Difference', in 'Signs', volume 23, No.1, pp. 23-39

Braverman Harry (1974), 'Labor and Monopoly Capital: The Degradation of Work in the Twentieth Century', New York, Monthly Review Press

Brown Carol (1981), 'Mothers, fathers, and children: from private to public patriarchy', in Sargent Lydia ed., 'Women and Revolution: The Unhappy Marriage of Marxism and Feminism', London, Pluto Press

Brownmiller Susan (1977), 'Against Our Will: Men, Women and Rape', Harmondsworth, Penguin

Brownmiller Susan (1986), 'Femininity', London, Paladin Grafton Books

Bruegel Irene (1979), 'Women as a Reserve Army of Labour: a Note on Recent British Experience', in 'Feminist Review', volume 3, pp. 12-23

Bryan Beverly et al. (1985), 'The Heart of the Race: Black Women's Lives in Britain', London, Virago

Bryman Alan (1995), 'Quantity and Quality in Social Research', London, Routledge

Bunch Charlotte and Myron Nancy eds. (1974), 'Class and Feminism: A Collection of Essays From the Furies', Baltimore (MD), Diana Press

Caldwell Lesley (1978), 'Church, State and Family: the Women's Movement in Italy', in Kuhn and Wolpe eds., 'Feminism and Materialism: Women and Modes of Production', London, Routledge and Kegan Paul

Carby Hazel (1982), 'White Women Listen! Black Feminism and the boundaries of Sisterhood', in Centre for Contemporary Cultural Studies, 'The Empire Strikes Back', London, Hutchinson, pp. 212-36

Castle Stephen and Kosack Godula (1985), 'Immigrant Workers and Class Structure in Western Europe', Oxford, Oxford University Press

Castelnuovo-Frigessi Delia (1978), 'La Condition Immigree', Lausanne, Editions d'En Bas

CENSIS '26th Rapporto sulla Situazione Sociale del Paese' (1992), Roma, Franco Angeli Editore

Centro Scalabrini di Londra, 'A Ricordo dell' Opera di Restauro' (1979), Vicenza, Editore Moro

Centro Scalabrini di Londra '25 Anni di Servizio' (1993), Vicenza, Editore Moro

Chabot Federici (1961), 'A History of Italian Fascism', Torino, Einaudi editore

Chianese Gloria (1980), 'Storia Sociale della Donna', Napoli, Guida Editori

Chistolini Sandra (1986), 'Donne Italoscozzesi', Roma, Centro Studi Emigrazione

Chodorow Nancy (1978), 'The Reproduction of Mothering: Psychoanalysis and the Sociology of Gender', Berkeley, University of California Press

Church Jenny et al. eds. (1995), 'Social Focus on Women', London, HMSO

Church Jenny et al. eds. (1997), 'Social Trends 27', London, The Stationary Office

Cixous Helene (1981), 'Sorties', in Marks and de Courtivron eds., 'New French Feminisms', Brighton, Harvester

Clark Alan (1967), 'What the Council Says About Marriage', London, The Incorporated Catholic Truth Society

Cockburn Cynthia (1983), 'Brothers', London, Pluto

Cockburn Cynthia (1991), 'In the Way of Women', London, Macmillan Education

Cohen Abner (1974), 'Two-Dimensional Man', London, Tavistock

Colpi Terri (1991), 'The Italian Factor', Edinburgh, Mainstream Publishing

Comer Lee (1974), 'Wedlocked Women', London, Feminist Press

Commissione Nazionale per la Parità e le Pari Opportunità tra Uomo e Donna (1993), 'Secondo Rapporto del Governo Italiano', Roma, Istituto Poligrafico dello Stato

Commissione Nazionale per la Realizzazione della Parità tra Uomo e Donna (1987), 'Il Sessismo nella Lingua Italiana', Roma, Istituto Poligrafico dello Stato

Cone James H. (1969), 'Black Theology and Black Power', New York, Seabury

Cone James H. (1991), 'Martin, Malcolm and America: a Dream or a Nightmare', New York, Orbis Books

Corea Ash (1990), 'Racism and the American Way of Media', in Downing John et al., 'Questioning the Media', California, Sage Publications

Cornelison Ann (1980), 'Strangers and Pilgrims', New York, Holt, Rinehart and Winston

Coward Rosalind (1982), 'Sexual Violence and Sexuality', in 'Feminist Review', no.11, pp. 9-22

Coward Rosalind (1992), 'Our Treacherous Hearts', London, Faber and Faber

Cox Oliver (1970), 'Caste, Class and Race: A Study in Social Dynamics', New York, Modern Reader Paperbacks

Craib Ian (1984), 'Modern Social Theory', Hemel Hempstead, Wheatsheaf Books

Crompton Rosemary and Mann Michael eds. (1986), 'Gender and Stratification', Cambridge, Polity Press

Crompton Rosemary and Sanderson Kay (1990), 'Gendered Jobs and Social Change', London, Unwin Hyman

Cross Malcolm (1983), 'Migrant Workers in European Cities', Birmingham, Social Sciences Research Council

Crowley Helen and Himmelweit Susan (1992), 'Knowing Women', Oxford, Blackwell Publishers

Cuff E.C., Sharrock W.W., Francis D.W. (1992), 'Perspectives in Sociology', London, Routledge

Dale A., Arber S., Procter M. (1988), 'Doing Secondary Analysis', London, Unwin Hyman

Daly Mary (1982), 'La Chiesa e il Secondo Sesso', Milano, Rizzoli

Davis Francis (1967), 'What The Council Says About The Church', London, The Incorporated Catholic Truth Society

De Beauvoir Simone (1952), 'The Second Sex', New York, Alfred A. Knopf

De Grazia Sebastian (1963), 'The Political Community', Chicago, University of Chicago Press

Delphy Christine (1984), 'Close to Home: A materialist analysis of Women's oppression', London, Hutchinson

Derrida Jacques (1976), 'Of Grammatology', Baltimore, Johns Hopkins University

Derrida Jacques (1981), 'Positions', Chicago, University of Chicago

Dinello Raimundo (1985), 'Adolescents Entre Deux Cultures', Paris, Editions L'Harmatan

Dinnerstein Dorothy (1978), 'The Mermaid and the Minotaur', London, Souvenir Press

Duke Vic and Crolley Liz (1996), 'Football, Nationality and the State', New York, Addison Wesley Longman Publishing

Durkheim Emile (1965), 'The Elementary Forms of Religious Life', New York, Free Press

Dworkin Andrea (1981), 'Pornography: Men Possessing Women', New York, Putnam

Eagleton Terry (1991), 'Ideology', London, Verso

Ehrenreich Barbara and English Deidre (1979), 'For Her Own Good: 150 Years of the Experts' Advice to Women', London, Pluto

Eisenstein Hester (1983), 'Contemporary Feminist Thought', Boston, G.K.Hall

Eisenstein Zillah R. (1979), 'Developing a theory of capitalist patriarchy and socialist feminism', in Eisenstein Zillah ed., 'Capitalist Patriarchy', New York, Monthly Review Press

Eisenstein Zillah R. (1986), 'The Radical Future of Liberal Feminism', Boston, North-Eastern University Press

Elshtain Jean Bethke (1981), 'Public Man Private Woman', Princeton, Princeton University

Engels Friedrich (1972), 'The Origin of the Family, Private Property and the State', New York, International Publishers

Erikson Thomas Hylland (1993), 'Ethnicity and Nationalism, Anthropological Perspectives', London, Pluto Press

Evans-Pritchard et al. (1954), 'The Institutions of Primitive Society: A Series of Broadcast Talks', Oxford, Blackwell

Eysenck Hans (1986), 'Decline and Fall of the Freudian Empire', Harmondsworth Penguin

Faludi Susan (1992), 'Backlash', London, Chatto and Windus

Fanfani Amintore (1935), 'Catholicism, Protestantism and Capitalism', London, Sheed and Ward

Felski Rita (1997), 'The Doxa of Difference', in Signs, volume 23, no.1, pp. 1-21

Fielding Steven (1993), 'Class and Ethnicity: Irish Catholics in England, 1880 - 1939', Buckingham, Open University Press

Fiori Giuseppe (1977), 'La Vie de Antonio Gramsci', Paris, Brodard et Taupin

Firestone Shulamith (1974), 'The Dialectic of Sex: The case for Feminist Revolution', New York, Morrow

Flannery Austin ed. (1975), 'Vatican Council II', Dublin, Dominican Publications

Fletcher Ronald (1970), 'The Family and Marriage in Britain', Harmondsworth, Pelican Books

Foerster R. (1919), 'The Italian Migration of Our Times', Boston, Harvard University

Fondazione Brodolini (1983), 'Gli Italiani Fuori D'Italia', Milano, Franco Angeli

Fondazione P.M.Loria (1963), 'L'Emancipazione Femminile in Italia', Florence, La Nuova Italia Editrice

Forgacs David (1990), 'Italian Culture in the Industrial Era 1880-1980', Manchester, Manchester University Press

Forman James D. (1974), 'Fascism', New York, Dell Publishing Co.

Foster Kate et al. eds. (1995), 'General Household Survey 1993', London, HMSO
Foucault Michel (1981), 'The History of Sexuality', volume 1: An introduction, Harmondsworth, Penguin
Foucault Michel (1989), 'The Archeology of Knowledge', London, Routledge
Frank Cedric (1967), 'The Anglican Church', London, The Incorporated Catholic Truth Society
Franklin Sarah, Lury Celia, Stacey Jackie (1991), 'Off-Centre', Birmingham, Centre for Contemporary Cultural Studies
Freud Sigmund (1934), 'The Future of an Illusion', London, Hogarth
Friedan Betty (1965), 'The Feminine Mystique', Harmondsworth, Penguin
Friedan Betty (1981), 'The Second Stage', New York, Summit Books
Friedman Jonathan (1990), 'Being in the World: globalization and localization', in Featherstone Mike ed., 'Global Culture', London, Sage
Fromm Erich (1934), 'The Dogma of Christ', New York, Holt
Gamarnikow Eva, Morgan David, Purvis June and Taylorson Daphne eds. (1985), 'Gender, Class and Work', Aldershot, Gower Publishing Company Limited
Garigue Philip and Firth Raymond (1956), 'Kinship Organization of Italianates in London', in 'Two Studies of Kinship in London', London, Athlone Press
Garnham Nicholas (1990), 'Capitalism and Communication', London, Sage
Gaskell Jane (1992), 'Gender Matters from School to Work', Buckingham, Open University Press
Gelles Richard (1972), 'The Violent Home', Beverly Hills. California, Sage
Gellner Ernest (1988), 'The Psychoanalytic Movement', London, Paladin Grafton
Gershuny J., Anderson M. and Bechhofer F. eds. (1994), 'The Social and Political Economy of the Household', Oxford, Oxford University
Giddens Anthony (1973), 'The Class Structure of the Advanced Societies', London, Unwin Hyman
Giddens Anthony (1989), 'Sociology', Cambridge, Polity Press
Gilroy Paul (1987), 'There Ain't No Black in the Union Jack', London, Hutchinson Education
Gilroy Paul (1993a), 'The Black Atlantic', London, Verso
Gilroy Paul (1993b), 'Small Acts', London, Serpent's Tail
Ginsborg Paul (1990), 'A History of Contemporary Italy', Harmondsworth, Penguin
Glazer Nathan and Moynihan David A. (1963), 'Beyond the Melting-Pot', Cambridge (MA), Harvard University
Good William (1963), 'World Revolution and Family Patterns', Glencoe, Free Press
Greer Germaine (1971), 'The Female Eunuch', London, Paladin
Griffin Susan (1981), 'Pornography and Silence', New York, Harper and Row
Hakim Catherine (1991), 'Grateful Slaves and Self-Made Women: Fact and Fantasy in Women's Work Orientations', in 'European Sociological Review', volume 7, no.2, September, pp. 100-121
Hakim Catherine (1994), 'Research Design', London, Routledge

Hakim Catherine (1996), 'The Sexual Division of Labour and Women's Heterogeneity', in 'British Journal of Sociology', volume 47, no.1, pp. 178-188

Hall, Hobson et al. (1980), 'Culture, Media, Language', Birmingham, Centre for Contemporary Cultural Studies

Hall Stuart and du Gay Paul eds. (1996), 'Cultural Identity', London, Sage

Hamilton Malcolm B. (1995), 'The Sociology of Religion, Theoretical and Comparative Perspectives', London, Routledge

Hamner Jalna and Saunders Sheila (1984), 'Well-founded Fear: A Community Study of Violence to Women', London, Hutchinson

Haralambos Michael ed. (1986), 'Sociology', Lancashire, Causeway Press

Harding Sandra (1986), 'The Science Question in Feminism', Ithaca, Cornell University Press

Harding Sandra ed. (1987), 'Feminism and Methodology', Bloomington, Indiana University Press

Hargrove Barbara (1979), 'The Sociology of Religion, Classical and Contemporary Approaches', Arlington Heights, AHM Publishing Corporation

Hartmann Heidi (1979), 'Capitalism, Patriarchy and Job Segregation by Sex', in Eisenstein Zillah ed., 'Capitalist Patriarchy', Monthly Review Press

Harvey David (1989), 'The Condition of Postmodernity', Oxford, Blackwell

Hawkes Seán J. (1996), Personal Communication, London

Healy Joseph (1993), 'Statistics, A Tool for Social Research', Belmont California, Wadsworth

Hearn Jeff (1987), 'The Gender of Oppression: Men, Masculinity and the Critique of Marxism', Brighton, Wheatsheaf

Hebblethwaite Peter (1967), 'Changes in the Church', London, The Incorporated Catholic Truth Society

Heidensohn Frances (1989), 'Crime and Society', London, MacMillan Press

Hobart C.W. (1972), 'Sexual Permissiveness in Young English and French Canadians', in 'Journal of Marriage and the Family', volume 34, pp. 292-303

hooks bell (1984), 'Feminist Theory: From Margin to Center', Boston, South End

Horney Karen (1973), 'Feminine Psychology', New York, W.W. Norton

Humphries Jane (1977), 'Class struggle and the persistence of the working class family', in 'Cambridge Journal of Economics', September, pp. 241-258

Hutchinson John and Smith Anthony eds. (1996), 'Ethnicity', Oxford, Oxford

Irigaray Luce (1985), 'This Sex which is Not One', Ithaca, Cornell University Press

Isaacs Harold (1975), 'Idols of the Tribe: Group Identity and Political Change', Cambridge (MA), Harvard University

Jackson Stevi (1978), 'On the Social Construction of Female Sexuality', London, Women's Research and Resources Centre

Jaggar Alison (1988), 'Feminist Politics and Human Nature', New Jersey, Rowman and Littlefield.

James Selma and Dalla Costa Mariarosa (1973), 'The Power of Women and the Subversion of the Community', Bristol, Falling Wall Press

Jary David and Julia (1991) 'Dictionary of Sociology', Glasgow, Harper Collins Publishers

Jeffreys Sheila (1990), 'Anti-Climax: A Feminist Perspective on the Sexual Revolution', London, Women's Press

Jowell Roger et al. eds. (1996/1997), 'British Social Attitudes - the 13th Report', Aldershot, Dartmouth Publishing Company

Kaplan Gisela (1992), 'Contemporary Western European Feminism', London, UCL

Kelly Liz (1988), 'Surviving Sexual Violence', Cambridge, Polity Press

Kemp Sandra and Bono Paola (1993), 'The Lonely Mirror', London, Routledge

Kemp Tom (1969), 'Industrialization in Nineteenth Century Europe', London, Longman Group

King Ursula (1993), 'Women and Spirituality', London, Macmillan Press Limited

King Ursula ed. (1995), 'Religion and Gender', Oxford, Blackwell Publishers

Kirkpatrick Jeanne (1974), 'Political Woman', New York, Basic Books

Knowles David (1968), 'Peter Has Spoken: The Encyclical without Ambiguity', London, The Incorporated Catholic Truth Society

Knowles David (1969), 'Authority', London, The Incorporated Catholic Truth Society

Koonz Claudia (1987), 'Mothers in the Fatherland', London, Jonathan Cape

Kristeva Julia (1986), 'The Kristeva Reader', ed. Toril Moi, Oxford, Blackwell

Kuhn Annette (1982), 'Women's Pictures: Feminism and Cinema', London, Routledge

'Labour Force Survey Quarterly Bulletin', no. 19, March 1997, London, HMSO

'Labour Market Quarterly', August 1998, London, DfEE

Lacan Jacques (1977), 'Ecrits: a selection, trans'., London, Tavistock

'Lambeth Conference Report' (1930), New York, Macmillan Company

Landry Donna and Maclean Gerald eds. (1996), 'The Spivak Reader: Selected Works of Gayatri Chakravorty Spivak', New York and London, Routledge

Lash Scott (1990), 'Sociology of Postmodernism', London, Routledge

Laslett Peter (1977), 'Family Life and Illicit Love in Earlier Generations: essays in historical sociology', Cambridge, Cambridge University Press

Layder Derek (1996), 'New Strategies in Social Research', Oxford, Blackwells

'La Voce degli Italian'i (1990), no. 831

Levi-Strauss Claude (1966), 'The Savage Mind', University of Chicago

Lieberson Stanley (1963), 'Ethnic Patterns in American Cities', New York, Free Press

Lincoln C. Eric (1961), 'The Black Muslims in America', Boston, Beacon Press

Little Daniel (1991), 'Varieties of Social Explanation', Oxford, Westview Press

Lombroso Gina (1927), 'La Donna nella Societa Attuale', Bologna, Nicola Zanichelli

Luckmann Thomas (1967), 'The Invisible Religion', New York, Macmillan

Lyotard Jean-Francois (1984), 'The Postmodern Condition: A Report on Knowledge', Manchester, Manchester University

Mafai Simona et al. (1980), 'Essere Donna in Sicilia', Rome, Editori Riuniti

Malamuth Neil M. and Donnerstein E. eds. (1984), 'Pornography and Sexual Aggression', Orlando Florida, Academic Press

Malinowski Bronislaw (1926), 'Crime and Custom in Savage Society', London, Kegan Paul

Mann Michael (1988), 'European Development: approaching a historical explanation', in Baechler J. et al. eds., 'Europe and the Rise of Capitalism', Oxford, Blackwells

Marin Umberto, (1975), 'Italiani In Gran Bretagna', Roma, Centro Studi Emigrazione

Marin Umberto (1991), 'Scalabrini', Vicenza, Editore Moro,

Martin Jean and Roberts Ceridwen (1984), 'Women and Employment: A Lifetime Perspective', London, HMSO

Marwick Arthur (1986), 'Class In The Twentieth Century', Brighton, Harvester Press

Marx Karl (1951), 'Capital', 3 volumes., London, Dent

Marx Karl (1971), 'A Contribution to the Critique of Political Economy', London, Lawrence and Wishart

Marx Karl and Engels Friedrich (1957), 'On Religion', Moscow, Progress Publishers

Marx Karl and Engels Friedrich (1964), 'The German Ideology', Moscow, Progress Publishers

McCutcheon Anthony (1996), Personal Communication, July, London

McDowell L. and Pringle R. (1992), 'Defining Women', Oxford, Blackwell

McGuire Meredith (1987), 'Religion: The Social Context', Belmont California, Wadsworth

McIntosh Mary (1978), 'The State and the Oppression of Women', in Kuhn and Wolpe eds., 'Feminism and Materialism', London, Routledge Publishing

McKinnon Catherine (1987), 'Feminist Unmodified: Discourses on Life and Law', Cambridge (MA), Harvard University Press

McNay Lois (1992), 'Foucault and Feminism', Cambridge, Polity Press

McReavy Rev. L.L. (1968), 'The Transmission of Life: An Explanation of the Encyclical 'Humanae Vitae'', London, The Incorporated Catholic Truth Society

Mermet Gerard (1993), 'Die Europaer, Länder, Leute, Leidenschaften', Munchen DTV Sachbuch

Merton Robert ed. (1957), 'Social Theory and Social Structure', New York, Free Press

Miles Robert (1982), 'Racism and Migrant Labour', London, Routledge and Kegan

Miles Robert (1989), 'Racism', London, Routledge

Miles Robert and Phizacklea Annie eds. (1979), 'Racism and Political Action in Britain', London, Routledge and Kegan Paul

Mill Harriet Taylor (1851), 'Enfranchisement of Women', in Rossi Alice ed. (1970), 'Essays on Sex Equality', Chicago, University of Chicago

Mill John Stuart (1869), 'The Subjection of Women', in Rossi Alice ed. (1970), 'Essays on Sex Equality', Chicago, University of Chicago

Millett Kate (1977), 'Sexual Politics', London, Virago
Mincer Jacob (1966), 'Labor-force Participation and Unemployment: a review of recent evidence', in 'Prosperity and Unemployment', Gordon Robert and Margaret, eds., New York, John Wiley
Mirrlees-Black Catriona (1995), 'Estimating the Extent of Domestic Violence: findings from the 1992 British Crime Survey', in 'Home Office Research and Statistics Department Research Bulletin', no.37, pp. 1-9
Missione Cattolica in Inghilterra (Paper dated 1996), 'Migranti Italiani in Gran Bretagna', Enfield
Mitchell Juliet (1975), 'Psychoanalysis and Feminism', Harmondsworth, Penguin
Modleski Tania (1991), 'Feminism Without Women', London, Routledge
Modleski Tania (1997), 'A Woman's Gotta do ... What a Man's Gotta Do?', in 'Signs', volume 22, no.3, pp. 519-544
Moerman Micheal (1965), 'Who are the Lue: ethnic identification in a complex civilization', in 'American Anthropologist', volume 67, pp. 1215-29
Moore Henrietta (1988), 'Feminism and Anthropology', Cambridge, Polity Press
Mouzelis Nicos (1995), 'Sociological Theory - What Went Wrong?', London, Routledge
Murphy Archbishop (1966), 'What The Council Says About The Office Of Bishops', London, The Incorporated Catholic Truth Society
Nietzsche Friedrich (1983), 'Ainsi Parlait Zarathoustra', Paris, Librairie Generale Francaise
Norusis Marija (1990), 'The SPSS Guide to Data Analysis', Chicago, SPSS Inc.
Nye Andrea (1988), 'Feminist Theory and the Philosophies of Man', Kent, Croom Helm
Oakley Ann (1974), 'The Sociology of Housework', Harmondsworth, Penguin
O'Dea Thomas F. (1966), 'The Sociology of Religion', New Jersey, Prentice-Hall
O'Riordan S. and Murphy J.J.W. (1949), 'Catholic Answers to Questions (put by some Protestants during the Clonard Missions for all Denominations)', Dublin, The Incorporated Catholic Truth Society
Paci Massimo (1982), 'La Struttura Sociale Italiana', Bologna, Edizione Mulino
Pahl Ray (1984), 'Divisions of Labour', Oxford, Blackwell
Park R.E. and Miller H.A. (1921), 'Old World Traits Transplanted', New York, Harper and Brothers Publishers
Parkin David (1974), 'Congregational and interpersonal ideologies in political Ethnicity', in Cohen Abner ed., 'Urban Ethnicity', London, Tavistock
Parolin Gaetano (undated paper), Foreign Catholics: 'The religious practice of the Emilian Community in London'
Parsons Talcott et al., eds. (1961), 'An Outline of the Social System', New York, Free Press
Patterson Orlando (1977), 'Ethnic Chauvinism. The Reactionary Impulse', New York, Stein and Day
Pawson Ray (1989), 'A Measure for Measures', London, Routledge
Paxton Robert (1975), 'Europe in the Twentieth Century', New York, Harcourt Brace Jovanovich

Petris Luigi (1996), 'The Italian Catholic Missions' (paper presented during the Italo-British Bilateral Meeting at MIGRANTES Foundation of the Italian Episcopal Conference), Rome

Phizacklea Annie ed. (1983), 'One Way Ticket: Migration and Female Labour', London, Routledge and Kegan Paul

Phizacklea Annie (1990), 'Unpacking the fashion industry', London, Routledge

Phizacklea Annie and Miles Robert eds. (1980), 'Labour and Racism', London, Routledge and Kegan Paul

Phizacklea Annie and Wolkowitz Carol (1995), 'Homeworking Women: Gender, racism and class at work', London, Sage Publications

Piccone Stella Simonetta (1979), 'Ragazze del Sud', Rome, Editori Riuniti

Piercy Marge (1976), 'Woman on the Edge of Time', New York, Fawcett Crest Books

Pizzey Erin (1974), 'Scream Quietly or the Neighbours Will Hear', Harmondsworth, Penguin

Plummer Kenneth (1975), 'Sexual Stigma: an interactionist account', London, Routledge

Pollert Anna (1996), 'Gender and Class Revisited; or the Poverty of Patriarchy', in 'Sociology', volume .30, no.4, pp. 639-659

Pope Paul VI (1967), 'Populorum Progressio Encyclical', London, The Incorporated Catholic Truth Society

Rabinow Paul ed. (1984), 'The Foucault Reader', London, Penguin

Radcliff-Brown A.R. (1959), 'Structure and Function in Primitive Society', London, Cohen and West

Ramazanoglou Caroline (1989), 'Feminism and the Contradictions of Oppression', London, Routledge

Ramazanoglou Caroline ed. (1993), 'Up Against Foucault', London, Routledge,

Raymond Janice (1986), 'A Passion for Friends', London, Women's Press

Redclift Nanneke and Sinclair Thea M. (1991), 'Working Women', London, Routledge

Rex John (1991), 'Ethnic Identity and Ethnic Mobilization in Britain', Coventry, Centre for Research in Ethnic Relations

Rex John and Mason David eds. (1986), 'Theories of Race and Ethnic Relations', Cambridge, Cambridge University Press

Rich Adrienne (1976), 'Of Woman Born: Motherhood as Experience and Institution', New York, W.W. Norton

Rich Adrienne (1981), 'Compulsory Heterosexuality and Lesbian Existence', London, Onlywomen Press

Roberts J.M. (1985), 'The Triumph of the West', London, British Broadcasting Corporation

Rowntree Derek (1981), 'Statistics Without Tears' , London, Penguin

Rueher Rosemary (1994), 'Christianity and Women in the World', in Sharma and Youngs eds., 'Today's Women in World Religions', New York, State University of New York

Russell Diana (1984), 'Sexual Exploitation: Rape, Child Abuse and Workplace Harassment', Beverly Hills, Sage

Russell Diana (1990), 'Rape in Marriage', Bloomington, Indiana University Press

Russell Ralph (1966), 'What the Council Says About Our Lady', London, The Incorporated Catholic Truth Society

Sahakian William (1968), 'History of Philosophy', New York, Barnes and Noble

Said Edward (1978), 'Orientalism', London, Routledge and Kegan Paul

Saltzman Chafetz Janet (1990), 'Gender Equity', London, Sage Publications

Sawicki Jana (1991), 'Disciplining Foucault', London, Routledge

Schneir Miriam ed. (1995), 'The Vintage Book of Feminism', London, Vintage

Shanley Mary Lyndon and Pateman Carole eds. (1991), 'Feminist Interpretations and Political Theory', Cambridge, Polity Press

Sharma Arvind ed. (1994), 'Today's Woman in World Religions', Albany, State University of New York

Sharpe Sue (1976), 'Just Like a Girl: How Girls Learn to Be Women', Harmondsworth, Penguin

Shorter Edward (1975), 'The Making of the Modern Family', New York, Basic Books

Showstack Sassoon Ann ed. (1987), 'Women and the State', London, Hutchinson

Siebert Renate (1991), 'E Femmina, pero E Bella', Torino, Rosenberg and Sellier

Sivanandan A. (1983), 'Challenging Racism: Strategies for the '80s', in 'Race and Class', volume .25, no.2, pp. 1-11

Smart Barry (1988), 'Michel Foucault', London, Routledge

Smart Carol (1984), 'The Ties Which Bind', London, Routledge

Smelser Neil (1959), 'Social Change in the Industrial Revolution: an application of theory to the Lancashire cotton industry', London, Routledge

Smith Anthony (1983), 'Theories of Nationalism', New York, Holmes and Meier

Smith Anthony (1996), 'Ethnicity', Oxford, Oxford University

Smith Leo (1963), 'The Priests and the People', London, The Incorporated Catholic Truth Society

Smith Reverend Michael ed. (1987) 'Southwark Catholic Directory' Catholic Children Society, by Authority

Spender Dale (1980), 'Man-Made Language', London, Routledge

Spivak Gayatri Chakravorty (1987), 'In Other Worlds', London, Methuen and Co.

Stanworth Michelle ed. (1987), 'Reproductive Technologies: Gender, Motherhood and Medicine', Cambridge, Polity Press

Taylor Edward (1964), 'The Church, The Pope and the Bishops', London, The Incorporated Catholic Truth Society

Thompson Clara (1964), 'Interpersonal Psychoanalysis: The Selected Papers of Clara Thompson', New York, Basic Books

Thompson Kenneth (1990), 'Emile Durkheim', London, Routledge

Therborn Göran (1995), 'European Modernity and Beyond', London, Sage

Tong Rosemarie (1993), 'Feminist Thought', London, Routledge

Treiman Donald and Hartmann Heidi eds. (1989), 'Women, Work, and Wages: Equal Pay for Jobs of Equal Value', Committee on Occupational Classification and Analysis of the Assembly of Behavioural and Social Sciences National Research Council, Washington DC, National Academy Press

Turner Bryan S. (1983), 'Religion and Social Theory', London, Heinemann Educational Books

Turner Bryan S. ed. (1990), 'Theories of Modernity and Postmodernity', London, Sage

Urwin Derek W. (1992), 'Western Europe since 1945', Harlow, Longman Group

Van den Bergh Pierre (1983), 'Class, race and ethnicity in Africa', in 'Ethnic and Racial Studies', volume 6 (2).

Villari Rosario (1973), 'Storia Contemporanea', Rome, Editori Laterza

Wach Joachim (1944), 'Sociology of Religion', London and Chicago, University of Chicago

Walby Sylvia (1986), 'Patriarchy at Work', Cambridge, Polity Press

Walby Sylvia (1989), 'Theorizing Patriarchy', in 'Sociology', volume 23, no.2, pp 213-234

Walby Sylvia (1990), 'Theorizing Patriarchy', Oxford, Basil Blackwell

Walby Sylvia (1994a), 'Methodological and Theoretical issues in the comparative analysis of gender relations in Western Europe', in 'Environment and planning', volume 26, pp. 1339-1354

Walby Sylvia (1994b), 'Is Citizenship Gendered?', in 'Sociology', volume 28, no.2, pp. 379-395

Walby Sylvia (1997), 'Gender Transformations', London, Routledge

Wallace Ruth A. (1989), 'Feminism and Sociological Theory', California, Sage

Watson L. James (1977), 'Between Two Cultures', Oxford, Basil Blackwell

Weatherford Doris (1986), 'Foreign and Female', New York, Schocken Books

Weber Max (1976), 'The Protestant Ethic and the Spirit of Capitalism', London, Allen and Unwin

Weber Max (1993), 'The Sociology of Religion', Boston, Beacon Press

Weedon Chris (1987), 'Feminist Practice and Poststructuralist Theory', Oxford, Blackwell

Weiner Gaby and Arnot Madeleine eds. (1987), 'Gender under Scrutiny', London, Unwin Hyman

Weiss John (1967), 'The Fascist Tradition', New York, Harper and Row Publishers

Weitzman Leonore (1985), 'The Divorce Revolution', New York, Free Press

West D.J, Roy C. and Nichols F.L (1978), 'Understanding Sexual Attacks', London, Heinemann

Westminster Year Book (1965-1996), Manchester, Gabriel Communications

Westwood Sally and Bhachu Parminder (1989), 'Enterprising Women', London, Routledge

'Whitaker's Almanack' (1993), 125th Edition, London, J.Whitaker and Sons

'Whitaker's Almanack' (1995), 127th Edition, London, J.Whitaker and Sons

Wilson Elizabeth (1983), 'What Is To Be Done About Violence Against Women?', Harmondsworth, Penguin

Williams Raymond (1983), 'Keywords: A Vocabulary of Culture and Society', London, Fontana

Wollstonecraft Mary (1992), 'A Vindication of the Rights of Women', Harmondsworth, Penguin

Yinger Milton (1994), 'Ethnicity', Albany, State University of New York

Young Michael and Willmott Peter (1975), 'The Symmetrical Family: A Study of Work and Leisure in the London Region', Harmondsworth, Penguin

Yuval-Davis Nira and Anthias Floya (1989), 'Woman - Nation-State', London, Macmillan Press

Yuval-Davis Nira (1997), 'Gender and Nation', London, Sage Publications

Zanuso Lorenza (1978), 'La ricerca del lavoro femminile', in 'Inchiesta' volume 32, pp. 16-18

Index